1 Timothy

1 Timothy

A Charge to God's Missional Household

Volume 2

Paul S. Jeon

☙PICKWICK *Publications* • Eugene, Oregon

1 TIMOTHY
A Charge to God's Missional Household
Volume 2

Copyright © 2017 Paul S. Jeon. All rights reserved. Except for brief quotations in critical publications or reviews, no part of this book may be reproduced in any manner without prior written permission from the publisher. Write: Permissions, Wipf and Stock Publishers, 199 W. 8th Ave., Suite 3, Eugene, OR 97401.

Pickwick Publications
An Imprint of Wipf and Stock Publishers
199 W. 8th Ave., Suite 3
Eugene, OR 97401

www.wipfandstock.com

PAPERBACK ISBN: 978-1-5326-1726-3
HARDCOVER ISBN: 978-1-4982-4185-4
EBOOK ISBN: 978-1-4982-4184-7

Cataloguing-in-Publication data:

Names: Jeon, Paul S.

Title: 1 Timothy : a charge to God's missional household : vol. 2 / by Paul S. Jeon.

Description: Eugene, OR: Pickwick Publications, 2017 | Includes bibliographical references.

Identifiers: ISBN 978-1-5326-1726-3 (paperback) | ISBN 978-1-4982-4185-4 (hardcover) | ISBN 978-1-4982-4184-7 (ebook)

Subjects: LCSH: Bible. Timothy, 1st—Commentaries. | Bible. Timothy, 1st—Criticism, interpretation, etc.

Classification: LCC BS2745.3 J4 2017 (print) | LCC BS2745.3 (ebook)

Manufactured in the U.S.A.   12/13/17

To James Forsyth, Bill Fullilove, and David Stephenson
—glad we can figure this out together.

Contents

Preface | ix
Acknowledgments | xi
Abbreviations | xiii

1 Synopsis of Volume 1 | 1
2 1 Timothy 3:1–16: Godly Leadership in God's Household (C Unit) | 3
3 1 Timothy 4:1–16: Preserving the Teaching and Promoting Godliness amidst Apostasy (C' Unit) | 93

Bibliography | 181

Preface

I HAD PLANNED TO COMPLETE this book on 1 Timothy not long after completing my dissertation on Titus. At the time, I figured that I had "academic momentum," a rhythm that one picks up from constantly researching and writing in the final season of a Ph.D. Given that I had worked with the 1 Timothy letter for many years and already developed what I thought was a solid outline, I thought that this book would be churned out in a matter of one or two years. That was the fall of 2011. Between then and now, much has transpired—so much that I wondered if I would ever be able to complete this project. Still, the unexpected delay gave me an extended season to dwell on the letter and gain certain insights that can come only with time. During the intervening years, I had ample opportunities both to lecture on 1 Timothy while teaching at Reformed Theological Seminary and to preach on it at my church (NewCity) and occasional conferences. Regular dialogue with students, colleagues, and parishioners opened new angles into understanding the message of 1 Timothy, a letter that unfortunately tends to be treated somewhat plainly as a sort of church-manual.

I write commentaries in hope that they might be of some service to those who want to better understand the Bible. My desire has never been to write *the* commentary on any given work in the New Testament. Rather, I see myself as entering into a dialogue that has been taking place for many centuries about the meaning of the text. In this sense, I feel deeply privileged to offer my brief comments on 1 Timothy. My goal is that the reader will feel like he or she has a better grasp of the meaning and import of the letter and, in turn, will experience a degree of the benefits that I have experienced from sitting down with this letter—indeed, sitting under it—for almost six years now.

Acknowledgments

First, as always, I want to thank my parents. They know that I have no idea how much they have sacrificed for me. Second, I want to thank my research assistant, Brian Forman, who meticulously reviewed the text and enhanced the overall commentary in more ways than I can fully express. Third, though we have never met, I want to readily acknowledge Philip Towner, who served as both my guide and conversationalist through his wonderful commentary for over six years. In more ways than I can count, he pointed me away from exegetical fallacies and towards more promising interpretations. Finally, I want to thank my church NewCity and my family—especially my wife, Geena—for making life and ministry a delight.

Abbreviations

1 Tim	1 Timothy
AB	Anchor Bible
ABCS	Africa Bible Commentary Series
AJPS	*Asian Journal of Pentecostal Studies*
ANTC	Abingdon New Testament Commentaries
BDAG	W. Bauer, W. F. Arndt, and F. W. Gingrich (3rd ed.; rev. by F. W. Danker), *Greek-English Lexicon of the New Testament*
BDF	F. Blass, A. Debrunner, and R. W. Funk, *A Greek Grammar of the NT*
Bib	*Biblica*
BSac	*Bibliotheca Sacra*
BT	*Bible Translator*
BTCB	Belief: A Theological Commentary on the Bible
BZ	*Biblische Zeitschrift*
CBC	*Cornerstone Biblical Commentary*
COP	Colloquium Oecumenicum Paulinum
EBib	Études bibliques
EKK	Evangelisch-katholischer Kommentar zum Neuen Testament
EQ	*Evangelical Quarterly*
ESV	English Standard Version
HNTC	Harper's New Testament Commentaries
HTKNT	Herders theologischer Kommentar zum Neuen Testament
ICC	International Critical Commentary

JBL	*Journal of Biblical Literature*
JETS	*Journal of the Evangelical Theological Society*
JSNT	*Journal for the Study of the New Testament*
JSNTSup	JSNT, Supplement Series
JSOT	*Journal for the Study of the Old Testament*
JTS	*Journal of Theological Studies*
KJV	*King James Version*
LXX	Septuagint
McMBSS	McMaster Biblical Studies Series
NASB	*New American Standard Bible*
NCBC	New Collegeville Bible Commentary
NCBNT	New Clarendon Bible, New Testament
NCCS	New Covenant Commentary Series
NEB	*New English Bible*
NIBC	New International Biblical Commentary
NICNT	New International Commentary on the New Testament
NIGTC	New International Greek Testament Commentary
NIV	*New International Version*
NT	New Testament
NTD	Das Neue Testament Deutsch
NTL	New Testament Library
NTM	New Testament Message
NTS	*New Testament Studies*
OBC	Oxford Bible Commentary
OT	Old Testament
PE	Pastoral Epistles
PS	Pauline Studies
PTMS	Princeton Theological Monograph Series
RNBC	Readings: A New Biblical Commentary
RST	Regensburger Studien zur Theologie
SANT	Studien zum Alten und Neuen Testament
SBJT	*Southern Baptist Journal of Theology*

SBLDiS	SBL Dissertation Series
SNT	Supplements to Novum Testamentum
TCGNT	B. M. Metzger, *A Textual Commentary on the Greek New Testament*
TLNT	C. Spicq and J. D. Ernest, *Theological Lexicon of the New Testament*
TorJT	*Toronto Journal of Theology*
UBS	United Bible Societies lexicon
WBC	Word Biblical Commentary
WMANT	Wissenschaftliche Monographien zum Alten und Neuen Testament
WUNT	Wissenschaftliche Untersuchungen zum Neuen Testament
ZNW	*Zeitschrift für die Neutestamentliche Wissenschaft*

1

Synopsis of Volume 1

IN VOLUME 1, CHAPTER 1, an overview of the 1 Timothy letter was provided regarding its main message, authorship, and historical background; in addition, my commentary's text-centered, literary-rhetorical, and audience-oriented approach to the 1 Timothy letter was explicated. Overall, the message of 1 Timothy is summarized in the title of this book, *1 Timothy: A Charge to God's Missional Household*. Regarding authorship and the historical background, the 1 Timothy letter was composed by the apostle Paul to address the problem of false teaching overseers within the mid-sixties Ephesian church. For the approach of my commentary, I demonstrated how the public, performative aspect of 1 Timothy as a first-century letter shapes the way in which a modern audience is to understand, experience, and analyze the apostle Paul's message.[1]

In volume 1, chapter 2, the performative aspect of 1 Timothy was analyzed according to the ancient linguistic structuring device of *chiasm*—a rhetorical method of organizing a letter's content to enable its oral delivery and aural comprehension. In ancient letters, a chiasm conveyed a parallel structure in language that intentionally led the audience through introductory themes toward a central point (or points); at the central point, the chiasm pivoted and moved the audience's attention toward a cumulative conclusion that recalled and developed aspects of the introductory themes. It was demonstrated that the 1 Timothy letter is organized into one overall chiastic arrangement, referred to in this commentary as a *macro*chiasm. It was also demonstrated that there are six literary units that comprise and arrange the 1 Timothy macrochiasm, which are referred to in this commentary as *micro*chiasms. Still, within each microchiasm of 1 Timothy, there are smaller literary units, referred to as *mini*chiasms. The aggregation of

---

1. For a detailed explanation of the main message, authorship, historical background, and performance of 1 Timothy as a communal letter, see volume 1, chapter 1.

the minichiasms, microchiasms, and macrochiasm of 1 Timothy effectively build and convey meaning to the audience.

Also in volume 1, chapter 2, an in-depth explanation of my translation methodology was provided. The basis of my English translation of 1 Timothy in this commentary seeks to maintain the dynamic sense of the original Greek words and to demonstrate how these Greek words were instrumental to the performance and rhetorical strategy of the letter.[2]

In volume 1, chapters 3 and 4, the first two microchiasms were analyzed according to their rhetorical organization, content, and themes. In volume 1, chapter 3, it was demonstrated that the first microchiasm—the A unit of the 1 Timothy letter (1:1–20)—established an inseparable link of authority from God and Jesus to Paul and Timothy (1:1, 2, 11, 18). In contrast, a group of "some" within the Ephesian church who "teach-different" (1:3) were identified by Paul as both the problem and motivation of the letter; over and against Paul, this group was teaching "some-thing different" that "lies-opposed to the sound teaching" (1:10b).

In volume 1, chapter 4, it was demonstrated that the second microchiasm—the B unit of the 1 Timothy letter (2:1–15)—highlighted the proper lifestyle of "godliness" (2:3, 10) that flows from Paul's sound teaching. Interrelated, there was a sustained emphasis on salvation—God's desire and activity to enable humans to be saved (2:3–6)—and the Ephesian church's missional duty to attract others to Jesus Christ for salvation. To this end, the apostle Paul identified the unique roles of men and women in the church (2:8–12, 15), which ulitimately derived from the creational roles of men and women by God (2:13–14).[3]

---

2. For the establishment of 1 Timothy as a macrochiasm, clarifications of terminology, and an explanation of my translation methodology, see volume 1, chapter 2.

3. For a detailed explanation of 1 Timothy 1–2, see volume 1, chapters 3 and 4.

2

1 Timothy 3:1–16: Godly Leadership in God's Household

(C Unit)

THIS CHAPTER EXAMINES THE C unit of the macrochiasm—the third of six microchiasms within the 1 Timothy letter.[1] Within this third microchiasm (3:1–16), two minichiasms are heard (3:1–5; 3:8–16).

The Third Microchiasm

The 3:1–16 microchiasm is composed carefully of four elements (A-B-B'-A'); linguistic parallels identifying chiastic arrangements are indicated by the Greek text:

> A. ³:¹ Faithful (πιστός) is the word: If someone aspires to overseer, a commendable work he longs-for. ² It is necessary, therefore, for the overseer to be irreproachable, man of one woman (μιᾶς γυναικὸς ἄνδρα), temperate (νηφάλιον), self-controlled, cosmopolitan, affectionate-of-stranger, able-to-teach, ³ not addicted-to-wine (πάροινον), not violent; rather kind, without-fighting, without-affection-of-money, ⁴ leading (προϊστάμενον) his own household (οἴκου) commendably, holding children (τέκνα) in submissiveness with all respectability, ⁵ but if someone does not know (οἶδεν) how to lead (προστῆναι) his own household (οἴκου), how (πῶς) will he care-for the church of God (ἐκκλησίας θεοῦ)?

---

1. For the establishment of 1 Timothy as a macrochiasm, clarifications of terminology, and an explanation of my translation methodology, see volume 1, chapter 2.

B. ⁶ Not a young-plant, that he might not—being-puffed-up—fall (ἐμπέσῃ) into the condemnation of the devil (διαβόλου).

B'. ⁷ But it is necessary to hold a commendable testimony from those-outside, so that he might not fall (ἐμπέσῃ) into disgrace and the snare of the devil (διαβόλου).

A'. ⁸ Likewise it is necessary for deacons to be respectable, not double-worded, not holding-toward much wine, not avaricious, ⁹ holding the mystery of the faith (πίστεως) in a pure conscience. ¹⁰ But they also must be-tested first; then let them serve-as-deacons, being blameless. ¹¹ Likewise it is necessary for women to be respectable, not devilishly-slanderous, temperate (νηφαλίους), faithful (πιστάς) in all things. ¹² Deacons must be the man of one woman (μιᾶς γυναικὸς ἄνδρες), leading (προϊστάμενοι) children (τέκνων) commendably and their own households (οἴκων). ¹³ For those who serve-as-deacons commendably acquire for themselves a commendable standing and much confidence in faith that is in Christ Jesus. ¹⁴ These-things to you I write, hoping to come to you in quickness; ¹⁵ but if I am delayed, that you might know (εἰδῇς) how (πῶς) it is necessary to behave in the household (οἴκῳ) of God, which is the church of the living God (ἐκκλησία θεοῦ), a pillar and foundation of the truth. ¹⁶ And confessedly great is the mystery of godliness: he was manifested in flesh, was declared-just in Spirit, was seen by angels, was proclaimed in the Gentiles, was counted-faithful in the world, was taken-up in glory.

1 Timothy 3:1–5: The Overseer

(A Element)

Within the introductory A element of the third microchiasm (3:1–5), the audience hear one minichiasm (3:1–5).

1 Timothy 3:1–5: A Minichiastic Unit

As a minichiasm in itself, verses 3:1–5 of the A element are composed carefully of five sub-elements ("a"-"b"-"c"-"b"-"a"); linguistic parallels identifying chiastic arrangements are indicated by the Greek text:

1 TIMOTHY 3:1–16: GODLY LEADERSHIP IN GOD'S HOUSEHOLD

> "a". ³:¹ Faithful is the word: If someone (εἴ τις) aspires to overseer, a commendable (καλοῦ) work he longs-for. ²ᵃ It is necessary, therefore, for the overseer to be irreproachable, man of one woman,
>
>> "b". ²ᵇ temperate, self-controlled, cosmopolitan, affectionate-of-stranger (φιλόξενον),
>>
>>> "c". ²ᶜ able-to-teach,
>>
>> "b'". ³ not addicted-to-wine, not violent; rather kind, without-fighting, without-affection-of-money (ἀφιλάργυρον),
>
> "a'". ⁴ leading his own household commendably (καλῶς), holding children in submissiveness with all respectability, ⁵ but if someone (εἴ τις) does not know how to lead his own household, how will he care-for the church of God?

The first minichiasm of the 3:1–16 microchiasm is framed by Paul's discussion of "someone" and the "commendable" activities that they must "commendably" do in the "a" and "a'" sub-elements. In the "b" and "b'" sub-elements, Paul focuses on the affections of the overseer. The minichiasm gravitates around the overseer being "able-to-teach" in the pivot "c" sub-element.

1 Timothy 3:1–2a: The Commendable Work of an Overseer

("a" sub-element)

The introductory "a" sub-element of the minichiasm begins with the declaration "Faithful is the word" (3:1). This recalls for the audience its prior occurrence in 1:15 of the first microchiasm. Several observations are worth noting. First, given the unity and flow of the overall macrochiasm—the 1 Timothy letter itself—the audience understand that the phrase "Faithful is the word" in 3:1 of the third microchiasm is to be understood consistently with its use in 1:15 of the first microchiasm, namely that it is "worthy of all acceptance" (1:15). Second, "Faithful is the word (λόγος)" was heard by the audience in the first microchiasm to stand in stark contrast to the "useless-words" (ματαιολογίαν, 1:6) of the false teachers. As such, from the outset of A element and "a" sub-element of the third microchiasm, the audience understand that whatever Paul says next is not to be heard in neutral terms but as an implicit polemic against those who desire to be law-teachers but fail to understand what they-are-saying and insisting (1:7).[2] In effect, the

---

2. See Swinson, *Letters to Timothy*, 60.

phrase in 3:1 is an affirmation that none of what the false teachers say is faithful or worthy of acceptance. As a polemical statement, then, the audience hear the phrase as a call to align themselves with the "faithful" (πιστός) word pertaining to the salvation of sinners (1:15). That is, in contrast to some who "regarding the faith (πίστιν) have become-shipwrecked" (1:19), the audience are to listen to Paul, who "was counted-faithful" (ἐπιστεύθην) with the sound teaching, the gospel (1:10b–11), who was considered "faithful" (πιστόν) by Christ Jesus (1:12), and was appointed a teacher "in faith" (ἐν πίστει, 2:7). The implication is that a rejection of Paul's words equates to a rejection of Christ and thus the faith.

A third observation is that the audience hears a seamless movement—via transitional words—from "in faith" (πίστει, 2:15) in the A′ element of the second microchiasm to "Faithful (πιστός) is the word" (3:1) in the A element of the third microchiasm.[3] Here, the overall theme of missional, godly behavior in the second microchiasm is carried into the third microchiasm.[4] At the same time, due to the immediate context of Paul's corrective statements for teaching and governing among godly men and women in the A′ element of the second microchiasm, the audience understand and expect to hear a continued discussion regarding teaching and governing in the A element of the third microchiasm. More specifically, given the sustained polemical quality of the letter, the continued discussion would likely be heard as a specific treatment against those whose teachings bring about the abdication of God's creational roles for godly men and women among the audience. Put positively, the audience understand that in the third microchiasm Paul has in view the proper observance of creational roles.

Fourth and lastly, the cascading, cumulative impact of the interconnected macrochiasm advances the phrase "Faithful is the word" in 3:1 as an indicator of Paul's sound teaching (1:10)—the gospel (1:11)—which brings-about "the household-law of God in faith" (1:4), namely "godliness" that results in the "child-parenting" of new believers "in faith" (2:15). On the one hand, the audience understand that salvation is at stake; Paul's teaching is God's own testimony that he himself saves sinners (1:15; 2:6–7). On the other hand, Paul's teaching is that, once saved, sinners lead lives of godliness (2:2, 3:10); thus the audience understand that Paul in 3:1 is still concerned with the proper lifestyle "in faith" (2:7, 15) that enables God's missional

---

3. Regarding the function of *transitional words*, see volume 1, chapter 2.

4. Swinson's observations are apt: "In the preceeding unit, Paul began to directly address the character and conduct of the believers in Ephesus, beginning with a broad directive and then shifting to more particular instructions to men and then to women. He continues in a similar vein . . . to develop the corrective teaching that has dominated the letter from 1:3" (*Letters to Timothy*, 60).

household to attract others to Christ. In this way, the progression of the macrochiasm further qualifies "Faithful is the word" in 3:1 with both saving connotations and behavioral implications. To summarize in full, the audience are ready to hear Paul's next words in the context of salvation, the godly behavior that accompanies it, and the sustained polemic against behavior that opposes it.[5]

Given the sustained polemic, the audience hear Paul's statement "if someone" in the "a" sub-element not simply as a generic reference to an individual.[6] Rather, "someone" (τις) in 3:1 recalls for the audience "some" (τισίν) who teach-different (1:3), "some" (τινες) who—swerving-from love, a pure heart, good conscience, and a without-hypocrisy faith (1:5)—have turned aside for useless-words (1:5–6), "someone" (τις) who does not know how to use the law lawfully (1:8b), and "some" (τινες) who—by rejecting faith and a good conscience—have become-shipwrecked regarding the faith (1:19). To be sure, Paul's statement is not neutral; given the unity of the macrochiasm, the consistent use of "some" to refer to the false teachers in the first microchiasm is undoubtedly carried forward here in the third microchiasm.[7] Yet, even in this context, Paul indicates that "someone" who "aspires to overseer" longs-for "a commendable work" (3:1), thus the generic reference would certainly be heard alongside the polemical connotation.

The duty of an "overseer" (ἐπισκοπῆς) itself assumes a role of authority.[8] Due to the immediate, uninterrupted movement from the concluding

---

5. It is possible to take the declaration "Faithful is the word" (3:1) with what has come before, namely that women will be-saved as they remain in faith (2:15) (e.g., Long, *1 & 2 Tim*, 84; Solevåg, *Birthing Salvation*, 132; Young, *Theology of the Pastoral Letters*, 56–59). This interpretation assumes in part that the phrase always pertains to an explicit mention of salvation, such as in 1:15 (e.g., Keegan, *First and Second Tim*, 17). Most scholars, however, take the statement with what follows (e.g., Towner, *PE*, 248; Ellingworth, "The 'True Saying' in 1 Timothy 3,1'" 443–45; Metzger, *TCGNT*, 572–73; Witherington, *Letters*, 203, 234; Knight, *PE*, 153). The macrochiastic understanding of the phrase—carrying forward the salvific implications of the second microchiasm while introducing the third microchiasm—naturally lends itself to the scholarly consensus without dismissing the relevance of salvation.

6. Contra Towner, *PE*, 248; Knight, *PE*, 153.

7. It is unlikely that Paul has women in view as the false teachers. Rather, the polemical use of the term "someone" (τις, 3:1) applies to "some" (τισίν, 1:3) who teach-different, namely men of whom are Hymenaeus and Alexander (1:20) who were likely influencing women to teach and govern in the church (2:12). See discussion in volume 1, chapter 4. Contra Belleville, "Teaching and Usurping Authority," 207.

8. It may be worth noting that many commentators view the terms "overseer" and "elder" interchangeably. Knight, *PE*, 175: "That 'elder' (πρεσβύτερος) was a synonym for ἐπίσκοπος is clear from Tit. 1:5, 7 and Acts 20:17, 28." See discussion in volume 1, chapter 1 regarding Acts 20. See also Köstenberger, "Interpreting the PE," 6; Barclay, *1 & 2 Tim*, 101–2; Ngewa, *1 & 2 Tim*, 60. Regarding the distinction between "overseer" and

A' element of the second microchiasm to the introductory A element of the third microchiasm, the audience would understand that the term "overseer" has in view Adam's creational leadership role to both teach and govern (2:12–13). Paul's mention of "overseer," therefore, would not only be addressed specifically to the men in the audience but would also function to identify—and likely to correct—specifically who among the men in the audience ought to teach and govern.[9] Given the use of the verb "aspires to" (ὀρέγεται), the apostle may be qualifying his earlier polemic against those "desiring to be (θέλοντες εἶναι) law-teachers" (1:7).[10] On the one hand, the audience would hear Paul's statement in 3:1 as an intensification, the sense being "some are *certainly not* to be overseers." For obvious reasons, the false teachers are unfit for such a leadership role that requires both teaching and governing—they do not even understand the things they-are-saying (1:7). On the other hand, the aspiration to be an overseer is not itself wrong.[11] In

---

"elder," see Coleman, *Connecting the Chasm*, 179–84; Long's discussion is also helpful (*1 & 2 Tim*, 86–87). For further analysis, see Merkle, *40 Questions about Elders and Deacons*, 76–83. Within this chapter, only the term "overseer" is used. For the connection between "overseer" and "elders" within 1 Timothy, see volume 3, chapter 2 regarding 1 Timothy 5:17a.

9. That Paul is specifically addressing men in the audience is clearly the case. Paul's concern in the immediately preceding A' element of the second microchiasm was for godly women to enable godly men in the audience to teach and govern (2:12–13). The continuous flow of Paul's speech directly into the A element of the third microchiasm would not be a break in thought: these same godly women in the audience would understand that Paul intends for godly men to oversee—to teach and govern—the congregation (3:1; cf. 2:12–13).

Not a few commentators argue against the notion that Paul is addressing only men in the audience for the role of overseer. Payne, *Man and Woman*, 445: "practically all English versions of 1 Tim 3:1 . . . give the false impression that Paul uses masculine pronouns, implying that these church leaders must be male. In Greek, however, there is not even one masculine pronoun or 'men only' requirement." This observation is apt; however, it does not consider what Paul has just said in the A' element of the second microchiasm concerning the roles of godly men and women in regard to teaching and authority in the congregation.

It is also worth noting that Payne interprets τις (3:1) as clear evidence that Paul is including women: "Paul affirms 'anyone' [τις] who desires the office of overseer desires a good work' (3:1, 5). Would Paul encourage women to desire an office, as these words do, if it were prohibited to them? . . . In fact, 3:1, 'Anyone desiring the office of overseer desires a good work,' encourages women to aspire to be overseers" (ibid., 448, 454, respectively). The problem with this observation is that it does not take into account the polemical quality with which Paul has consistently ascribed to the term τις throughout the letter (1:3, 6, 8, 19) in reference to the group of false-teaching men (1:20).

10. In passing, not only connected conceptually, the audience may have also heard an aural cadence between ὀρέγεται and θέλοντες εἶναι.

11. The further significance of the phrase "Faithful is the word" (3:1a) may be worth noting here. Towner, *PE*, 248: "The additional weight of affirmation it lends to the office

1 TIMOTHY 3:1–16: GODLY LEADERSHIP IN GOD'S HOUSEHOLD 9

fact, Paul states that it is exactly the opposite—"a commendable work he longs-for."[12] In the arrangement of Paul's full statement, the terms "aspires to" (ὀρέγεται) and "longs-for" (ἐπιθυμεῖ) should be treated basically as synonyms, thus making clear that the "commendable work" in view is synonymous with the duty of an "overseer."[13] The rhetorical effect would highlight both the aspiration to oversee and the duty thereof. The audience are to understand that it is in no way wrong to aspire—indeed it is commendable—to be an overseer because the leadership position itself is commendable.

Still, an important rhetorical implication would likely not go unnoticed by the audience. Though the sense of Paul's statement in 3:1 is conditional and hypothetical—"*If* (εἴ) someone aspires to overseer"—Paul's specific use of the rhetorically loaded term "some" would simultaneously—and significantly—highlight a situational reality in Ephesus. In the same way that "some" currently teach-different (1:3), "some" have turned aside for useless-words (1:6), "someone" does not know how to use the commendable law lawfully (1:8), and "some" have become-shipwrecked regarding the faith (1:19), so too is "someone" not only aspiring but has already aspired to an overseer (3:1). In other words, the implication is that Paul is addressing a situation wherein "some"—the false teachers—are already overseers. Indeed, Paul's earlier use of the phrase "If (εἴ) some-thing (τι) different lies-opposed to the sound teaching (διδασκαλίᾳ)" in 1:10b underscored a present—not hypothetical—situation in Ephesus, namely regarding "some" (τισίν) who "teach-different" (ἑτεροδιδασκαλεῖν) in the Ephesian church (1:3).[14] In this way, particularly given the rhetorical combination of "if" (εἴ, 1:10b; εἴ, 3:1) and cognate terms of the indefinite pronoun "some-thing" and "someone" (τι, 1:10b; τις, 3:1), it would be apparent to the audience

---

may have been intended to shore up support for the church, whose leadership had come under attack from a failure to address the heretical movement or because some of its membership had gone over to the opposition." Such an endorsement may have been necessary if the heresies fomented a distrust for leaders that, in turn, discouraged current and future leaders from fulfilling the role; see Marshall, *PE*, 476.

12. Knight, *PE*, 154: "Here καλοῦ ἔργου ἐπιθυμεῖ shows that the aspiration is being commended."

13. See Knight, *PE*, 154.

14. Paul's use of the term "if" (εἴ) in the first microchiasm was undoubtedly factual; the parallel arrangement of the first microchiasm would function to emphasize this implication:

A element: "charge some (τισίν) not to teach-different (ἑτεροδιδασκαλεῖν)" (1:3);

A' element: "if some-thing (τι) different (ἕτερον) lies-opposed to the sound teaching (διδασκαλίᾳ)" (1:10).

See volume 1, chapter 3 regarding 1 Timothy 1:10. Particularly in relation to "someone" (3:1), it would be evident that Paul's use of "If" (εἴ) in 3:1 has already happened and is currently happening in the Ephesian church.

that Paul's use of the phrase "If (εἴ) someone (τις) aspires to overseer" in 3:1 underscores the same, present situation in Ephesus regarding "some" who teach-different, that is, "some-thing" that lies-opposed to the sound teaching of Paul (1:3, 10b). In short, Paul intends the audience to know that there are false-teaching overseers in Ephesus.[15]

The descriptive phrase "commendable work" (καλοῦ ἔργου) recalls several of Paul's previous statements. In the A' element of second microchiasm, Paul's instructions to the women were to cosmetic themselves in "good works (ἔργων)" (2:10) in order to visibly exhibit the inward impact of the gospel on their hearts and consciences and to fulfill their critical, missional role in the Ephesian church to attract others to have-faith upon Christ (1:16). In the A element of the third microchiasm, the audience now hear Paul's declaration to the godly men, which specifically concerns their "commendable work (ἔργου)" (3:1) in view of an "overseer."[16] Thus as in the second microchiasm, Paul continues his concern for godly men and women to do what is uniquely proper for those in God's missional household. Moreover, the adjective "commendable" (καλοῦ, 3:1) recalls for the audience the overall progression of the macrochiasm: the law is "commendable" (καλός, 1:8); the war to preserve the sound teaching, the gospel, is "commendable" (καλήν, 1:19); and the audience's prominent activity to pray on behalf of all humans and to exhibit a missional life in all godliness is "commendable" (καλόν, 2:3). In all these instances, the connotations are good, honorable, and fitting. Here in the third microchiasm, then, Paul's use of "commendable" would certainly be heard in the same way, effectively underscoring that

---

15. The implication here is reminiscent of Paul's final statement to the Ephesian church in Acts 20:29–30, where Paul, specifically addressing the "overseers" (ἐπισκόπους, v. 28) in Ephesus, declared: "I know that with my departure fierce wolves will come into you-all, not sparing the flock, and *from you-all yourselves will arise men saying twisted-things* pulling-away the disciples after themselves" (my emphasis). Paul indicated that *men*—new overseers—would arise from among the overseers to whom Paul was speaking. Indeed, such seems to be the case here and thus the cause for Paul's letter: "If someone aspires to overseer (ἐπισκοπῆς)" in 3:1 would have in view the new overseers about whom Paul foretold in Acts 20:29–30. For further discussion, see volume 1, chapter 1 regarding Acts 20:28–30; see also volume 3, chapter 2 regarding 1 Timothy 5:17–20 and volume 3, chapter 3 regarding 1 Timothy 6:9–10.

16. Although similar, the plural "works" (ἔργων) applicable to women in 2:10 and the singular "work" (ἔργου) applicable to men in 3:1 indicates a distinction. Knight, *PE*, 154: "ἔργον is not being used in its more general sense of work as deed or action, but either in the sense of work as 'occupation' or 'task,' perhaps even 'office.'" Given the connectedness and flow of the second and third microchiasm, the official leadership position of "overseer" (3:1) may be analogous to Adam's official role as "first" in regard to teaching and governing (2:12–13).

the duty of "overseer" is nothing but "a commendable work."[17] Further still, the movement of the macrochiasm affirms that when an overseer is both qualified and selected to lead—as when the law is used lawfully, when the sound teaching is preserved, and when godliness is demonstrated—there is an overall positive impact on others, including those within and outside of the church. The work of the overseer, then, is to be heard in this way: it is an admirable task that exists to benefit the audience, has a missional impact, and merits the respect both of those who aspire and those who benefit.

In sum, the audience understand that the polemical edge of the statement "If someone aspires to overseer" is not directed against the aspiration to oversee nor the duty of an overseer but rather—and only—against the aspirant in view, namely "someone." The problem, therefore, resides in those who are unqualified yet aspire to oversee the entire congregation in teaching and governing. Specifically, then, the audience hear both a qualifying and disqualifying aspect to Paul's statement in 3:1. Undoubtedly, Paul has a high view of the leadership role of an overseer and encourages those who aspire toward it to become overseers. At the same time, Paul has a low view of false teachers and discourages them from any aspirations to oversee. With these words, Paul challenges the audience to consider—or reconsider—whether or not "someone" is fit to teach and govern as "overseer" of the church.[18]

Given Paul's concern with the actual *person* who aspires to the commendable work of overseer, the audience understand that aspiration—though commendable—alone is insufficient to be an overseer. Rather, given the significance of the position as analogous to Adam's leadership role, a high view of the overseer's position must be reflected in the high standards required of those who aspire to fill it.[19] Such is the import of Paul's next

---

17. Marshall, *PE*, 475: "The statement must surely imply that some people thought it undesirable."

18. Swinson suggests that Paul has in view "those who already hold positions of responsibility in the churches as well as upon those who aspire to such positions. In other words, this unit is not chiefly concerned with appointing individuals to office or with establishing new offices" (*Letters to Timothy*, 60). This is likely the case, given that the church had been in existence for at least ten years prior to the composition of 1 Timothy (see volume 1, chapter 1). Patterson and Kelley, "1 Tim," 667: "The church in Ephesus was well-established and already had elders [overseers]." As such, Paul's challenge to the audience in 3:1 would include "someone" who is already teaching and governing as an overseer, the sense being, "If a false teacher is currently in the office of overseer, it is commendable for them not to be an overseer any longer."

19. Barclay, *1 & 2 Tim*, 102: "The importance of the office of overseer means that rigorous qualifications must be imposed on those who seek it." Marshall, *PE*, 476: "There probably never was a situation in which people functioned as leaders purely on a charismatic basis."

statement, "It is necessary, therefore, for the overseer to be irreproachable."[20] The conjunction "therefore" (οὖν) highlights the tie between an "overseer" and the high standards of the "commendable work." The verb "It is necessary" (δεῖ) also reiterates the significance of an "overseer," communicating to the audience that there should be no relaxation of the standards that are "necessary" to complete all that is involved in the "commendable work." At the same time, "It is necessary" suggests an urgency, likely stemming from the progression of the macrochiasm to the immediate situation: "some" who teach-different in the Ephesian church (1:3)—indeed, "someone" who already is an overseer in the Ephesian church (3:1)—bring-about results that are antithetical to "the household-law of God in faith" (1:4), such as influencing women to do what is improper (2:9-12) and thus hindering the missional "child-partenting" of new believers "in faith" (2:9-15). In such a context, the audience hear "It is necessary" in 3:2 of the "a" sub-element as a summary call of the entire macrochiasm so far: qualified men in the audience must teach and govern as overseers in order to bring-about the true household-law of God that exists "in faith," thus promoting proper, missional godliness among the entire congregation (2:1-15).

The overarching adjective that describes a qualified overseer is "irreproachable" (ἀνεπίλημπτον), which connotes blameless, without fault, or above criticism.[21] That is, the audience understand that the aspiring individual must command the respect of all the audience through his observable lifestyle.[22] This recalls the overarching concern of the second microchiasm, wherein Paul underscored the missional necessity for believers to lead a life in all godliness and respectability (2:2) and, to that end, gave specific instructions for the men (2:8) and women (2:9-15). The overseer, then, is not only in a leadership role to teach and govern, but he also functions as an observable model of godliness for "all"—those "in faith" (1:2, 4; 2:7, 15) and "those who would-inevitably-come to have-faith" (1:16).[23] In other words,

---

20. The effect of the verbal couple ("It is necessary . . . to be") continues through 3:7.

21. That "irreproachable" (ἀνεπίλημπτον) functions as an umbrella term for the qualities that follow in 3:2-3, see Barcley, *1 & 2 Tim*, 102; Knight, *PE*, 155-56; Wall with Steele, *1 & 2 Tim*, 104; Ngewa, *1 & 2 Tim*, 61.

22. See Fee, *1 & 2 Tim*, 43. Note that the nuanced emphasis on respectability through conduct does not connote perfection. Ngewa's explanation (*1 & 2 Tim*, 61) is helpful: "Although overseers' lives must not leave any loophole for criticism, this does not mean that they must be totally free from both internal and visible sin. If this were the requirement, then no one in Ephesus or anywhere else would qualify, for the New Testament explicitly states that we all sin (1 John 1:10). Nor must the overseers be hypocrites, disguising their own sinfulness. Rather than being show-offs who parade their righteousness, they must have solid character and must deserve their reputation."

23. Marshall, *PE*, 472: "it is expected that they will actually show the qualities which

the duty of "overseer" is "a commendable work" (3:1) in direct relation to "the overseer" himself (3:2): in order for his work as overseer to be commendable, the overseer himself must reflect a commendable lifestyle.²⁴ This same pattern was heard by the audience in the second microchiasm, where Paul's teaching in "truth" (2:7) was related to "a knowing-embrace of truth" (2:4a), that is, the corresponding lifestyle. Moreover, the movement of the overall macrochiasm here presents a fundamental litmus test for the audience as well as—indeed much more—for the overseer. On the one hand, the sound teaching—the gospel—results in "godliness" (2:2, 10). On the other hand, a "without-godly" life (1:9b) is indicative of "someone" who does not know the lawful use of the law (1:8b) as a result of teaching some-thing different that lies-opposed to the sound teaching (1:10b). In effect, for "some" among the audience who were incorrectly teaching and governing as overseers in the Ephesian church, the qualifying standard "to be irreproachable" would likely intend affirming looks of disapproval by the surrounding men and women in the audience who adhere to the sound teaching of the apostle Paul who established the church.²⁵ The qualification for an overseer is not only a person who "aspires" but also a person who is "irreproachable" in the eyes of others. To be sure, such approval would not be restricted to only those in the audience. Rather, just as the second microchiasm called upon the congregation to participate in God's missional purpose for all humans to be-saved through their exemplary lifestyles of godliness in the Ephesian community, so too must the overseer in the third microchiasm. As the model of godliness, then, observable missional piety is not only required but is all the more "necessary."²⁶

Paul goes on to specify a concrete example of how the overseer is to be missionally irreproachable: "man of one woman" (3:2).²⁷ The first-century

---

are desirable for all believers." Malherbe, "Overseers," 81: "The delineation of the overseer's character and actions is adequate for its paraenetic purpose; the modeling of the behavior suffices."

24. Kierspel captures the nuance well: "The quality of the work depends on the character of the worker!" (*Charts*, 244).

25. That false-teaching overseers are in view, see volume 1, chapter 1 regarding Acts 20.

26. Wall with Steele, *1 & 2 Tim*, 106: "The motive of Paul's instructions is not a social program of domestication according to which the administrator is put forward as an exemplary citizen; rather, the administrator is an exemplary believer whose 'good work' personifies the redemptive will of God for all to see."

27. The subject of Paul's address is a "man" (ἄνδρα). Still, not a few commentators argue that Paul is also addressing women, thus including women in his discussion of overseers. The basis for this interpretation mostly has 1 Timothy 5:9 in view, wherein Paul indicates that a widow must be a "woman of one man" (ἑνὸς ἀνδρὸς γυνή); see

Ephesian audience would have understood the phrase "man of one woman" as a reference to marital fidelity and devotion.[28] What is highlighted from the outset of what "is necessary," therefore, is how a man manages his own marriage: the public duty of "the overseer" in the church depends directly on his personal family life.[29] Two observations are worth noting. First, Paul's reference to a "man (ἄνδρα) of one woman (γυναικός)" (3:2) in the introductory A element of the third microchiasm recalls for the audience Paul's prior discussion of men in general (ἄνδρας, 2:8; ἀνδρός, 2:12) and women in general (γυναῖκας, 2:9; γυναιξίν, 2:11; γυνή, 2:11, 13; γυναικί, 2:12) in the concluding A' element of the second microchiasm. On the surface, the reference to a married man and woman in 3:2 seems to be an odd—or even

---

e.g., Belleville, "1 Tim," 68; Wall with Steele, *1 & 2 Tim*, 106–7. While this is an apt observation, it does not take into consideration the rhetorical grounding of 3:2, namely its immediate placement after 2:11–14 of the preceding A' element in the second microchiasm, which specifies such teaching and governing authority in the church to men.

Though Paul strictly has in view a "man" for the role of overseer on the basis of God's design in 2:13, Patterson and Kelley's observation ("1 Tim," 667) may be helpful for understanding how everyone in the first-century Greco-Roman audience—Christian or not—would have understood Paul's discussion of an overseer: "Paul presupposed that the elders [overseers] in Ephesus were both male and married, as would be expected in the patriarchal culture of the Greco-Roman world."

That Paul presupposes a "man" (ἄνδρα) in view of the overseer (3:2), see Paul's final statement to the Ephesian overseers in Acts 20, wherein Paul specifies that "from you-all yourselves will arise men (ἄνδρες) saying twisted-things pulling-away the disciples after themselves" (Acts 20:30). Here in 1 Timothy, Paul's specification may be remedial and oriented toward these false-teaching "men" whom Paul had predicted ten years prior. With this connection, it is clear that the false teachers whom Paul is addressing in 1 Timothy are men. See volume 1, chapter 1.

28. See Fee, *1 & 2 Tim*, 80–81; Patterson and Kelley, "1 Tim," 667; Trummer, "Einehe nach den Pastoralbriefe," 471–84. Where marital fidelity is in view, Ngewa suggests an inclusion of unmarried men: "Paul was focusing more on the person's moral integrity than on their marital status . . . What Paul is saying is that those overseers who are married (as most of them are) must be faithful, and that those who are not married must display purity of character" (*1 & 2 Tim*, 62). Similarly, Madsen, "Ethics of the PE," 231: "The overseer must be faithful or abstinent, as the case may be." See MacArthur, *1 & 2 Tim*, 35.

In passing, it has been variously suggested that this phrase refers to a rejection of: polygamy (e.g., Payne, *Man and Woman*, 445–46), remarriage after the death of a spouse (e.g., Verner, *Household of God*, 130–31; Wall with Steele, *1 & 2 Tim*, 106), divorce (e.g., Belleville, "1 Tim," 68), and unmarried men (e.g., Dibelius and Conzelmann, 52). For a summary of responses to these alternative positions, see Towner, *PE*, 250 n. 42; Knight, *PE*, 157–59.

29. Though not specific to 3:2, Tellbe's comment is applicable: "Not improbably, the 'false' teachers had neglected to manage their own family and/or they had encouraged others to neglect their family responsibilities" (*Christ-Believers in Ephesus*, 162). Beginning with Paul's concern for an overseer's wife, the apostle removes any possible reason for the neglect of family.

arbitrary—switch from men and women in general. However, given the consistent rhetorical movement of the macrochiasm, the audience would hear a natural progression in Paul's rhetoric. Beginning with the A element of the second microchiasm, Paul moves from the audience's general missional calling in the household of God—both men and women (2:1-2)—to men and women's specific missional roles in the household of God within the parallel A' element (2:8-15); now in the immediately connected A element of the third microchiasm, Paul moves on to specify one missional role concerning one specific man—the overseer of God's missional household (3:1-2). In other words, Paul's concern for "all" (πάντων, 2:2, 3; πάντας, 2:4) is met by "one" (μιᾶς, 3:2)—the person capable of leading all, namely the overseer. The singular role of "the overseer" is thus appropriately described by the relationship of a singular man to a singular woman. For a man who teaches and governs to bring-about "the household-law of God in faith" (1:4), Paul's nuance would not be a heard as a sudden departure from his prior references to all men in general but as a specification of what "is necessary" for one man—out all the godly men in the congregation—to be able to do, namely to lead all who live within the household of God, the realm "in faith."

Second, therefore, given both the sustained movement of "in faith" throughout the entire macrochiasm (1:2, 4; 2:7, 15) and the familial language associated with those who are "in faith" (1:2, 4, 18; 2:15), it comes as no surprise to the audience that Paul is concerned with the way in which an aspiring overseer is faithful to his own individual family, namely his wife. The audience understand the implication: negatively, a man who is unfaithful to his wife will be an unfaithful leader for the household of God; positively, a man who is faithfully married would lead the household of God in the same way. In short, a man's irreproachable relationship with his wife reflects his overall irreproachable standing in life. Part of the overseer's qualification is not only to be the model of godliness—to be "irreproachable"—but also—and specifically—to be the model of marital fidelity for all those "in faith" as well as missionally for "all humans" in general outside of the church. The audience understand that a man is qualified to oversee—to teach and govern, that is, bring-about "the household-law of God in faith" (1:4)—only insofar as his teaching and governing is rooted in faithfulness to his wife. This is quite significant and would not go unnoticed: more than a man's self-assessment of his marriage, Paul is directing and inviting the audience to give greater voice to a man's wife who alone can determine whether or not her husband is fit to lead. To be sure, the clear implication to all the men and all the women is that Paul cares very much not only for the health of marriages in the church but also—and quite noticeably—for wives to experience the health, joy, and contentment that proper teaching and governing is intended to bring. In this way, just as the overseer is called to be a model of life "in faith" for all men and women, so too is the wife's experience of her husband to represent what the blessed life "in faith" is intended to be. The overseer would not only be a corrective model for any unfaithfulness by men in the audience—adultery, abuse, or abandonment—but also by his wife's happiness in marriage would attract many to the Christian life "in faith." In sum, prior to benefiting the audience, "It is necessary" for the overseer's teaching and governing to be experienced, enjoyed, and evidenced by "one woman"—his wife. Only then is he "irreproachable."[30]

Paul's attention to the relationship of a man and woman in marriage may have reminded the audience of a metaphor that Paul used in a prior letter to the Ephesian congregation to illustrate the relationship of Christ and the church.[31] In Ephesians 5:25–26, Paul instructs men (ἄνδρες) to love their wives (γυναῖκας) in the same way that Christ loved the church, that is, by giving-over himself on behalf of her (ἑαυτὸν παρέδωκεν ὑπὲρ αὐτῆς) in order to present the church to himself as spotless and without blemish—in a word, irreproachable. The apparent connection is telling about the way in which the overseer is to be a "man (ἄνδρα) of one woman (γυναικός)" in 3:2. Just as Christ selflessly loved the church to purify her, so a man must selflessly love his wife for the same purpose. The overseer, then, is called to teach and govern in a way that protects, guides, and encourages godliness in his wife, just like Adam was formed to do (2:13). Yet, this is not all. Not only did Christ love the church, but he also "gave-over himself on behalf of her" (ἑαυτὸν παρέδωκεν ὑπὲρ αὐτῆς) (Eph 5:26); this language is remeniscient of Paul's statement in the second microchiasm of 1 Timothy that Christ "gave himself (δοὺς ἑαυτόν) as a ransom on behalf of (ὑπέρ) all" (2:6). The implication for the audience would be clear: an overseer's fidelity and love toward his wife is irreproachable insofar as he is willing to lead by giving

---

30. As Payne aptly observes, it is most unlikely that Paul is completely excluding unmarried men from the role of an overseer: "if this [marriage] were a requirement for all overseers ... not even Paul, as single, would qualify to be an overseer ... even though his actions epitomize church oversight" (*Man and Woman*, 446). See Schreiner, "Overseeing," 96. As such, where the qualification of marital fidelity is in view, an unmarried man's faithfulness to his singleness would function in a similar way as the married man—not only modeling fidelity in all circumstances of life for the congregation but also attracting many to Christ by his honorable treatment of all women.

31. Both Paul's letter to the Ephesians and 1 Timothy are dated to the early to mid-sixties; see Carson and Moo, *Introduction*, 486–87, 571–72, repectively. See also Knight, *PE*, 54. In the event that the letter to the Ephesians was received prior to 1 Timothy, its contents would be freshly in their minds and the connection would easily be made between Ephesians 5:22–33 and 1 Timothy 3:2.

himself up for his wife, just like Adam should have done (2:14).³² A man's fidelity to such a degree would not only merit respect from the congregation and those outside the church but also—and indeed most importantly—his wife. In effect, then, a godly woman who experiences the faithfulness of her husband—and thus by her own accord follows her husband's loving lead, just like Eve was formed to do (2:13)—is a woman who has qualified her husband to be an overseer of the church.³³

1 Timothy 3:2b: Irreproachable in a Positive Sense

("b" sub-element)

In 3:2b, the "b" sub-element in the third microchiasm, Paul elaborates further on the personal qualities expected of a prospective overseer. He is to be "temperate, self-controlled (σώφρονα), cosmopolitan (κόσμιον), affectionate-of-stranger." A few initial comments are in order. First, this certainly would recall Paul's discussion in the A' element of the second microchiasm for women "to cosmetic (κοσμεῖν) themselves in cosmopolitan (κοσμίῳ) apparel with . . . self-control (σωφροσύνης)" (2:9–10). The strong echoes of Paul's instructions to women (2:9–15) communicate to the audience that Paul holds the men who profess godliness to the same standard of self-control and proper conduct as the women. Moreover, given the progression of the macrochiasm, the description of godly women is now qualified by the overseer: as the lead teacher and governor of the entire congregation—the model of "irreproachable" godliness for men and women—the audience understand that the women's missional behavior is the direct outworking of the overseer's—and thus his wife's—example.³⁴

32. Cochran, *As Though It Were Actually True*, 214: "Adam's response should have been to bring her before God and offer Him his own life in place of his wife's—not to follow her into sin. This is the love Christ shows to His Church."

33. It may be worth noting that Eve's role to follow Adam's loving lead equally corresponds to Paul's statement in Ephesians: "Wives, submit to your own husbands, as to the Lord" (5:22, *ESV*), that is, to the Lord "who gave-over himself on behalf of her" (5:25). Here, then, the clear implication of God's design for Eve to follow Adam's lead in 1 Timothy 2:13—and thus for women in the church to follow the teaching and governing of men in the church (2:12)—is not in any way misogynistic, subjugating, or demeaning (contra Bufe, *Provocations*, 79). Rather, Paul's point in Ephesians 5 and 1 Timothy 2:12–13 is that God's design for men is to exhibit sacrificial love—as evidenced by Jesus Christ—and for women to receive the benefits of such leadership—as evidenced by the church.

34. Payne interprets this as evidence that the "qualifications for the office of overseer apply to women as well as to men. First Timothy mentions verbal or conceptual parallels to each of the overseer requirements in passages specifically regarding women.

The first quality that the audience hear in the "b" sub-element is that the overseer is to be "temperate" (νηφάλιον)—not given to excesses but marked by sobriety in thought and decision. The term is referring neither to a general sense of balance nor to a specific sense of moderation in the use of wine, although the connotation of the former is more accurate than the latter. To be sure, Towner is correct in stating that the "overseer is to maintain command of his reason, to be watchful and observant of things going on around him, and balanced in his assessments."[35] But this still begs the question of what framework or standard Paul has in mind when using the term. The context of what has come before makes clear that to be "temperate" has in view the framework of God's saving activity in Christ Jesus's entrance into the world to give himself as a ransom (1:5; 2:6).[36] That is, the building progression of the macrochiasm pushes forward "the gospel" (1:11), namely that "Christ Jesus came into the world to save sinners" (1:15), that God "desires all humans to be-saved," and that such salvation was accomplished and freely offered by the one human mediator Christ Jesus "who gave himself as a ransom on behalf of all" (2:4–6). It is in this framework that the overseer is to be "temperate"—sober in his interpretation of events that surround him.[37] In short, the gospel-framework concerning

---

Close to half of these parallels use nearly identical terminology... These show that in Paul's thinking at the time he writes this letter, these qualifications not only can, but in fact do, apply to women" (*Man and Woman*, 449). While Payne's literary observations are apt, the conclusion does not seem to follow the leadership qualifications that are grounded in creation and established in the immediately preceding microchiasm (see volume 1, chapter 4 regarding 1 Tim 2:13).

35. Towner, *PE*, 251. Marshall, *PE*, 478: "most commentators hold that the word has the broader metaphorical sense of sober-mindedness or sound judgment." See Knight, *PE*, 159; MacArthur, *1 & 2 Tim*, 35; Merkle, *Why Elders?*, 73.

36. In full, this framework has at its opposite ends the first and second coming of Christ; see 1:15 in tandem with 6:14. This framework is also made explicit in Titus 2:11–13; see Jeon, *To Exhort and Reprove*, 76–82.

37. The qualifications here in 1 Timothy 3 are similar or nearly identical to the Greco-Roman virtue and vice lists that would have been recognizable to Paul's audience (see e.g., Thielman, *Theology of the New Testament*, 420–21; Wilson, *Pauline Parallels*, 414; Thatcher, "Deacon in the Pauline Church," 59). Ho comments: "most of the qualities are general ethical virtues valued in Greco-Roman society and are in themselves not particularly Christian ... the positive and negative traits are found in typical lists of virtues and vices ... The convergence of the leadership traits prescribed in 1 Tim 3:1–7 with the values of the wider society stem from an underlying concern for credibility and respectability vis-à-vis those outside the church" ("Mission in the PE," 252). This rightly captures the forward missional movement from the second microchiasm (2:1–15); however, it is too limiting to conclude that Paul's concern is to assimilate with Greco-Roman culture. To be sure, Paul's fundamental concern is "godliness" (2:2, 10)—a lifestyle that accords with the realm "in faith." Secondarily and as a corollary, a godly lifestyle will be credible and respectable to those not "in faith."

Christ Jesus, as it is contained in Paul's sound teaching, must command, shape, and guide the overseer's reasoning, sensitivities, and assessments.[38] Significantly, as the teacher and governor of the congregation, undoubtedly the "temperate" overseer will lead and influence the godly men and women to view all of life in the same framework. For the benefit of all, the audience are to look for godly men whose minds are fully saturated in the gospel and who, in turn, express "gospel-temperance" in their actions and pursuits.

The next quality that Paul lists in the "b" sub-element is "self-controlled" (σώφρονα), which would likely be the materialization of the overseer's temperance. The occurrences of the cognate "self-control" (σωφροσύνης) in 2:9 and 2:15 of the A' element within the second microchiasm make clear that Paul is not merely concerned with observable behavior that would have been acceptable to the surrounding Greco-Roman community. Rather, in the second microchiasm, Paul describes the missional calling of the church: men and women are to conduct themselves in a manner that will attract all people to the one God who desires all humans to be-saved (2:4) and to the one mediator Christ Jesus who gave himself as a ransom on their behalf so they could be-saved (2:5). Specifically, the women's participation in this calling is displayed in the way they cosmetic themselves with "self-control"—paying careful attention to their apparel, that is, their lifestyle in accordance to what is proper for their role as godly women "in faith." Having this in the background, the audience hear the term "self-controlled" applied to the overseer as a summons to focus on missional living in accordance to what is proper for his role as a godly man "in faith." In effect, Paul raises the following question to the audience: does the aspiring overseer reflect a lifestyle that communicates—especially through his actions—a commitment to God's mission to save all people through the one mediator Christ Jesus? Such a man is qualified to lead the missional household of God.

As with "self-controlled," the next term "cosmopolitan" (κόσμιον) recalls the earlier reference "cosmopolitan" (κοσμίῳ) in 2:9 of the A' element within the second microchiasm, wherein Paul instructs the women in the audience to consider whether their manner of dress is appropriate as those who profess godliness. Such was a call to modesty for the missional purpose of attracting others to Christ and—being unhindered by luxurious spending—of devoting their attention, efforts, and resources to good works (2:10).

---

38. The sense of balance that Paul is speaking of is perhaps best illustrated in his instructions in 1 Thessalonians 4:13–14, where he informs believers not to grieve like those who do not have hope. Paul is not suggesting here a form of asceticism, as if believers should not cry when tragedy hits. Rather, even their weeping must be tempered in view of "Christ Jesus our hope" (1:1), that is, controlled by what Christ has done on their behalf, namely securing freedom and salvation from sin (1:15; 2:6).

Applied to the overseer, then, the nuance of the adjective "cosmopolitan" appears to focus on a man's tangible possessions in distinction to his "temperate" thought-processes and his "self-controlled" conduct. Furthermore, the term takes on a specific missional connotation as the macrochiasm pushes the concern for "all humans to be-saved" (2:4a) from the second microchiasm into the third microchiasm. The question Paul's audience are to consider, especially the women who have just received explicit instructions in regard to being "cosmopolitan"—respectably fitting with his role as overseer—is whether the aspiring overseer's acquisitions or "spending habits" align with his missional leadership of the congregation. A man who lives modestly—along with the resultant example of his wife—is capable of leading all godly women to do what is proper, namely the missional "child-parenting" of new believers "in faith" (2:15).

Paul further specifies that an overseer must be hospitable, "affectionate-of-stranger" (φιλόξενον)—a compound term of the adjective "affection" (φίλος) and the noun "stranger" (ξένος).[39] The reference may have in mind Genesis 18:1–8, where Abraham shows abounding hospitality to three traveling men,[40] but this was also a common practice in Hellenistic culture.[41] Yet, again, Paul has more in view than meeting the surrounding Greco-Roman standard.[42] Rather, it undoubtedly was evidence of a personal experience of the gospel by which God is affectionate toward the stranger—but much more, toward a blasphemer, persecutor, and hubristic-person (1:13).[43] An overseer who evidences a generous disposition is a man who displays the gospel in a concrete measure to all.[44] Still, hospitality

---

39. Not at all contrasting this translation, Koenig aptly nuances its scope: "*philoxenia*, the term for hospitality used in the New Testament, refers literally not to a love of strangers per se but to a delight in the whole guest-host relationship" (*New Testament Hospitality*, 8). Ibid., 13 n. 7: "*Philoxenia* is an intensification of the basic noun that stresses the love of or attraction to hospitality (see Rom. 12:13; Heb. 13:2). *Philoxenos*, its adjectival form, has the same connotation (see 1 Tim. 3:2; Titus 1:8; 1 Pet. 4:9)."

40. Jipp, *Hospitality to Strangers*, 134: "we see that Abraham does considerably more than provide water and bread for the guests . . . That Abraham's hospitality is ideal and proper is indicated by the haste with which Abraham prepares the meal and the generous amount of food offered." See also Genesis 19:1–3.

41. See O'Gorman, "Dimensions of Hospitality," 20–22.

42. Belleville, "1 Tim," 69: "the church cultivated hospitality, thereby distinguishing it from the rugged individualism and popular stoic philosophy of the surrounding culture."

43. Ngewa, *1 & 2 Tim*, 63: "this [open] house is simply the outward manifestation of an open heart." That hospitality is to be seen as a common Christian duty, see Marshall, *PE*, 478; Knight, *PE*, 159.

44. The qualification to love showing hospitality to strangers certainly does not

was all the more necessary for the proper functioning of God's missional household;[45] in Acts there are multiple instances when Paul and his companions depended on the kind provision of converts (e.g., Acts 16:15; 21:7; 28:14).[46] The term "affectionate-of-stranger," therefore, not only has in view a giving disposition but also a reception of traveling missionaries—his very own home thus being the model missional household. For the audience, a man whom they regard as generous with his time, resources, and home is qualified and capable of leading God's entire household to be missionally "affectionate-of-stranger"—a house that warmly welcomes all and supports its itinerant workers.[47]

As the "b" sub-element concludes, the audience hear the complementary nature and forward progression of all the qualifications: stemming from his "temperate" gospel-thinking that results in missional "self-controlled" conduct, an overseer is marked by a modest "cosmopolitan" living that frees up his resources to use for the benefit of others because he is "affectionate-of-stranger."

1 Timothy 3:2c: Able-to-Teach

("c" sub-element)

The pivot "c" sub-element of the minichiasm (3:2c) centers and hinges upon the qualification "able-to-teach."[48] The adjective "able-to-teach" (διδακτικόν) highlights a sustained movement throughout the entire macrochiasm. In the first microchiasm, the A and A' elements established Paul's

---

require wealth. Trebilco, *Early Christians in Ephesus*, 410 n. 34: "We also note that one of the qualifications looked for in an overseer was that they were hospitable (φιλόξενος; 1 Tim 3:2; Tit 1:8). This might suggest that the person had to have some financial means, but we should beware of thinking that only the rich can be hospitable and clearly poorer people can also demonstrate hospitality . . . It is therefore not an indicator of wealth."

45. Quinn, *Letter*, 90–91.

46. Denaux, "Stranger on Earth," 91: "In the Book of Acts, the Early Christian mission is often performed within a network of hospitality: evangelists wandering about in Meditarranean areas receive hospitality in local churches . . . and prosperous Christians place their houses at the disposal of the local churches for their meetings."

47. Belleville, "1 Tim," 69: "the church cultivated hospitality, thereby distinguishing it from the rugged individualism and popular stoic philosophy of the surrounding culture." Ngewa, *1 & 2 Tim*, 64: "A hospitable overseer spreads a spirit of hospitality, so that hospitality is also offered by the members of the congregation."

48. Smith, *Pauline Communities*, 74: "Outside the NT, the adjective διδακτικός is found only in Philo, in relation to Abraham's moral excellence 'attained by means of teaching.' Within the NT it occurs twice as a predicative adjective, regarding qualifications of leaders within the Christian community (1 Tim. 3:2; 2 Tim. 2:24)."

firm concern related to teaching: Timothy must charge "some" not "to teach-different" (ἑτεροδιδασκαλεῖν, 1:3), namely "some" who are desiring to be "law-teachers" (νομοδιδάσκαλοι) though not understanding either what they-are-saying or regarding some-things they-are-insisting (1:7); indeed, they are teaching "some-thing different" that lies-opposed to "the sound teaching (διδασκαλίᾳ)" of the apostle Paul (1:10b). In the second microchiasm, Paul highlighted that he himself was divinely appointed as a "teacher" (διδάσκαλος) of the Gentiles in faith and truth (2:7), namely concerning the inclusive message of salvation—the testimony that Christ Jesus gave himself as a ransom on behalf of all (2:6). As the authorized teacher "in faith" (2:7) to bring-about "the household-law of God in faith" (1:4), Paul instructs from Genesis what is proper for men and women living in God's household, specifying that women are not "to teach" (διδάσκειν) nor to govern a man (2:14). The implicit call for men to teach in the second microchiasm, then, is made explicit in the third microchiasm where the audience hear Paul declare that a man who oversees the congregation must be "able-to-teach" (διδακτικόν, 3:2). The cumulative effect of the overall macrochiasm upon the audience underscores not only the importance of teaching but specifically what is taught and who is teaching. That is, the phrase "able-to-teach" conveys a dual qualification for an aspiring overseer: positively, it is meant to identify and qualify a person whose teaching is in line with Paul's (1:10; 2:7) and who is a man (2:12–13); negatively, it is meant to identify and disqualify a person whose teaching is not in line with Paul's (1:3, 7, 10)—man or woman (2:12, 14). In other words, the qualified overseer is a person who not only has "come to a knowing-embrace of truth" (2:4b)—a life a godliness that accords with the realm "in faith"—but also has specifically embraced Paul's teaching "in faith and truth" (2:7)—all of "the sound teaching" and none of "some-thing different" (1:10b).

As the macrochiasm has conveyed, when a person accepts Paul's teaching, they accept the person who appointed him and whom he represents, Christ Jesus (1:1, 12); the opposite applies, too: a rejection of Paul's teaching is a rejection of Christ. To be sure, only a man who accepts Paul's teaching is "able-to-teach" the men and women in the congregation about the testimony concerning Christ Jesus and what it means to live "in faith" (1:2, 4; 2:7, 15), that is, "in Christ" (1:14). Rather than ability, skill, or talent, the audience understand that Paul has allegiance in view—to him and, therefore, to Christ Jesus. Significantly, therefore, Paul's statement here in the pivot "c" sub-element of the minichiasm concerning overseers would be heard as a sustained polemic against "some" who "teach-different" (1:3), "some" who teach "some-thing different" that lies-opposed to "the sound teaching" with which Paul was counted-faithful (1:10b) and to which Paul was appointed as a "teacher" (2:7), "some" who have turned-aside from a without-hypocrisy faith (1:5–6), and "some" who—by rejecting faith—regarding the faith have become-shipwrecked (1:19). The rhetorical force of the qualification for an overseer is clear: "some" in the Ephesian church are not "able-to-teach" and should not be overseers.

As the minichiasm has moved the audience toward and now around the pivot "c" sub-element, they have no doubts about who is qualified to oversee and bring-about the household-law of God in faith. On the one hand, the simple rejection of Paul's teaching renders all people unable to teach the congregation. On the other hand, the acceptance of Paul's teaching—Christ's teaching—does not render all men able-to-teach but only a man whose life is irreproachable, whose wife is nourished with his sacrificial love, who thinks of the gospel at all times, who is missional in all circumstances, who is modest with his possessions so that what he has may benefit others, and who aligns himself with the sound teaching of the divinely appointed teacher, Paul. Only this man is "able-to-teach."

1 Timothy 3:3: Irreproachable in the Negative Sense

("b'" sub-element)

Having reached the pivot, the "b'" sub-element of the minichiasm moves the audience forward by contrasting the qualities of the parallel "b" sub-element: "not addicted-to-wine, not violent; rather kind, without-fighting, without-affection-of-money" (3:3). The twice-repeated emphasis of the negative particle "not" (μή) recalls its earlier occurrences in the first microchiasm in association with the activities of the false teachers who are "not (μή) to teach-different" (1:3), "nor (μηδέ) to hold-toward myths and genealogies without-limit" (1:4), "not (μή) understanding either (μήτε) what they-are-saying or (μήτε) regarding some-things they-are-insisting" (1:7), and might learn "not" (μή) to blaspheme (1:20). Here, then, the audience most likely understand that Paul is identifying and using the false teachers in Ephesus as a deliberate contrast against men who are qualified overseers. Furthermore, the audience hear obvious conceptual echoes of the "b" sub-element expressed negatively. Paralleling how the aspiring overseer must be "temperate," having his mind controlled by the gospel—God's desire to save all humans (2:4a) and Christ Jesus's activity to save sinners (1:15; 2:6)—he is therefore to be "not addicted-to-wine" (μὴ πάροινον)—not controlled by wine. Thus, similar to the audience's understanding of "temperate" in the "b" sub-element, they might hear 3:3 of the parallel "b'" sub-element as a negative restatement of Paul's concern for the aspiring overseer to avoid devotion to anything other than the gospel. Yet, given both the progression from the preceding A' element of the second microchiasm into the A element of the third microchiasm, as well as the movement of the 3:1–5 minichiasm around the pivot "c" sub-element, most likely the audience hear that Paul is not restating the same point but is qualifying it: the phrase "not addicted-to-wine" is referring specifically to an overseer's drunkenness as a hindrance to what is proper for godly men and women and thus a hindrance to the missional calling of God's household.[49] Notably, then, Paul is not stating that a qualified overseer is to "to avoid wine" or "to not drink wine"; rather, the clear focus of the qualification is imbibing wine in excess and repeatedly.[50] As the model and leader for the entire congregation, an overseer leads all people toward the same end; in order for the godly men and women in the audience to be led in gospel-thinking, they understand that it is necessary, therefore, for an overseer to be "not addicted-to-wine." Furthermore, in the same way that "temperate" gospel-thinking in the "b" sub-element began an interconnected chain of ensuing missional behavior, so too does Paul's specification "not addicted-to-wine" in the parallel "b" sub-element begin an interconnected chain of ungodly behavior.[51]

Paul goes on to state that the overseer is to be "not violent." The audience hear several connections. First, an association between the terms "not addicted-to-wine" (μὴ πάροινον) and "not violent" (μὴ πλήκτην) would be heard as intentional, given the repetition of the negative particle "not" (μή). Second, therefore, understood as a negative coupled pair in the "b" sub-element, "not addicted-to-wine" and "not violent" would be heard in relation to the positive coupled pair in the parallel "b" sub-element: just as an overseer's "temperate" quality is expressed in his missional "self-control," so too "not addicted-to-wine" is expressed by being "not violent." An overseer's commitment to avoid drunkenness is therefore demonstrated by the absence of violence.[52] The term "violent" (πλήκτην), especially in connection with the term "addicted-to-wine" (πάροινον), indicates a pugnacious,

---

49. Knight, *PE*, 160: "The parallel tips the scales in favor of this literal meaning over a figurative interpretation." In a missional setting, drunkenness may have been unnattractive to the surrounding Greco-Roman community; see Cook, *Alcohol, Addiction, and Christian Ethics*, 37; Jamir, *Exclusion and Judgment*, 18–20.

50. See below regarding 3:8; see also discussion in volume 3, chapter 2 regarding 1 Timothy 5:23.

51. Cook *Alcohol, Addiction, and Christian Ethics*, 48: "the association of drunkenness with other items in some of the lists may be taken as suggesting that the author (usually Paul) was concerned with the problems and vices to which drunkenness leads."

52. See Marshall, *PE*, 162.

confrontational person who has filled himself with too much alcohol.[53] Yet, given the movement of macrochiasm's polemical tone toward the false teachers into the current minichiasm, "violent" may also allude to "some" who do not bring-about the household-law of God in faith but rather bring-about controversial-speculations (1:3–4), and "some" who have turned-aside from a pure heart, good conscience, and a without-hypocrisy faith and are thus without love (1:5–6). In other words, "someone" (3:1) who is "violent" (3:3) quite aptly describes "some" who have no love, no concept of family, nor any concept of faith. In effect, then, the audience hear a dual sense of the "b'" sub-element: not only are qualified overseers described in negative terms— "not violent"—but also the unqualified, false-teaching overseers are identified in positive terms—"violent."[54] The reverse applies to the qualifications listed in the parallel "b" sub-element. To be sure, as much as the audience are to understand the positive qualifications of an overseer, Paul wants his audience to equally identify the qualifications of a false-teaching overseer: "someone" who is not irreproachable, not nourishing his wife with sacrificial love, not gospel-thinking, not missional, not moderate nor generous with his possessions, not able-to-teach.

At this point in the "b'" sub-element, the audience hear the abrupt statement "rather kind, without-fighting, without-affection-of-money." The disjunction "rather" (ἀλλά) likely has the force "much rather." Combined with the next two terms Paul intends a contrast to the immediately preceding quality.[55] That is, much rather than merely being "not violent," it is necessary for an aspiring overseer to be actively "kind, without-fighting" (ἐπιεικῆ ἄμαχον). The first term "kind" (ἐπιεικῆ) connotes patience and occurs in the OT to describe God's forbearance (e.g., Ps 86:5).[56] Such a theologically rich term undoubtedly recalls for the audience God's response of gracious, patient kindness not only toward Paul who was formerly a blasphemer, persecutor, and hubristic-person (1:12–13) but also toward all among the audience who have themselves experienced the same grace as fellow believers of "our" hope and Lord Christ Jesus (1:1, 2, 12). Paul's implication would not be unclear: for any aspiring overseer who professes to know such kindness from God—the salvific blessings of grace and mercy

---

53. Ibid., 479.

54. See discussion in volume 3, chapter 2 regarding 1 Timothy 5:1: "do not (μή) rebuke-violently (ἐπιπλήξῃς)."

55. See Knight, *PE*, 160. Contra Ngewa, *1 & 2 Tim*, 65: "The presence of the word *but* after the words 'not violent' suggest that this characteristic should be linked to gentleness, the characteristic that follows it, not the one that precedes it."

56. Psalm 86:5 *ESV*: "For you, O Lord, are good and forgiving (ἐπιεικής), abounding in steadfast love to all who call upon you."

(1:2, 13, 14, 16)—it is necessary for him to substantiate his claim by being "kind," that is, showing patience and forgiveness toward others. At the same time, then, its absence would convey an association with "some." Due to the parallel "b" sub-element, the audience may hear the term as giving further voice to the man's wife, who better than anyone could vouch for or discredit his "kind," daily fidelity toward her. Moreover, heard in parallel to the term "cosmopolitan," the audience would understand that it is necessary for an overseer not only to have experienced God's kindness but also to missionally cosmetic himself with kindness toward all. Such a man would be qualified to teach and govern the godly men and women in God's kind, missional household by his daily example.

The second term of the pair, "without-fighting" (ἄμαχον), connotes a person who is peaceable and not quarrelsome.[57] This certainly aligns with the peaceful, godly behavior of both the entire congregation (2:2) and the men (2:8) in the second microchiasm. Yet, given the polemic in the minichiasm, the audience would likely hear a subtle reference to "some" whose teachings bring-about controversial-speculations—a lack of solidarity and unison—rather than the single, unified household-law of God in faith (1:3–4). Still, the overall progression of the macrochiasm undoubtedly indicates that the apostle is not suggesting that future overseers should never engage in controversy. Rather, the audience recall the A' element of the first microchiasm in which Paul makes clear directly to Timothy and indirectly to the audience that they are to war the commendable war specifically against "some" who teach-different (1:18). In other words, the man "without-fighting" in view here is not to be equated with a man without any convictions. To be sure, the progression of the macrochiasm removes any uncertainty: the God-appointed apostle Paul (1:1, 12; 2:7) affirms and commends that sound teaching (1:10)—the gospel (1:11)—concerning Christ Jesus and the salvation of sinners (1:15)—all humans (2:4a, 6)—is not only worth defending but must be defended (1:18). In light of the cumulative impact of the 3:1–5 minichiasm concerning overseers, the audience understand that the quality "without-fighting" is a descriptor of a "temperate" man who, being controlled by the fundamental concern of the gospel, is able to distinguish between primary and secondary matters—what is worth a war and what is not—and thus avoid needless, meaningless, divisive controversies (1:4). Significantly, then, in the immediately preceding A' element of the second microchiasm, the audience heard Paul address and engage the matter of women teaching the congregation (2:11–14). As the macrochiasm advances into the A element of the third microchiasm, what becomes clear to the

---

57. See Marshall, *PE*, 479; Knight, *PE*, 160.

audience is that the apostle distinguished it as a primary matter concerning the gospel: Christ Jesus came into the world (1:15) as a result of a man abdicating his responsibility to teach and to govern (2:13–14). In other words, where the proper roles that would enable women to "remain in faith" (2:15) are challenged, Christ Jesus and the salvation he effected—the gospel—are challenged. To preserve the sound teaching and promote godliness as God's missional household, therefore, the audience understand that an overseer must be willing to lead the entire congregation in defense of the teaching that Christ Jesus himself taught to Paul.[58]

The "b'" sub-element concludes with the term "without-affection-of-money" (3:3). The term "without-affection-of-money" (ἀφιλάργυρον) highlights its linguistic contrast to "affection-of-stranger" (φιλόξενον) in the parallel "b" sub-element. In effect, the parallel symmetry brings into focus the question of the overseer's affections: is he generously affectionate toward the stranger and use his resources upon them, or is he generously affectionate toward his resources? Furthermore, echoing Jesus's own teaching that no person can simultaneously serve and love two masters (Matt 6:24; Luke 16:13), the parallelism in the "b" and "b'" sub-elements calls the audience not only to examine *what* but also *whom* the overseer serves. That is, a qualified overseer who is "without-affection-of-money" is not only "affectionate-of-stranger" but, in effect, is positively "affectionate-of-Christ." Thus the audience understand that Paul's concern is not about money itself—as though it were evil.[59] Rather, the full picture conveyed by the minichiastic movement is whether or not the aspiring overseer exemplifies a love for Christ, namely by sharing the Savior God's missional affection for all strangers to-be-saved, that is, by tangibly demonstrating his affection

---

58. The relevance of Paul's discussion about qualified men for an overseer to Paul's prohibition in 2:12 for women not to teach nor to govern a man in church cannot go unnoticed. That is, as the apostolic teacher appointed to service by Christ Jesus and by the command of God (1:1; 12; 2:7), Paul clearly would expect his audience to both accept his teaching—Christ and God's teaching—and defend it against attacks. Regarding the response of the women in Paul's audience, Cochran's comments are helpful: "If one imagines she is being called to something to which God has already said no, she is wrong—it is as simple as that. It does not matter if it ends up 'working out' or if it brings about any great things . . . Unlike God, Christians are not in the business of bringing about anything, but rather are in the business of loving God with all our hearts, minds, and souls regardless of the consequences. One cannot love Him with all her mind if she uses her mind to ignore or explain away what He has told her" (*As Though It Were Actually True*, 207). Ultimately, Paul intends for his audience to understand that they live within "the household-law *of God*" (1:3)—not *of humans*. Those "in faith," therefore, submit to God the Father's loving, familial leadership (1:2) and to Christ Jesus's sacrificial Lordship (1:2, 15; 2:6).

59. See also discussion in volume 3, chapter 3 regarding 1 Timothy 6:10.

through his generous use of money. Still, given the sustained polemic, the audience likely hear an implicit description of the false-teaching overseers in Ephesus: "some" are not "without-affection-of-money" precisely because they are "without-love-of-Christ."[60]

1 Timothy 3:4–5: Leading His Household and Knowing How to Lead

("a'" sub-element)

The concluding "a'" sub-element of the minichiasm (3:4–5) begins by moving the audience toward the climactic qualification for an overseer to be "leading his own household commendably" (3:4). Several observations are worth noting. First, the term "household" (οἴκου) recalls "household-law" (οἰκονομίαν) in the first microchiasm, wherein Paul has in view the familial aspect of the entire congregation "in faith" (1:4). Thus as the macrochiasm progresses into the third microchiasm, the audience are to understand that Paul has the realm "in faith" in mind. Second, however, the audience hear a distinction between the scope of the two households: in the first microchiasm, it is the household-law "of God" (θεοῦ, 1:4) while in the third microchiasm, it is a man's "own" (ἰδίου, 3:4) household. That is, not only are the audience to understand that the two households are inseparably related but also that a qualified overseer's relationship specifically with his "own" household impacts his qualifications within the household "of God."[61] Third, accordingly, a man's relationship with his "own" household is defined by whether or not he is "leading . . . commendably." The notion of a household in the first century would refer not only to the overseer's wife and children but also to his slaves, property, and significant relationships

---

60. Given the historical situation in Ephesus recorded in Acts 19, it is worth noting the contextual significance of Paul's word choice here in 1 Timothy. Where the riot in Ephesus was caused by those who clearly did not worship God—namely, a "silversmith" (ἀργυροκόπος) who made temple "silver" (ἀργυροῦς)" for the worship of Artemis (Acts 19:24)—Paul's specification that a qualified overseer is "without-affection-of-money" (ἀφιλάργυρον, 3:3)—literally, "without-affection-of-silver"—would likely be highly meaningful to the Ephesian audience. As was Demetrius's motivation in Acts 19, Paul may be underscoring that the false teachers's motivation is for "abundant-prosperity" (Acts 19:25). See discussion in volume 1, chapter 1. See esp. volume 3, chapter 3 (1 Tim 6:5, 9, 10, 17).

61. Indeed the priority of the overseer's "own household" is hinted at by the sequence of Paul's words, literally, "his own household commendably leading " (τοῦ ἰδίου οἴκου καλῶς προϊστάμενον). Where the grammatical arrangement of the phrase is not necessary, it therefore seems intentional.

that would have impacted the reputation and well-being of the household.⁶² Thus by Paul's use of the term "leading" (προϊστάμενον), the audience would hear the emphasis on the overseer's ability to apply his teaching and governing over a myriad of responsibilities in an effective manner—"leading," therefore, would connote the sense of "effective managing."⁶³ Moreover, Paul's specification that an aspiring overseer's leading at home must be done "commendably" (καλῶς) in the "a'" sub-element would recall Paul's description of the duty of an overseer itself as "a commendable (καλοῦ) work" (3:1) in the parallel "a" sub-element. The audience are to understand the connection: only a man who is leading "commendably" in his own household is qualified to perform the "commendable work" of leading God's household. Still, the movement of the minichiasm into the "a'" sub-element—carrying with it the qualifications in the "b" and "b'" sub-elements—indicates that a qualified overseer is "leading his own household commendably" insofar as his overall leading is "irreproachable" (3:2) in view of the "a," "b," "b'," and now "c'" sub-elements. What is more, as the minichiasm progresses, Paul seems to be further removing an aspiring overseer's own estimation of his qualifications: just as he is qualified by his wife's assessment of his fidelity in 3:2 of the "a" sub-element, so too is he qualified by the assessment of all who live under his leading in 3:4 of the parallel "a'" sub-element.⁶⁴

The concluding "a'" sub-element of the minichiasm ends with a specific example of effective household management: "holding children in submissiveness with all respectability" (3:4). Paul's intention is certainly not to limit

62. Verner, *Houshold of God*, 133; Strobel, "'Hauses,'" 91–100; Towner, *Letters*, 254; Betsworth, *Reign of God*, 28. For more information about slaves in the first-century Greco-Roman setting, see Bartchy, *First-Century Slavery*.

It may be worth noting that although Paul uses familiar Greco-Roman "household" language, there are key differences in Paul's application in 3:4 to an overseer. For example, regarding a man's leadership in relation to his wife, Jeffers notes: "Aristotle says that the husband's rule over the wife is like an aristocracy, because he is more capable to rule and thus superior to her . . . By contrast, the New Testament passages . . . do not assert that the husband is in any way superior to his wife or more capable of making decesions; rather they say that God has put him in this position" (*Greco-Roman World*, 87). To be sure, Paul's application of the "household" is based on 2:13, wherein God—not man—determined the roles of men and women in the household of God (2:8–15) and in their individual households (3:2, 4). Furthermore, even if, as Torjesen suggests, the notion of a household manager in Greco-Roman culture functionally involved women (*When Women Were Priests*, 53–87), Paul does not base the household on a Greco-Roman model but on God's model.

63. See Marshall, *PE*, 480.

64. MacArthur's balanced observations are worth noting: while affirming that "the issue is not the elder's martital status" in view of 3:2, in view of 3:4 he comments that "issues of divorce should be related to this matter. A divorced man gives no evidence of a well-managed home . . ." (*1 & 2 Tim*, 35–36).

the assessment of effective management to this criterion. Nevertheless, the participle phrase "holding children in submissiveness with all respectability" expresses a measure of an overseer's leadership qualification and echoes for the audience several important themes.[65] First, in 1:2 and 1:18 of the first microchiasm, Timothy is identified as "child" (τέκνῳ, 1:2; τέκνον, 1:18) in relation to Paul; notably, Paul has in view the familial realm "in faith" (1:2, 4), that is, in the realm where Christ Jesus is considered to be "our Lord" (1:2, 12). In the second microchiasm, Paul—the teacher "in faith" (2:7)—instructs the women in the audience that their missional activity to bring new people into God's household—"child-parenting" (τεκνογονίας)—is evidence that they themselves are remaining "in faith" (2:15), that is, in God's household. Thus as the macrochiasm progresses into the third microchiasm, the necessity for an overseer "holding children (τέκνα) in submissiveness" (3:4) is undoubtedly connected with the realm "in faith." Yet, the nuance that the "children" here belong to an overseer's "own household" (3:4) intends a distinction: in the same way that the leading of his "own" household informs the way in which he would lead the household "of God" (1:4), the submissiveness of his own children to his leadership informs the way that the children of God's household "in faith" will respond to his leadership.

Second, then, the prepositional phrase "in submissiveness" (ἐν ὑποταγῇ, 3:4) recalls the tranquil disposition in which women in the church are to learn "in all submissiveness" (ἐν πάσῃ ὑποταγῇ) (2:11) in the immediately preceding A' element of the second microchiasm. Thus in the third microchiasm, "in submissiveness" highlights for the audience that an aspiring overseer's children are to learn from his teaching in the same way as missional women who profess godliness remain "in faith" (2:10, 15). Yet also—and perhaps more significantly—that his children are "in submissiveness" demonstrates their admiration for his teaching and governing. In a word, a qualified aspiring overseer is held in high regard in his own household—the implication being that if his own children do not follow his

---

65. Given Paul's discussion in the previous microchiasm—particularly his discussion on the proper relations between men and women in view of God's creational design (2:12–13)—it is surprising that some commentators take the language here almost exclusively as Paul's appropriation of the Greco-Roman cultural norms of his time (e.g., Towner, *Letters*, 255; Tellbe, *Christ-Believers in Ephesus*, 162–63). To be sure, MacDonald rightly observes the missional importance of "upholding values cherished by Greco-Roman society . . . [as a] means of stabilizing relations with that society and protecting the vision of universal salvation" (*Pauline Churches*, 214); yet, it seems to be too limiting to conclude that only "the Greco-Roman household provided important leadership patterns for the organization of the community" (ibid., 220). While indeed it may be that the language and instruction here in 3:4 reflects the Greco-Roman cultural norms, Paul has already made clear that his perspective stems from the creational norms of God's doing (2:13).

teaching, it is expected that neither will the children of God's household "in faith" (1:4). The audience are called to examine the conduct of an aspiring overseer's children as a measure of his qualification to lead in the teaching and governing of their own conduct.

Third, given the sustained polemic of the overall macrochiasm and the current minichiasm, the participle "holding" (ἔχοντα) would certainly recall for the audience Paul's charge in the first microchiasm for Timothy to war the commendable war by "holding (ἔχων) faith and a good conscience" (1:19). As in the first microchiasm, then, the participle in the third microchiasm connotes holding tightly—to "faith" in 1:19; to "children" in 3:4—specifically amidst the shipwrecking danger of "some" who teach-different and "hold-toward" (προσέχειν) myths and genealogies without-limit, thus bringing about controversial-speculations (1:3–4). The phrase "holding children," then, would be understood as the aspiring overseer's unfailing and irreproachable commitment to both preserve the sound teaching and promote godliness in his own children. As the "aʹ" sub-element of the minichiasm insists, a man such as this would do the same for each and all of the children "in faith." Moreover—and significantly—the audience understand the dual implication of Paul's statement. On the one hand, children "in submissiveness" indicates their allegiance to the qualified overseer and thus to Paul's, that is, Christ's teaching and governing. Conversely, on the other hand, any person not "in submissiveness" to a qualified overseer implies that they are, in fact, not children "in faith," that is, not considering Christ as "our Lord" (1:2, 12). Here, then, it seems that Paul intends for the audience to have in view Timothy—Paul's "child" (1:2, 18)—in stark contrast to "some" who, by their litany of opposing activities throughout the entire macrochiasm, prove themselves to not have any familial relation to Paul. As such, the audience understand that any qualified aspiring overseer will not only align themselves with Paul and Timothy but also, like Paul and Timothy, will join in the preservation of the sound teaching and promotion of the corresponding godliness thereof.

Fourth and finally, it is possible that the audience understand the concluding prepositional phrase "with all respectability" (μετὰ πάσης σεμνότητος) as having multiple implications. On the one hand, it may be heard as a description of the submissive children of an aspiring overseer.[66] On the other hand, the audience may hear it as a description of the way in which the aspiring overseer leads his own children.[67] Yet, given Paul's dual

---

66. In support of this interpretation, the phrase "with all respectability" is in immediate proximity to the term "children" (3:4). See e.g., Fee, *1 & 2 Tim*, 82.

67. In support of this interpretation, the focus of the overall minichiasm pertains to the "irreproachable" qualities an overseer's leadership. See e.g., Belleville, "1 Tim,"

concern throughout the minichiasm about an aspiring overseer's impact upon his own household and ultimately God's household, the audience may very well understand that both are in view: by leading his children "with all respectability," the children in turn will respond to him and live "with all respectability."[68] Moreover, the term "respectability" (σεμνότητος) in 3:4 of the third microchiasm recalls the missional, godly life of "respectability" (σεμνότητι) in 2:2 of the second microchiasm that is expected for all those in the realm "in faith." Thus where "respectability" describes the life of an aspiring overseer and the resulting impact upon his own children, the audience understand that such a man is qualified to oversee and bring about the "respectability" of all children "in faith" (2:2).

The progressive effect of the minichiasm up to this point is worth noting. The "commendable (καλοῦ) work" of an overseer in 3:1 of the "a" sub-element requires a man that is already leading his own household "commendably" (καλῶς), as demonstrated by his wife's experience of his fidelity (3:2) and by his children's submissiveness.[69] The overall message is that leading commendably amounts to exhibiting such respectable, irreproachable authority in the household—mainly in the form of teaching and governing—that his wife and children gladly follow his lead. The apostle's focus is less on wives and children being submissive and more on the man's role in leading his own household commendably. In other words, the audience understand that it is by a man's commendable leadership that his wife and children willingly enable and support him to be their leader.

In light of this, Paul concludes the "a'" sub-element of the minichiasm with a rhetorical question: "but if someone does not know how to lead his own household, how will he care-for the church of God?" (3:5). The question itself is heard as a climactic summary statement of the minichiasm. The phrase "if someone" (εἰ τις) here in 3:5 of the "a'" sub-element recalls Paul's

---

68–69; Marshall, *PE*, 480; Merkle, *Why Elders?*, 71.

68. This appears to be the position taken by Witherington: "The children of the overseer must be 'in order,' or submissive, with all seriousness or respect. Notice that nothing is said about forcing them to submit; rather, it is assumed that the conduct of the family life will be such that the children will be encouraged, and even want, to behave" (*Letters*, 238). Witherington's position, however, may need to be qualified if it is interpreted as a somewhat passive approach to parenting ("nothing is said about forcing them to submit"). The participle "leading" (προϊστάμενον) does not suggest any sort of passivity.

69. The question may arise as to whether a man may be qualified to lead the church if he has no children at home to manage. By analogy, the same may be said regarding a man who does not have a wife. Where fidelity and faithfulness to being a good husband and father are in view, the lack of children does not seem to disqualify a man from the role of an overseer. Still, it cannot be overlooked that Paul considers a man's children to be a proper measure of his qualification to lead the "children" in God's household.

statement in 3:1 of the parallel "a" sub-element: "If someone" (εἴ τις) aspires to overseer." Notably also, Paul's rhetorical use of the conditional phrase "if someone" (εἰ τις) in 3:5 recalls Paul's use of the conditional phrase "if something (εἴ τι) lies-opposed to the sound teaching" in 1:10b. To be sure, given Paul's specific use of "if" (εἴ, 1:10b; εἴ, 3:1) in combination with the rhetorically loaded connotation of the indefinite pronoun cognates "some-thing" and "someone" (τι, 1:10b; τις, 3:1), the audience understand that Paul's consistent use of the formulaic phrase "If someone (εἴ τις)" in 3:5 is also highlighting a situational reality in Ephesus. That is, in the same way that "some" currently teach-different (1:3), "some" have turned-aside for uselesswords (1:6), "someone" does not know how to use the commendable law lawfully (1:8), "some" have become-shipwrecked regarding the faith (1:19), and "someone" aspires—indeed, has already aspired—to overseer (3:1), the implication is that Paul is addressing a situation wherein "someone"—the false teachers—are leading the church of God as overseers but "does not know how to lead his own household" (3:5). Thus as the minichiasm concludes, Paul emphasizes that his description of a qualified overseer is to be understood as a sustained polemic against "some." Paul's point is that while men who are qualified for an overseer will fit the description (3:1-5), "someone" clearly does not. Paul wants his audience to understand that—beyond all certainty—"some" are not qualified to teach and to govern as overseers in the Ephesian church.

What is more, the progression of the minichiasm from the "a" sub-element to the "a'" sub-element has included criteria by which it is made even clearer as to why "some" are disqualified from filling the authoritative position of an overseer. Specifically and most immediately, the polemical statement "if someone" in the "a'" sub-element is heard in the context of "holding children in submissiveness." Given the warring connotation of "holding" (ἔχων, 1:19; ἔχοντα, 3:4) and the association of being "in submissiveness" as being "in faith," the obvious absence of the false teachers's submission to Paul—the overseeing authority and teacher who is qualified by God and by Christ Jesus (1:1, 11, 12; 2:7)—plainly indicates that they themselves are unfit to lead the congregation toward "submissiveness" because—more significantly—they themselves are not "in faith."

Second, the audience hear "does not know (οἶδεν)" in 3:5 of the third microchiasm as an echo of Paul's polemical, declarative statements in 1:8-9 of the first microchiasm, where in contrast to "some" who are desiring to be law-teachers and "someone" who does not know the lawful use of the law (1:7, 8b), Paul states, "But we know (οἴδαμεν) that the law is commendable . . . knowing (εἰδώς) this . . ." In short, "not understanding" (1:7) and not knowing are defining qualities of the false teachers. Implied further is that by not knowing the lawful use of the "commendable" law (1:8), the false-teaching overseers in Ephesus are incapable of knowing how to fulfill "a commendable work" (3:1). Hence, the rhetorical question "how will he care-for the church of God?" is an implicit indictment that "someone" cannot care for the church of God because their ignorance cannot but produce more ignorance, both in their own household and among the men and women in the audience. Furthermore, "to lead his own household" (τοῦ ἰδίου οἴκου προστῆναι) in 3:5 recalls the immediately preceding qualification "leading his own household commendably" (τοῦ ἰδίου οἴκου καλῶς προϊστάμενον) in 3:4. Here, the arrangement of the minichiasm conveys Paul's polemic in full effect. In the "a'" sub-element, wherein the false-teaching overseers are ignorant about how to lead (3:5), they are most definitely incapable of leading commendably (3:4) and thus incapable of fulfilling the commendable work of an overseer according to the parallel "a" sub-element (3:1).

Verse 3:5b concludes the minichiasm by affirming that only a commendable man who has proven to be an effective, commendable leader in his own household is fit to "care-for (ἐπιμελήσεται) the church of God."[70] Such ability to "care-for" the church indicates to the audience that a qualified overseer does not merely teach and govern (2:12) out of principle of the sound teaching (1:10b) but rather oversees and issues charges on the basis of love (1:5)—his whole purpose being to bring-about the household-law of God in faith (1:4).[71] Still, Paul's phrase "the church of God" pushes the minichiasm toward a climactic focus. While the term "church" (ἐκκλησίας) itself refers to those who are literally "called-out," the term "of God" (θεοῦ) indicates that it is the same sustained macrochiastic activity of "God (θεοῦ) our Savior" (1:1), "God (θεοῦ) the Father" (1:2), "the blessed God (θεοῦ)" (1:11), the "only God (θεῷ)" (1:17), "our Savior God (θεοῦ)" (2:3), the "one God (θεός)" (2:5) who has called the audience to be his church. Thus the audience are not only to remember and consider God's unique, saving activity in each of their individual lives but also that collectively, as those

---

70. Towner suggests that the use of a different verb "expands the scope of 'management,' which might be limited to a rather mechanical view of supervision, to include the more compassionate view of 'caring for'" (*Letters*, 256). This may be the case, although it is difficult to imagine how anyone could lead his own household effectively by adopting such a mechanical supervisory approach.

71. The way that overseers are to "care-for" (ἐπιμελήσεται) the church of God is reminiscent of Luke 10:35—"Take care (ἐπιμελήθητι) of him, and whatever more you spend, I will repay you when I come back" (*ESV*)—wherein the context is specifically about love (Luke 10:27). Knight, *PE*, 163: "The personal and thorough care given by the Good Samaritan, the only other NT occurrence of the verb, cannot help but serve as a pattern, even though the contexts differ."

called-out by God, they have been brought "in faith"—the familial realm of "the household-law of God" (1:4). Here, then, the connection between an overseer who is able to lead "his own household" and care-for "the church of God" becomes explicit: overseers and the audience are to view "the church" in the same light as their "own household"—as a family of children (1:2, 19; 2:15; 3:4) with God as the Father, the head of the household (1:2), and with qualified men as appointed overseers to lead the church under God's divine supervision.[72] In this way, Paul's discussion on the qualifications of overseers affords him with an opportunity to strengthen in the minds of the audience how they are to view themselves as "the church"—in relation to one another, to the apostles and qualified leaders, and to God himself. As the audience would care for the repute, health, and leadership of their own households, so now they are summoned to find qualified men—indeed, the qualified men are summoned to step forward—to care for the good repute, health, and leadership of the household of God.[73]

Overall, in the first minichiasm of the third microchiasm—the introductory A element (3:1–5)—Paul provides the audience with a memorable arrangement for discerning qualified men for an overseer. The pivot point for any qualified overseer is his ability to teach ("c" sub-element); his ability to teach is demonstrated by his irreproachable qualities ("b" and "b'" sub-elements); his irreproachable qualities are expressed by his commendable fidelity and leadership in his own household ("a" and "a'" sub-elements). That is, the evidence for a qualified overseer should be readily observable according to the validation of his wife and behavior of his children.

In passing, it may be worthwhile to ask why Paul felt it necessary to include the rhetorical question of verse 3:5. In keeping with the entire minichiasm, it certainly would have a noticeable, dual effect. Negatively, the audience would hear it as an indictment against the false-teaching overseers who were aspiring to lead others while they themselves were refusing to submit to Paul's authority and teaching. Positively, it was heard as a way to bring-about the household-law of God. Yet, the flow of the macrochiasm suggests another purpose. In the preceding A' element of the second microchiasm, Paul's rehearsal of the creation and fall narrative (2:13–14) was a

---

72. Barcley's comments are apt: "This requirement is directly related to the New Testament language for the church as family. A man who does not lead his personal family well will not be able to lead the church family well" ("1 Tim," 367).

73. Merkle captures Paul's point regarding the inseparability of caring for one's one family as a requisite for being qualified to care for God's family: "In addition, by neglecting his family—even for the sake of 'the ministry'—a man can become disqualified to serve as an elder [overseer]. Family life must take precedence over the ministry: God first, family second, ministry third" (*Why Elders?*, 72).

subtle rebuke toward the men for failing to protect the women among them from the deceptive influence of "some." The immediate movement into the A element of the third microchiasm—the 3:1–5 minichiasm—suggests a similar rebuke by the apostle. That anyone among the audience would follow "some" who bring-about controversial-speculations and who have a low view of submission (cf. 2:11; 3:4) to Paul's authority and teaching (1:1, 10b–11, 12; 2:7)—thus a low view of God and Christ Jesus who commanded and appointed Paul (1:1, 12; 2:7)—has severe implications in regard to their salvation. Furthermore, for those in the audience who bear the foremost responsibility—to be sure, the men (2:13)—for accepting unqualified men to lead the church in teaching and governing as overseers, Paul's climactic, rhetorical question in 3:5 would be heard with full effect: had the men in the Ephesian church been more attentive, and had the qualified men in Ephesus actually stepped up to teach and govern the church as overseers—thus to preserve the sound teaching and promote godliness as God's missional household—then the problem of the false-teaching overseers in the Ephesian church would never have gained any traction nor any influence among the men and women in the church of God.

1 Timothy 3:6: Not A Young-Plant, That He Might Not Fall

(B Element)

The B element (3:6) of the third microchiasm moves the audience toward a greater understanding of the household-law of God as Paul continues his multifaceted qualifications of an aspiring overseer, adding the negative qualification: "Not a young-plant." The term "young-plant" (νεόφυτον) would not only connote a person who recently converted to Christianity but also, therefore, a person who has not had time to mature in their faith upon Christ."[74] Given the second microchiasm's climactic emphasis on missional activity of "child-parenting" by women "in faith" (2:15)—conversions of new believers—and given the "household" context in the prior verse (3:5), the term "young-plant" (3:6) would carry the sense of, "a young child

---

74. See Marshall, *PE*, 482. The term occurs in LXX Isaiah 5:7.
It may be worth noting that two other words in 1 Timothy 3:5–6 (οἴκου and κρίμα) seem to find an allusion to the same OT text: "For the vineyard of the LORD of hosts is the house (οἶκος) of Israel, and the men of Judah are his pleasant planting (νεόφυτον); and he looked for justice (κρίσιν), but behold, bloodshed; for righteousness, but behold, an outcry" (Isaiah 5:7 *ESV*). In the case that Paul intentionally references Isaiah 5:7, it seems likely that Paul has God's judgment for unfaithfulness in the background.

in faith." Paul's point would be apparent to the audience: such newly born children into the realm "in faith," that is, within God's familial household, are not yet mature enough to lead or care-for the entire church of God (3:5) and, therefore, should not be considered for an overseer, even if he aspires to it (3:1).[75] Simultaneously, the positive implication of Paul's statement is that there are, in fact, older, mature men "in faith" who are not only capable to lead and care-for the church of God but also to specifically lead, care-for, and nurture these "young-plant" children "in faith" so that their roots can grow deep.[76] Given the sustained polemic against "some" who are unqualified, false-teaching overseers in the Ephesian church, Paul's stipulation here would not only have been responsive and corrective but also remedial and preventative. In short, Paul's implication is that "some" are young-plants whose roots "in faith" have not had enough time to grow deep and ground them in the sound teaching concerning Christ Jesus. Moreover, as much as Paul is addressing a real problem among the church in Ephesus, he clearly intends to draw the audience's attention—particularly qualified, mature men in the Ephesian church—toward resolving it.

Continuing the B element, the apostle Paul further explains the purpose for why Timothy and the audience should refrain from selecting a young-plant for an overseer: "that he might not—being-puffed-up—fall into the condemnation of the devil" (3:6). While the phrase "that he might not" (ἵνα μή) seems to convey a possibility, namely the negative outcome of what will happen if the audience enable "a young-plant" to aspire to an overseer, the sustained implication of Paul's letter is that he is addressing an actual, present reality in the Ephesian church. Indeed, given that the negative particle "not" (μή) recalls its prior occurrences and association with "some" who are negatively engaged in the church (1:3, 4, 7, 20), the implication strongly suggests not only that the current false teachers are in view but also that Paul is using them as specific examples of an unqualified overseer. Indeed, where the phrase "that he might not" (ἵνα μή) here in 3:6 recalls Hymenaeus and Alexander whom Paul had given-over to Satan "that they might . . . not" (ἵνα . . . μή) blaspheme in 1:20, the audience understand that Paul's statement in 3:6 is a reference to a current situation.

---

75. The sense is that "a young-plant" does not have deep-rooted faith (Ngewa, *1 & 2 Tim*, 69). Gench aptly describes the connotation as "'seedlings' still searching for roots" (*Faithful Disagreement*, 92).

76. Marshall, *PE*, 482: "This requirement presupposes that the church has been in existence for a few years." Schreiner, "Overseeing," 99: "The churches in Ephesus had been established for some time, and hence recent converts should not be selected as leaders." Recall that the Ephesian church was about ten years old (e.g., Belleville, "1 Tim" 12, 69; Ngewa, *1 Tim*, 69) and possibly even fifteen years old (e.g., Merkle, "Biblical Qualifications for Elders," 255).

In this case, Paul is clearly identifying that "some" who teach-different are currently "a young-plant," are "being-puffed-up," and "fall into the condemnation of the devil" (3:6).

The term "being-puffed-up" (τυφωθείς) carries a dual nuance. Pertaining to "someone" aspiring to an overseer (3:1), the term is heard in the immediate context of "a young-plant"—a recently converted person who is not deeply grounded "in faith." As such, the audience understand that "being-puffed-up" is the result of being elevated to a leadership position in the church too quickly, that is, without having roots to ground them in a solid foundation.[77] Indeed, where the false-teaching overseers are "a young-plant," it is evident that they are "being-puffed-up" due to their current positions as overseers in the Ephesian church. Still, and related, the phrase "being-puffed-up" also speaks to the effects of pride, connoting "blinded" or "deluded."[78] In short, the audience hear that a person who is "a young-plant" runs the risk of "being-puffed-up," thus blindly leading others if elevated to the leadership duties of an overseer, namely to teach and to govern, but also to care-for the church of God. Thus the implicit but nevertheless clear fact is that the "young-plant," false-teaching overseers in the mid-sixties Ephesian church are not only "being-puffed-up" but due to their ensuing pride are decidedly refusing to accept the sound teaching (1:10b) to which Paul was appointed as a teacher (2:7). That is, rather than growing their roots "in faith and truth" with Paul (2:7), "some" have instead grown upward in pride and chosen to teach-different (1:3)—specifically to teach something different that lies-opposed to the sound teaching with which Paul was counted-faithful by God (1:10b–11). Such pride by "some" is not only antithetical to an existence in the realm "in faith" (1:2) and also a personal disregard for God and Christ Jesus who appointed Paul as a teacher (2:7), but its results are disastrous, as Paul has identified throughout the letter—controversial-speculations rather than the household-law of God (1:4), not understanding instead of knowing (1:7–9a), rejecting faith and becoming shipwrecked regarding the faith instead of holding faith (1:19). Indeed, the pride of "some" who disregard the sound teaching of Paul (1:10b–11), thus Paul as a teacher (2:7), thus God and Christ who appointed Paul (1:1, 11,

---

77. Long, *1 & 2 Tim*, 90: "To put a new convert into the bishop's seat of wisdom could easily create the delusion that he actually *had* some seasoned wisdom, an almost certain misconception that is an equally sure path to puffery and conceit." Ngewa, *1 & 2 Tim*, 149: "False teachers ... have too high an opinion of themselves ... It is easy for recent converts to fall into the trap of thinking like this, particularly if they are pushed into positions of leadership too soon (3:6). These people have no real grounds for their conceit, for despite their claims to know it all, they actually *understand nothing*."

78. See Marshall, *PE*, 482.

12; 2:7) has dangerously influenced others in the church to also disregard the household-law of God in faith (1:4)—impropriety instead of what is proper for a profession of godliness (2:9–10), an abdication of God's creational roles for men and women rather than approving of God's design (2:11–14). What is apparent, then, is that the problem of the young-plant, being-puffed-up false-teaching overseers is not only a matter of teaching some-thing different and its ungodly effects thereof but is also a matter of their personal character and disposition thereof, as exhibited in their lifestyle and low view of those who have higher authority (cf. 2:2), such as the apostle Paul, Christ Jesus the Lord, and God the Father of the whole household "in faith" (1:1–2). Paul is undoubtedly emphasizing the need for mature, seasoned men to lead—to teach and govern—not only the entire church of God but also "some" who are immature, young-plants. Without qualified men to lead commendably as overseers, care-for the church, and model the lifestyle and behavior for men and women in the church, the situation in Ephesus will not only persist but get worse: "someone" who is "a young-plant" overseer will lead "being-puffed-up," thus instilling the same quality among all whom he oversees.

The full gravity of the situation, however, is not heard until the concluding scenario in the B element. It is necessary for an overseer to not be a young-plant, both so that he will not—being-puffed-up—become a false teacher and also—more significantly—so "that he might not . . . fall into the condemnation of the devil" (3:6). In other words, as much as it is necessary to protect the audience from the dangers of young-plant overseers, it is equally necessary to prevent a young-plant "in faith" from endangering himself by aspiring to an overseer (3:1). Again, the aspiration itself is not wrong, but the danger of leading without deep roots "in faith" is that it results in "being-puffed-up" and, worse yet, a certain "fall into the condemnation of the devil." Similar to "being-puffed-up," the verb "fall" (ἐμπέσῃ) relates to blindness by which a person or animal falls into a hidden trap. It is thus by "being-puffed-up" that "a young-plant" will "fall." It is possible that the phrase "condemnation of the devil" is heard by the audience in two ways. If the genitive "of the devil" (τοῦ διαβόλου) is taken objectively, the phrase refers to the condemnation of punishment that the devil himself received for being-puffed-up against God.[79] Yet, if the genitive is heard subjectively, the phrase refers to the condemnation that the devil himself issues as God's

---

79. Not a few commentators suggest that Paul still has Genesis 3 in mind from the second microchiasm (2:14). Knight, *PE*, 164: "Genesis 2 and 3, particularly Gn. 3:14, 15, would seem to provide the background for our text. In Genesis the serpent receives condemnation because he tempted Eve to be like God (Gn. 3:5)." See Barcley, *1 & 2 Tim*, 108; Schreiner, "Overseeing," 99.

provocateur, as he did in the story of Job.[80] Moreover, the term "devil" is reminiscent of Paul's earlier statement in the first microchiasm concerning Hymenaeus and Alexander, whom Paul had given-over to Satan (1:20). The connection may be significant. In 1:20 it was Paul's own authoritative action that intended their restoration to the faith that they had rejected (1:19), that is, "that they might be-disciplined not to blaspheme." In 3:6, it is the audience's action of not enabling an unqualified, young-plant, puffed-up-man to aspire to an overseer so "that he might not . . . fall into the condemnation of the devil." In both cases, the purpose is missional, restorative, and for the sake of their salvation. Thus not only are the false teachers clearly in view in 3:6, but also the dual nature of the B element is highlighted. On the one hand, Paul's burden is to prevent the church from repeating the error of elevating immature and unqualified men who are especially vulnerable to fall—either into the condemnation given to the devil (punishment for pride) or into the condemnation that the devil gives (enticement to pride). On the other hand, Paul is reiterating that the young-plant, being-puffed-up men who are currently false-teaching overseers in the Ephesian church should not be counted as leaders in God's household.

1 Timothy 3:7: It Is Necessary to Hold a Commendable Testimony from Those-Outside

(B' Element)

In the B' element (3:7) of the third microchiasm, Paul concludes his discussion on the qualification of aspiring overseers and begins to move his audience toward an enhanced understanding of the preceding B and A elements. First, the audience hear the final qualification: "But it is necessary to hold a commendable testimony from those-outside" (3:7). The combination of the terms "But" and "it is necessary" would be heard as a concluding formula. The verb "it is necessary" (δεῖ) in 3:7 of the B' element recalls for the audience Paul's opening words on the topic in 3:2 of the A element: "It is necessary (δεῖ)." The the repetition of the verb clearly brackets the apostle's discussion on an overseer—its latter occurrence signifying a conclusion. Thus rather than a contrast, the proximal conjuction "But" (δέ) functions to emphasize Paul's conclusion. In this way, the sense of the opening statement of the B' element would be heard by the audience to the effect of, "Finally, now, it is necessary."[81] Still, the progression of microchiasm from

---

80. E.g., Spicq, *Les Épîtres Pastorales*, 437; Towner, *Letters*, 257–58.

81. Marshall, *PE*, 483: "The emphatic conjuction and the repetition of δεῖ from 3.2

the A element, to the B element, and now to the B' element has a cumulative impact. That is, with the repetition of "it is necessary" in the B' element, the audience understand that everything the apostle has said so far concerning overseers must be carefully taken into consideration.

The emphatic, concluding qualification for an aspiring overseer into which the entire microchiasm funnels is "to hold a commendable testimony from those-outside." The verb "to hold" (ἔχειν) recalls for the audience its occurrence in the A element—"holding (ἔχοντα) children in submissiveness" (3:4)—and also its occurrence in the first microchiasm— "holding (ἔχων) faith and a good conscience" (1:19). Given the polemical context in each of these prior two instances, the audience hear that Paul intends the verb to be understood in the same, consistent manner here in the B' element. That is, over and against "some" who are rejecting the faith that Timothy is "holding" (1:19) and who instead "hold-toward" (προσέχειν) myths and genealogies without-limit (1:4), Paul indicates that it is necessary for a qualified overseer "to hold a commendable testimony from those-outside" (3:7).

The term "commendable" (καλήν) recalls its occurrences throughout the macrochiasm. The audience would certainly recall how the term bracketed the 3:1–5 minichiasm—"a commendable (καλοῦ) work" (3:1); "leading his own household commendably (καλῶς)" (3:5). Thus as the final qualification of an overseer in 3:7 of the B' element, the term also brackets Paul's entire discussion. Here, then, the audience hear an emphatic summary and purpose of the overseer's qualifications, namely his missional presence among "those-outside" (3:7). It is the "commendable (καλήν) testimony from those-outside" (3:7) pertaining to his "leading . . . commendably (καλῶς)" (3:4) that qualifies a man for the "commendable (καλοῦ) work" of an overseer (3:1). Paul's point is to remove any uncertainty for the audience: a man who aspires to the commendable work of an overseer must have a commendable reputation—he must be considered irreproachable by all. Still, given the sustained polemic of Paul's discussion regarding overseers, the qualifiying phrase "a commendable testimony" (3:7) would certainly also have "some" in view, recalling "the commendable (καλήν) war" that Timothy is to war against "some" who teach-different (1:19). To be sure, combined with the sustained connotation of the term "holding" throughout the macrochiasm, the audience understand the full force of the B' element: as the final qualification, it is necessary for an overseer to fight tooth and nail—and never cease—"to hold a commendable testimony" as

---

is meant to underline the importance of this particular requirement."

part and parcel of "the commendable war" against some-thing different that lies-opposed to the sound teaching (1:10b, 19).

The term "testimony" (μαρτυρίαν) recalls for audience Christ Jesus in the second microchiasm, "who gave himself as a ransom on behalf of all, the testimony (μαρτύριον) at his own times" (2:6). Moreover, it recalls Paul who was appointed by God as a proclaimer, apostle, and teacher to publically announce the testimony concerning Christ Jesus (2:7). Thus where both the subjective testimony—Christ's own action—and the objective testimony—Paul's affirmation of Christ's action—were equally bound together in the second microchiasm, certainly the audience expect to hear the same in the third microchiasm. To be sure, where "it is necessary to hold a commendable testimony" (3:7), subjectively, the overseer's own actions must be proof that he is commendable, and, objectively, this must be accompanied by others affirming that his actions are commendable.[82] Again, what Paul appears to be doing is focusing the audience on the empirical lifestyle of both current and aspiring overseers in the church. The audience understand that if no one can validate an overseer as commendable, then he is not qualified for the commendable work of an overseer. That is, without a "commendable testimony" (3:7), there is no proof that a man is "leading... commendably" (3:4) and thus no reason to appoint him to such "a commendable work" (3:1).

Up to this point in the third microchiasm, Paul has highlighted that it is necessary for a man who aspires to an overseer to be irreproachable; presumably, the audience understood that this validation was to come from them, that is, the church. However, here in 3:7 Paul highlights that it is not ultimately the audience who are to prove that an aspiring overseer is commendable; rather, at the emphatic conclusion of the qualifications for an overseer, Paul states that it is necessary for the commendable testimony to come specifically "from those-outside" (3:7).[83] Given that the sustained theme of the macrochiasm concerns the realm "in faith"—the household of God—the audience clearly understand "those-outside" (ἔξωθεν) as a reference to those not yet living in God's household, that is, not yet "in faith"—the surrounding non-Christian Ephesian community.[84] On the one

---

82. Towner, *Letters*, 258, helpfully describes the objective aspect as a "truthful evidence given by one person in assessment of another... ongoing 'evidence' about people that attaches to them in the sense of a reputation."

83. Ho, "Mission in the PE," 252: "the whole text (vv. 3–7) is directed toward and culminates in the concern for the overseer's reputation with those outside the church (v. 7)."

84. Knight, *PE*, 164: "Since the discourse in this passage is speaking of the church (vv. 5, 15), those who are outside are 'those outside *the church*' (*NASB*), or non-Christians

hand, the obvious implication is that a qualified overseer is a man who is involved and has a presence in the local non-Christian community: "those-outside" the church must know the aspring overseer well enough to prove that he is commendable.[85] On the other hand, given that such a man is aspiring to or already leads as an overseer in the missional household of God—the "Savior God, who desires all humans to be-saved" (2:4b)—the audience understand that a qualified overseer's involvement with "those-outside" intends a missional effect. That is, "a commendable testimony" is not merely meant to validate his qualification but to attract and welcome "those-outside" into the household of God.

Significantly, then, the audience hear the movement of the overall macrochiasm: the missional lives of prayer and godliness by the entire church in the second microchiasm (2:1–15) are to flow from the irreproachable, commendable leadership of the qualified, mature overseer in the third microchiasm (3:1–6). To be sure, in accordance with the sound teaching of Paul who was appointed by God to be a missional "teacher of the Gentiles (ἐθνῶν) in faith and truth" (2:7), the audience are not only to look for a man who is "able-to-teach" (3:2) but who also is missional toward "those-outside" (ἔξωθεν).[86] As the model and leader of the church, then, the audience understand that the overseer's influence is multifaceted, having both a direct and indirect missional impact. Indirectly, by his own missional example of godliness, he influences the church to live purposeful lives of missional godliness, thereby attracting those-outside to Christ (2:8–15). Directly, he himself attracts those-outside to Christ by his commendable life, leadership, and maturity (3:1–6).[87] Indeed, those inside and outside of

---

(BAGD; *NEB*: 'the non-Christian public')." See MacArthur, *1 & 2 Tim*, 36; Marshall, *PE*, 483–84.

85. To be sure, "those-outside" includes all humans outside of God's household, but Paul's concern for the church in Ephesus is certainly for all the people living immediately in Ephesus. The focus on the local community seems to have in view Jesus's summons to "love your neighbor as yourself" (Matt 22:39; Mark 12:31; perhaps also the allusion to Luke 10:27, 35, see above regarding 1 Tim 3:5). The overseer in Ephesus would "hold a commendable testimony" simply through his normal, everyday interactions with his immediate neighbors. Paul's point seems to underscore to the Ephesian church that, as the missional household of God in Ephesus, their overseer will lead them to live godly, missional lives among "those-outside" in their immediate community.

86. Certainly, there is the connotation that "the Gentiles" were once "those-outside." Significantly, the majority of those in the Ephesian church were "the Gentiles" and thus were once "those-outside." The aural similarity between ἐθνῶν and ἔξωθεν would likely be heard by the audience, thus strengthening Paul's implication: the Ephesian church must remember that they themselves were brought inside God's household through missional activity.

87. Hutson, "Ecclesiology in the PE," 184: "the conduct of Christian leaders must

the church are to see and testify to his sacrificial love and fidelity to his wife as a missional model of Christ Jesus's fidelity to the church (3:2; Eph 5:25). In a word, the qualified overseer preserves the sound teaching and promotes godliness—inside God's household—in order for the entire church to be missional—outside God's household. Thus as the final qualification for an aspiring overseer, the audience hear the unified progression of the macro-chiasm concerning the sound teaching, godliness, and missions: a man who views "those-outside" (3:7) as "those who would-inevitably-come to have-faith upon [Christ]" (1:16) is qualified to lead them "to come to a knowing-embrace of truth" (2:4b), that is, an acceptance of "the testimony" (2:6) that "Christ Jesus came into the world to save sinners" (1:15), thereby inviting "those-outside" to enter into the realm "in faith" (1:2, 4; 2:7, 15). Furthermore, the opening statement concerning the qualifications of overseers—"Faithful is the word" (3:1a)—is now understood with its full significance: by a qualified overseer's missional godliness, he enables "those-outside" to not only *hear* and consider that "Faithful is the word . . . that Christ Jesus came into the world to save sinners" (1:15) but to *experience* and personally testify that in view of the overseer's commendable life, "the word" concerning Christ Jesus is undoubtedly "worthy of all acceptance" (1:15).[88]

The B' element concludes with the purpose clause: "that he might not fall into disgrace and the snare of the devil" (3:7). Given the focus on those-outside, to fall into "disgrace" (ὀνειδισμόν) likely means to fall into public ridicule and shame for living according to a standard of conduct less than that of society.[89] Such "disgrace" would certainly hinder the missional calling of the church, not only affecting the church's internal godliness but also its reputation among "those-outside." Moreover, the phrase "that he might not" (ἵνα μή) and the terms "fall" (ἐμπέσῃ) and "devil" (διαβόλου) here in 3:7 of the B' element recall their occurrence in 3:6 of the parallel

---

be not only exemplary for insiders but recognizably and undeniably good to outsiders, especially to those who are suspicious or critical of a religious movement that is new, outlandish, or threatening." Long, *1 & 2 Tim*, 87: "What endures are the two basic trajectories of the Pastor's wisdom about leadership. First, he is concerned with integrity and trustworthiness inside the household of God, and second, he is attentive to the public face of the church, with the church's reputation for virtue among its neighbors."

88. Ngewa, *1 & 2 Tim*, 70: "The church is surrounded by a non-believing society that watches everything it does. Overseers with a bad reputation are a stumbling block to the gospel, for they will give outsiders a negative image of the church and its leaders (3:7). The outsiders will then be unwilling to listen to the message of the gospel proclaimed by the overseer."

89. Ho indicates that the term here in 3:7 refers to a "loss of credibility as a result of some spiritual and/or moral failure of the leader . . . There is a missional impetus that should not be overlooked" ("Mission in the PE," 253).

B element where Paul's concern was for a young-plant who was being-puffed-up, namely "that he might not (ἵνα μή) . . . fall (ἐμπέσῃ) into the condemnation of the devil (διαβόλου)." Thus the audience understand that "to hold a commendable testimony" certainly concerns a man holding on to his faith (cf. 1:19). Still, the phrase "the snare of the devil" here in 3:7 of the B' element would enhance the audience's understanding of the parallel phrase "the condemnation of the devil" in 3:6 of the B element. The term "snare" (παγίδα) epitomizes deception; it would be set in place by an effective hunter, who hides and conceals the snare—purposefully disguising the trap—so that the victim will ignorantly step into it. Thus where the "snare" is "of the devil" (τοῦ διαβόλου), the audience clearly understand that the genitival form "of the devil" is to be heard as subjective, thus indicating that it is the devil who sets an elusive "snare" (παγίδα) for the overseer to fall into.[90] In this way, given the parallelism of the B and B' elements, Paul is conveying to the audience a corresponding activity: "the devil" (3:6, 7) is present and active, employing a variety of methods—"the condemnation" (3:6) and "the snare" (3:7)—to stumble and make overseers fall, thus causing the entire household of God—along with its missional purpose—to stumble and fall.[91] Though a young-plant is most susceptible, Paul highlights that all overseers—as well as the church itself—must be active and vigilant against the elusive trap—"the snare"—of the devil. By implication, therefore, Paul is identifying that the false-teaching overseers have failed to do so: the snare of the devil has already deceived them.

Furthermore, given the polemical concern of the overall macrochiasm regarding "some," the repetition of "the devil" again recalls for the audience Hymenaeus and Alexander, whom Paul had given-over to "Satan" (1:20). Here, the connection makes clear to the audience that these false teachers have already fallen into the elusive snare of the devil (3:7); it is for this reason that they are currently blaspheming and why Paul intends for them to be-disciplined (1:20).[92] In other words, in the B' element of the third microchiasm, Paul conveys the explicit reason for giving both men over to Satan in the first microchiasm. On the one hand, the false-teaching overseers

---

90. Marshall, *PE*, 484: "the reference here is to the trap laid by the devil."

91. Barclay, *1 & 2 Tim*, 109: "The devil's desire is to discredit the church and the gospel of Jesus Christ. One of the primary ways he seeks to do that is by discrediting the church's leaders."

92. Marshall notes that "'the devil's snare' refers to his capturing people to use them for his own ends" (*PE*, 483). In this way, given the sustained polemic against the false teachers, Paul may be implying that "some" who have ignorantly fallen into the devil's snare are, in fact, currently ensnared as they attempt to lead the church toward something different (1:10), namely a place where the result is shipwrecked faith (1:19).

have unknowingly fallen into the snare of the devil (3:7) and, still without knowing their dire situation, are actively working against the household-law of God in faith (1:4). On the other hand, by publically giving them over to Satan, Paul intends to jolt them from their ignorance: the false teachers need to know they have fallen into the devil's snare "that they might be-disciplined not to blaspheme" (1:20) and thus be restored to the faith they are rejecting and about which have become-shipwrecked (1:19). Again, as in 3:6 of the B element, the preventative measure of the audience to select a qualified man for an overseer in 3:7 of the parallel B' element is for the sake of the overseer's salvation.

In sum, in the final qualification of an overseer carries the entire force of the third microchiasm and overall macrochiasm. Paul's concern is not only for the individual who might fall into disgrace (3:7) but also for the entire church's reputation. More specifically, Paul's concern is for the impact that a leader's failure will have on the church's ability to fulfill its missional calling. In the first microchiasm, Paul sought to maintain the integrity of the sound teaching, namely the truth of its content concerning Christ Jesus and salvation. In the second microchiasm, Paul underscored the importance of upholding a life in all godliness and respectability as a means of attracting all humans to the truth concerning Christ Jesus and salvation. Here in the third microchiasm, Paul articulates that the success of the missional household of God—that is, the preservation of the sound teaching and the promotion of godliness—depends directly upon the overseer, who is not only responsible for teaching, governing, leading, and caring-for the church of God but also for modeling and representing godliness for the entire church and to those-outside. The audience understand that the qualifications for an overseer are to be accepted as part of the faithful word (3:1a) because salvation is at stake—the salvation of the overseer himself (3:6–7), the salvation of the church of God (3:5), and the salvation of "those-outside" (3:7).

1 Timothy 3:8–16: Deacons and the Household of God

(A' Element)

Within the concluding A' element of the third microchiasm (3:8–16), the audience hear one minichiasm (3:8–16).

1 TIMOTHY 3:1–16: GODLY LEADERSHIP IN GOD'S HOUSEHOLD

1 Timothy 3:8–16: A Minichiastic Unit

As a minichiasm in itself, verses 3:8–16 are composed carefully of six sub-elements ("a"-"b"-"c"-"c'"-"b'"-"a'"); linguistic parallels identifying chiastic arrangements are indicated by the Greek text:

> "a". ⁸ Likewise it is necessary for deacons to be respectable, not double-worded, not holding-toward much wine, not avaricious, ⁹ holding the mystery (μυστήριον) of the faith in a pure conscience.
>
> > "b". ¹⁰ But they also must be-tested first; then they must serve-as-deacons (διακονείτωσαν), being blameless.
> >
> > > "c". ¹¹ Likewise it is necessary for women (γυναῖκας) to be respectable, not devilishly-slanderous, temperate, faithful in all.
> > >
> > > "c'". ¹² Deacons must be the man of one woman (γυναικός), leading children commendably and their own households.
> >
> > "b'". ¹³ For those who serve-as-deacons (διακονήσαντες) commendably acquire for themselves a commendable standing and much confidence in faith that is in Christ Jesus. ¹⁴ These-things to you I write, hoping to come to you in quickness; ¹⁵ but if I am delayed, that you might know how it is necessary to behave in the household of God, which is the church of the living God, a pillar and foundation of truth.
>
> "a'". ¹⁶ And confessedly great is the mystery (μυστήριον) of godliness: he was manifested in flesh, was declared-just in Spirit, was seen by angels, was proclaimed in the Gentiles, was counted-faithful in the world, was taken-up in glory.

The second and final minichiasm of the 3:1–16 microchiasm is framed by a parallel concern for "the mystery" in the "a" and "a'" sub-elements. Within this linguistic framing, Paul's concern is for those who "serve-as-deacons" in the "b" and "b'" sub-elements. The minichiasm gravitiates around Paul's concern for a deacon's family life in the "c" and "c'" sub-elements.

1 Timothy 3:8–9: Deacons, Holding the Mystery of the Faith

("a" sub-element)

The introductory "a" sub-element (3:8–9) of the 3:8–16 minichiasm begins the A' element of the third microchiasm and initiates Paul's discussion on a second leadership role in the church: "Likewise it is necessary for deacons to be..."[93] The specification of the term "deacons" (διακόνους) in distinction from an "overseer" leaves no doubt for the audience that Paul is speaking now of a different role.[94] Moreover, recalling the cognate term that Paul used to describe his own appointment for "service" (διακονίαν, 1:12), the role of "deacons" (διακόνους, 3:8) would likely be understood in terms of serving rather than oversight.[95] To be sure, the adverb "likewise" (ὡσαύτως, 3:8) recalls "likewise" (ὡσαύτως, 2:9) in the A' element of the second microchiasm, wherein Paul conveyed that the women were to have similar yet distinct roles from the men in the congregation. In this way, the audience understand that the phrase "Likewise ... deacons" (διακόνους ὡσαύτως) communicates two nuances. On the one hand, men qualified for deacons must exhibit the same qualities listed for the aspiring overseer in 3:1–7.[96] On the other hand, these same qualities are to be carried out in a distinct

---

93. The Greek here does not include the terms "it is necessary" (δεῖ) or "to be" (εἶναι). Rather, they are implied by the term "Likewise" (ὡσαύτως). Knight, PE, 168: "ὡσαύτως ... requires that a verb be understood or supplied (see 2:9). Both here and in v. 11 the verb is that found at the beginning of, and presumed throughout, the list of qualifications for the bishop [overseer], i.e., δεῖ εἶναι (v. 2)." See Marshall, PE, 489 n. 59.

94. Merkle, "Ecclesiology in the PE," 191: "It is striking that Paul does not explain the duties of this office, which suggests that the Ephesian church already had experience with deacons. Paul simply lists the qualifications and assumes the church will use these officers in the appropriate manner."

95. The exact meaning of the term διάκονος is difficult to narrow down because of the different ways the term is used in the NT; see Collins, *Diakonia Studies*, 57–164; Marshall, *PE*, 486–87. In the context of 1 Timothy 3, however, it is clear that the term is used to describe a role in the church that is distinct from an overseer yet complementary in nature. For further discussion, see Thatcher, "Deacon in the Pauline Church," 53–57.

96. Witherington, *Letters*, 240: "Notice that of the nine traits or virtues of the deacon, six are directly parallel to that of the overseer." See also Mounce, PE, 195; Marshall, PE, 485, 487. Still, not a few commentators observe that the qualification "able to teach" (3:2) applies only to aspiring overseers and suggests a distinction between the two roles; see e.g., Barclay, *1 & 2 Tim*, 104; Knight, PE, 150; Merkle, "Ecclesiology in the PE," 191.

Given that an overseer pertained to men (see 3:1–5 above), Paul's discussion of deacons would most likely be understood by the audience as a continued list of qualifications for men.

role as deacons.⁹⁷ Like a qualified overseer, then, the fundamental concern for the deacon is to be irreproachable. In other words, the audience are not to consider the qualifications for deacons to consist of a lower standard of character.⁹⁸

The first qualification for a deacon is to be "respectable" (σεμνούς), which recalls the qualified overseer who is "holding children in submissiveness with all respectability (σεμνότητος)" in 3:4 of the parallel A element.⁹⁹ Thus the audience understand that both deacons and overseers are expected to share and model the same quality of "respectability."¹⁰⁰ Moreover, similar to the function of the umbrella term "irreproachable" for overseers (3:2), the initial quality "respectable" would be understood as a summary description of the men who are qualified for deacons. The meaning of the term undoubtedly echoes Paul's exhortation to the entire congregation, who are to pray for all humans and to live in all godliness and "respectability" (σεμνότητι, 2:2). Both in 2:2 of the second microchiasm and here in 3:8 of the third microchiasm the main idea is living an observably respectable life that stems from God's calling to participate in his mission for all humans to be-saved by coming to a knowing-embrace of truth concerning the one God and one mediator Christ Jesus (2:4-6). In this way, the audience understand that qualified deacons, similar to men who are qualified for an overseer, are

---

97. Knight, *PE*, 168: "The adverb ὡσαύτως (see 2:9) with its meaning of 'likewise' both distinguishes the διάκονοι from the ἐπίσκοπος and compares the two. The διάκονοι, like the ἐπίσκοπος, must 'likewise' have qualifications."

98. It may be worth noting that deacons would most likely be understood as secondary to overseers, functioning to enable the overseer(s) to teach and govern. Towner, *Letters*, 261-62: "Probably with the position(s) of overseers and elders already in existence, the need for greater specialization in some churches of more significant size and longer history led to the establishment of a group commissioned to support the ministry overseen by the *episkopoi* and *presbyteroi* . . . we should probably understand the deacon's task as being that of assisting the overseer/supervisor in administration, leadership, and teaching within the church. The arrangement in Ephesus was apparently that of a group of deacons (note the plurality) serving the church as assistants either to the overseer (singular) or team of overseers." Marshall, *PE*, 488: "The deacon's relation to the overseer is unclear, but the order of mention in both passages and the comparative brevity of the description may well suggest a subordinate appointment."

99. Wall with Steele, *1 & 2 Tim*, 109: the linguistic parallel "suggests that a servant's [deacon's] chores are in relation to the 'children' who belong to the household of faith and pertain to cultivating the faith of God's extended family."

100. In passing, the flow of the microchiasm recommends that "with all respectability" in 3:4 of the A element is to be understood primarily as a description of the overseer's leadership. This, of course, does not change the dual implication but rather affirms it: as a direct result of the overseer's "leading . . . with all respectability," his children will be "in submissiveness with all respectability."

men who embody and represent for the audience the missional calling of the household of God.

Paul goes on to unpack the overarching qualification of deacons with with three attributes, expressed negatively: "not double-worded, not holding-toward much wine, not avaricious" (3:8). Due to the repetition of "not" (μή), the audience understand that all three attributes are to be categorized together. Also, similar to the qualifications for overseers, the negative qualities would be understood as a positive association with "some" who are "not" (μή) to teach-different (1:3) and their influence thereof.[101] The first negative descriptor "not double-worded" (διλόγους), connotes "two-faced, insincere."[102] This quality must have been particularly piercing, given the repeated declaration, "Faithful is the word (λόγος)" (1:15; 3:1a). To be "double-worded," then, is to pursue a manner of life that has the opposite effect of the sound teaching, the gospel concerning Christ Jesus (1:10b–11a). In connection with the false-teaching overseers, the obvious suggestion is that such men are not living according to the realm "in faith" but rather according to their decision to turn-aside from a without-hypocrisy faith for "useless-words" (ματαιαλογίαν)" (1:5–6). Indeed, in contrast to "some" who are desiring to be law-teachers but not understanding what "they-are-saying" (λέγουσιν, 1:7), qualified deacons are not to be "double-worded (διλόγους, 3:8). Similar to the qualified overseers, the audience understand that qualified deacons are to be nothing like the false teachers in the Ephesian church.

Paul lists the second negative qualification for deacons as "not holding-toward much wine." The phrase "not . . . much wine" (μὴ οἴνῳ πολλῷ) here in 3:8 of the A' element recalls Paul's qualification for overseers as "not addicted-to-wine" (μὴ πάροινον) in 3:3 of the parallel A element. The audience not only hear Paul's parallel expectations of the overseer and deacons but also his parallel polemic against the false teachers. In short, Paul is underscoring that all respectable leadership in the church is qualitatively unlike the leadership of "some." To be sure, in light of the overall concern for deacons to be "respectable," the specification of "wine" (οἴνῳ) is not surprising to the audience, given that excessive drinking often leads to conduct that is anything but respectable. Moreover, the adjective "much" (πολλῷ) is significant, communicating to the audience that Paul is not at all suggesting asceticism—as though abstinence from wine is required—but rather is warning against excesses that would distract God's household from

---

101. See 1:4, 7, 20; 2:9; 3:3, 6, 7.

102. The term is a *hapax legomenon*. Knight, *PE*, 168: "διλόγους . . . must mean here 'double-tongued' in the sense of 'insincere.'"

remembering what is important, namely the fact of their own salvation and their corresponding missional purpose. Furthermore, the notion of "holding-toward" (προσέχοντας) recalls "some" in 1:4 of the first microchiasm who "hold-toward" (προσέχειν) myths and genealogies without-limit. In this way, the positive implication is that men who are qualified deacons do not "hold-toward" things that destabilize the household-law of God (1:4) or hinder its missional participation with the Savior God (2:3–4).

Still, with the cumulative progression of the macrochiasm, the term "holding-toward" in 3:8 highlights a significant point of contrast in the letter. Rather than "holding (ἔχων) faith and a good conscience" (1:19), "holding (ἔχοντα) children in submissiveness" (3:4), and "to hold (ἔχειν) a commendable testimony" (3:7), the activities associated with the false teachers conveys the opposite—the connotative sense of "hold-toward" (προσέχειν, 1:4) and "holding-toward" (προσέχοντας, 3:8) effectivingly referring to a deviated devotion, "giving themselves to" rather than "clinging tightly to." Thus in contrast to those aligned with Paul who are "holding"—clinging tightly—it is evident that those associated with the false teachers are doing the exact opposite by "holding-toward"—devoting themselves to some-thing different (1:3–4, 1:10b). Paul's point seems to indicate that there is an absence of neutrality in the Ephesian church. Furthermore, the audience hear that Paul is not merely pointing out a contrast. Rather, in line with the themes of restoration that were emphasized in the parallel B and B' elements, Paul's intention is for "some" to stop "holding-toward" (3:8; cf. 1:4) and to begin "holding," namely faith and a good conscience (1:19), children in submissiveness with all respectability (3:4), and commendable lifestyles (3:7). Undoubtedly, Paul has the unity of the church in view—its restoration from division (1:4). The audience are to understand that the end of his charge, indeed, is love (1:5).

The last negative descriptor "not avaricious" (μὴ αἰσχροκερδεῖς) is a conceptual echo of an aspiring overseer's call to be "without-affection-of-money" (ἀφιλάργυρον, 3:3).[103] The term "not avaricious" itself is not altogether very different from the term "without-affection-of money"—"avaricious" referring to an excessive desire for money, a desire that results in illegitimate gain. To be sure, the apostle's concern is not financial gain or money itself but a strong desire for it that leads to sordid profits. Given the sustained polemic against the false teachers, there may be some suggestion to the audience that those associated with the false teachers—likely some of the deacons—were themselves were guilty of greed.[104]

---

103. See Marshall, *PE*, 489.

104. Barclay, "1 Tim," 368: "This probably reflects the deacon's role of handling, at least in part, church financial resources."

While the adjective "able-to-teach" (διδακτικόν, 3:2) suggests that the overseer plays the primary role in teaching—and in combating false teaching—Paul indicates in 3:9 of the A' element that deacons also play an important role in preserving the sound teaching within God's household. The qualification of the participle phrase "holding the mystery of the faith in a pure conscience" is formally distinct from the previous attributes, which suggests its particular importance. Moreover, the phrase recalls for the audience Timothy's own call to war the commendable war in 1:19 of the first microchiasm by "holding faith and a good conscience."[105] The repetition of "holding" (ἔχοντας), the sustained contrast in the macrochiasm between those who hold on to faith (1:19; 3:4, 7) and those who give up faith (1:4; 3:8) is evident. Moreover, augmented from the fact that Timothy is "holding faith" (1:19), the audience hear "holding the mystery of the faith" (3:9) to convey the deacon's alignment and support of Timothy's task in the Ephesian church to war the commendable war against "some" (1:18). The additional term "the mystery" (τὸ μυστήριον) would certainly draw the audience's attention. Although the audience have not yet heard this term, its placement in connection with "of the faith" (τῆς πίστεως) would make its meaning clear. Throughout the macrochiasm, the audience heard the cognate terms for "faith" (1:2, 4, 5, 11, 14, 16, 19; 2:7, 15) as references to the familial realm where God is the Father and Christ Jesus is Lord (1:2, 12), namely the household of God (1:4; 3:5), which is entered by coming to have-faith upon Christ (1:16). Upon hearing the phrase "holding the mystery of the faith" in 3:9, then, the audience understand that qualified deacons are men who cling to that which aligns with their existence "in faith," namely the sound teaching (1:10)—the gospel (1:11)—concerning the testimony that Christ gave himself as a ransom on behalf of all (2:6).[106] In short, qualified deacons are aligned with Paul, the authoritative apostolic teacher "in faith and truth" (2:7).[107] As such, the fact that the deacons are men who hold tightly to Paul's teaching indicates that they embody the preservation of the sound teaching as they live and operate "in faith," thereby promoting

---

105. Note the similarities in Greek:
3:9: "ἔχοντας τὸ μυστήριον τῆς πίστεως ἐν καθαρᾷ συνειδήσει";
1:19: "ἔχων πίστιν καὶ ἀγαθὴν συνείδησιν."

106. The apparent association (uniqueness of the article τό) between τὸ εὐαγγέλιον ("the gospel," 1:11) and τὸ μαρτύριον ("the testimony," 2:6) and τὸ μυστήριον ("the mystery," 3:9) may be worth noting. Where a linguistic connection is intended, each of the terms further links together the first, second, and third microchiasms.

107. In the phrase "the mystery of the faith," the genitive expresses apposition; see BDF §167. Marshall, *PE*, 490: "apposition: 'the mystery which is the faith,'" faith being "the content of what is believed rather than the act or disposition characterized by faith." See also Barclay, *1 & 2 Tim*, 112–13; Spicq, *Les Épîtres Pastorales*, 99.

godliness. Thus even though the deacons may not play an active role in teaching within the church, it is difficult to imagine how their commitment to the gospel—the mystery of the faith—would not function as a formidable force to counter the deliberately rebellious activities of "some" who teach some-thing that lies-opposed to the sound teaching (1:3, 1:10b).[108] Along with Paul, Timothy, and the qualified overseers, the audience understand— and perhaps are comforted—that qualified deacons are men who will never give up and will always be holding "the faith" (τῆς πίστεως, 3:9). Indeed, such men are anchors for the church to preserve the sound teaching and promote godliness—men who can be trusted to prevent others from becoming shipwrecked regarding "the faith" (τὴν πίστιν, 1:20).

Paul concludes the "a" sub-element of the minichiasm by adding that deacons are to hold the mystery of the faith "in a pure conscience" (3:9). The adjective "pure" (καθαρᾷ) recalls for the audience its earlier occurrence in the first microchiasm to describe a "pure (καθαρᾶς) heart" (1:5). In the former instance, Paul has in mind a heart that has been cleansed by God.[109] The term "conscience" (συνειδήσεως) would recall its earlier occurrences in 1:5 and 1:19 of the first microchiasm to signify the human faculty that applies truth to actual life. Here, then, the combination of both terms in the phrase "in a pure conscience" would indicate that qualified deacons are men whom God has enabled to pursue ethical behavior as a direct result of "having the mystery of the faith."[110] To be sure, the ethical life that qualifies a man for a deacon requires an unwavering commitment of holding the mystery of the faith—doing so is the very lifeline by which he is "respectable" (3:8). In sum, the audience understand that the tangible sign that deacons have come to a knowing-embrace of truth (2:4), namely of the gospel (1:11), is their life of godliness and conduct thereof—both informed and empowered by the mystery of the faith (3:9), that is, by the content of the sound teaching of the apostle Paul (1:10b).[111]

---

108. Perhaps the best example of a deacon playing a formidable role in promoting the truth of the gospel is Stephen (Acts 6:1—7:60).

109. Regarding καθαρᾷ as activity of God, see Marshall, *PE*, 491. See also volume 1, chapter 3 regarding 1 Timothy 1:5.

110. Given the connection of "the mystery of the faith" to the sphere of existence "in faith" (see above), the preposition "in" (ἐν) is likely an allusion to same sphere and the lifestyle that corresponds.

111. Long's observations may be helpful: "When the Pastor urges deacons to 'hold fast to the mystery of the faith with a clear conscience,' he means not simply purity of belief but also purity of action and integrity in the performance of their ministry. If, as many have argued, the deacons were administrators of the day-to-day operations of the financial care of widows [Acts 6:1–3; 1 Tim 5:3, 5, 9, 10], then this would be a practical place where their true creed would find expression. If they are 'greedy for money,'

1 Timothy 3:10: Deacons Must Be-Tested First, Then They Must Serve-As-Deacons

("b" sub-element)

The "b" sub-element of the minichiasm (3:10) moves the audience toward a deeper understanding of the role of deacons as Paul continues his discussion of the qualifications: "But they also must be-tested first; then they must serve-as-deacons, being blameless." Both the construction and style of verse 3:10 are somewhat jarring. It is possible that the dual conjunctions "But also" (καὶ ... δέ) would have been understood by the audience in different ways.[112] Yet, the force of the conjuctions may have been heard as "However, indeed they must be tested," suggesting that the audience were accepting not only unqualified men as deacons (3:8) but, specifically, untested men. Given the further context of the "b" sub-element (3:10), this was likely the case, and in response the audience hear Paul underscoring the need and importance for men to undergo an assessment process. In addition to the conjunctions, Paul's audience hear the shift from "It is necessary ... to be" (δεῖ ... εἶναι; 3:2) to the use of the imperatives: "they also must be-tested ... they must serve-as-deacons" (δοκιμαζέσθωσαν ... διακονείτωσαν). This sudden change in style would likely be understood as Paul's way of drawing attention to the fact that this assessment of deacons is not optional but should be received as an authoritative instruction. Furthermore—and most significantly—the emphasis on testing is highlighted by the juxtaposition of the adverbs "first; then." The term "first" (πρῶτον) recalls the consistent, interconnected progression of the entire macrochiasm: in the first microchiasm Paul was the "first" (πρῶτός, 1:15b; πρώτῳ, 1:16a)—lead, prominent—sinner; in the second microchiasm, both the "first" (πρῶτον, 2:1)—lead, prominent—duty of the church was to pursue missional prayer and a life in all godliness, and Adam was the "first" (πρῶτος, 2:13)—lead, prominent—teacher and governor. Here in the third microchiasm, therefore, the audience understand that Paul is speaking of prominence, not sequence. That is, the "first"—lead, prominent—qualification for deacons is their testing, not their serving. To be sure, given the entire third microchiasm's focus on the importance of men's qualifications to lead the church as overseer and deacons—not to mention the consistent use of "first" throughout the entire macrochiasm as a reference to prominence—it would be most unfitting for Paul to use "first" in 3:10 as a temporal, sequential marker. In

---

["avaricious," 3:8] then their actions could easily lead to shipwreck" (*1 & 2 Tim*, 93).

112. For various suggestions, see Fee, *1 & 2 Tim*, 87; Towner, *Letters*, 264–65; Marshall, *PE*, 485.

the same way, it would be equally unfitting on the part of the audience to perceive such a sudden, ungrounded change in meaning. Thus Paul's point is not to articulate a sequence to enable men to serve-as-deacons but rather to emphasize the prominence of men's qualifications as that which enables them to serve-as-deacons. In short, if men are unqualified according to 3:8–9, there is no reason to enable them to serve-as-deacons according to any sequence of activities.

Indeed, the force of Paul's statement is strengthened by the term "then." In the same way as "first, then" (πρῶτος . . . εἶτα) in 2:13 of the second microchiasm was understood, the simple phrase "they also must be-tested first" in 3:10 of the third microchiasm would have sufficiently communicated that the lead qualification for deacons is their testing; the additional tag "then they must serve-as-deacons" is unnecessary for Paul to make his point. The rhetorical emphasis would therefore be intentional and heard as "they also must be-tested *first*; *then* they must serve-as-deacons." Thus as in 2:13, that Paul felt compelled to make this emphasis suggests its corrective function for the audience; more than likely, there was a misunderstanding in Ephesus regarding deacons and the relationship between testing and serving. Furthermore, given the polemical context of the macrochiasm—even more, of the immediate third microchiasm—such a misunderstanding may have been the result of the different teaching of "some" (1:3, 10b). Moreover, as in the second microchiasm, the audience understand that if the arrangement of prominence "first; then" is reversed for deacons in the third microchiasm—first serving, then being tested for qualifications—there is a direct impact on the sound teaching and godliness. Therefore, in line with Paul's divine authority as an apostle (1:1; 2:7) and his divine appointment as a teacher (2:7), the audience understand that his corrective instructions here in 3:10 are meant not only to safeguard the Ephesian church but also to emphasize that the selection of men to serve-as-deacons naturally follows from their qualification thereof.

As much as men's qualifications "must be-tested first," the audience must understand what it means to "be-tested." The verb "must be-tested" (δοκιμαζέσθωσαν) means to be examined and proven true. Although its Greco-Roman connotations would indicate a selection methodology,[113] the OT use of the term would likely also have been intended. For instance, LXX Psalm 16:3: "You have tested (ἐδοκίμασας) my heart . . . and unrighteousness has not been found in me"; LXX Psalm 65:10: "For you, O God, have tested

---

113. Collins, *1 & 2 Tim*, 88–89: "This was a technical term used in the Athenian court to refer to the screening of a candidate for public office."

(ἐδοκίμασας) us; you have tried us as silver is tried."[114] In Paul's letter, then, the verb "must be-tested" in 3:10 is to be understood with at least two nuances. First, men qualified to be deacons must pursue a righteous life. The righteousness in view has the gospel—the mystery of the faith (3:9)—as its source: because deacons know that Christ Jesus came into the world and gave himself as a ransom on their behalf in order to save them (1:15; 2:6), so now they hold on to the lifestyle that "Christ Jesus our Lord" (1:2, 12) expects, the lifestyle that "God the Father" (1:2) expects, the lifestyle consistent with "the household-law of God in faith" (1:4), that is, consistent with their mode of existence "in faith" (1:2, 4; 2:7, 15). In a word, deacons are to demonstrate a life of godliness (2:2; cf. 2:10) that accords with their knowing-embrace of truth (2:4b). Second, the audience understand that "must be-tested" entails more than a cursory evaluation. Rather, as fine metals are exposed to high heat, pressure, and fire to prove their worth, so too qualified deacons are men who undergo careful assessment and come out unscathed.[115]

Still, given the polemic of the microchiasm, the audience likely understand "must be-tested" as a way to distinguish qualified men from those who associate with "some" or who support "some-thing different" that lies-opposed to the sound teaching (1:10b). Namely, given that deacons are to be models of "holding the mystery of the faith" (3:9), the testing of men's qualifications to be deacons involves an observation of their responses to the "fires" of life. The audience are to consider: in the midst of life's difficulties, does a man hold the mystery of the faith—the gospel, the testimony—that Christ Jesus entered into the world to save him from sin and that he is part of God's familial realm "in faith"? Is the mystery of the faith so tightly clutched in his grip? Or does he respond like the false teachers by holding-toward some-thing different—have his hands relaxed and let go? The audience understand that men who have been tested and still hold the mystery of the faith are qualified to be models for the church. Indeed, for the sake of God's missional household—to preserve the sound teaching and promote godliness—men such as these "must serve-as-deacons" (διακονείτωσαν).[116]

In the concluding phrase of the "b" sub-element, Paul describes qualified deacons as "being blameless." The term "blameless" (ἀνέγκλητοι) identifies the condition of men who have been tested and are qualified to

---

114. The LXX passages (Pss 16:3; 65:10) are referenced in modern English translations as 17:3 and 66:10, respectively.

115. Paul seems to use the term similarly in 1 Corinthians 3:13: "the fire will test (δοκιμάσει)."

116. To be sure, the verb διακονέω has the broader sense of "to serve or minister," but it is obvious that in the immediate context of deacons (3:8) that Paul has in mind the specific meaning "to serve-as-deacons."

serve-as-deacons. The aural similarity between deacons who are "blameless" (ἀνέγκλητοι, 3:10) and overseers who are "irreproachable" (ἀνεπίλημπτον, 3:2) would most likely be heard by the audience, suggesting not only that the two terms are synonymous but also highlighting again that the same high standards apply to both leadership duties. Such repeated emphasis to the audience probably was necessary, given Paul's concern in the third microchiasm that they had allowed unqualified men to be overseers and deacons. What is more, the participle "being" (ὄντες) recalls for the audience Paul's description of his life "in unfaithfulness," namely as "being (ὄντα) a blasphemer and a persecutor and a hubristic-person" (1:13). As a point of contrast, then, in 3:10 the audience likely understand that "being blameless" is indicative of deacons being "in faith"; such a connection would strengthen and affirm Paul's emphasis that qualified deacons are men who constantly model godliness and thus preserve the sound teaching that motivates it. At the same time, this connection would be yet another polemical assertion: any men associated with those "in unfaithfulness"—the false teachers who have become-shipwrecked regarding the faith (1:19)—are disqualified from serving as deacons, as their behavior would indicate.

1 Timothy 3:11: It Is Necessary for the Wives of Deacons to be Respectable

("c" sub-element)

In the "c" sub-element (3:11) Paul progresses his discussion on the qualifications for deacons: "Likewise it is necessary for women to be respectable."[117] It is possible that the audience would hear "women" (γυναῖκας) as a general reference—all women in the congregation. However, due to the natural progression of Paul's rhetoric from the second to the third microchiasm, it is more than likely that the audience would not hear "women" as a general term but rather as the specific term "wives."[118] In the A element

---

117. The Greek construction of 3:11 is literally, "Women likewise respectable" (γυναῖκας ὡσαύτως σεμνάς). Noticeably, the Greek does not include the terms "it is necessary" (δεῖ) or "to be" (εἶναι); rather, they are implied by the term "Likewise" (ὡσαύτως). See discussion above regarding 3:8.

118. There is disagreement over whether γυναῖκας in 3:11 means "wives" or "women," and the difference is not at all insubstantial. In short, the latter position would not only allow but also prescribe the ordination of women as deacons. That "wives" are in view, see Knight, PE, 170–72; Mounce, PE, 202–4; Krause, 1 Tim, 69–70; that "women" are in view, see Towner, Letters, 265; Blackburn, "The Identity of the 'Women' in 1 Tim 3.11," 303–19; Patterson and Kelley, eds., "1 Tim," 669; Marshall, PE, 492–94; Long, 1 & 2 Tim, 94–95; Hutson, "Ecclesiology in the PE," 180.

Either position is defensible. My inclination, however, is that the text—particularly its notable rhetorical movement from men and women in general (2:8-15) to specific men and women (3:2)—is referring to the wives of deacons. Towner argues for the opposite position: "(1) in similar parenetic contexts, the adverb ὡσαύτως ... that changes the topic to 'women' serves to introduce a new but related case ... (2) ... the term 'deaconess' ... did not exist, and within a code listing requirements for an office, a reference to 'women' (γυναῖκας) would have sufficed to direct attention to female candidates for the post. (3) ... if 'wives of deacons' was meant, it would have been more common to indicate this with either a possessive pronoun or the definite article ... (4) The omission of a parallel instruction to wives of overseers makes it still less likely that 'wives of deacons' would be singled out. (5) Finally, the reference to Rom 1:1 to 'Phoebe, a deacon of the church at Cenchreae' ... demonstrates both the existence of women deacons and the use of the masculine term to refer to a female deacon" (*Letters*, 266 n. 28).

These are strong arguments. However, one must also consider arguments for the opposite position. First, as Towner himself notes: "The most convincing argument that wives rather than women deacons are in view is the abrupt placement of the reference in the midst of qualifications for male deacons" (ibid.); see 3:12. If, indeed, ὡσαύτως is being used "to introduce a new but related case" (ibid.), it is odd that Paul would suddenly return to the case of male deacons in 3:12. Second, the occurrences of γυνή in the context of this microchiasm (3:2, 11), particularly 3:2, would likely orient the audience to hear the term as "wives." Moreover, given the apostle's explicit instructions in 2:12 that it is improper for a woman to have authority over a man in the context of the household of God, and given that this third microchiasm concerns itself with offices of leaders, it is unlikely that Paul is suddenly allowing women to candidate as deacons. Towner notes, perhaps rightly so, that Paul's concern here is to limit "the *excess* of some women" (*Letters*, 266, italics mine). Similarly, the reference to the creation account in 2:13-14, specifically to the dynamic between Adam and Eve, suggests that redemption in 1 Timothy is to be understood in part as a restoration of what was lost in creation wherein Adam was called to lead Eve in love and service. Third, as Towner himself observes, the term διάκονος has various usages (ibid., 265 n. 27; see also Moo, *Romans*, 913 n. 7). It is, to be sure, a sound hermeneutical principle to use clear texts to illuminate less clear texts. But in this case it is not at all clear that the reference to "Phoebe, a deacon of the church," means that Phoebe functioned in the capacity of a deacon as described in 3:8-11. Moo observes that in Rom 16:1, "Paul may ... simply be highlighting the fact that Phoebe has effectively 'served' the church to which she belongs" (ibid., 913-14). Thus, it is not at all the case that Rom 16:1 "*demonstrates* the existence of women deacons" (Towner, *Letters*, 266 n. 28, italics mine). Others, in fact, go so far as to argue that Rom 16:1 indicates Phoebe was a leader and preacher of the church (e.g., Ellis, "Paul and His Co-Workers," 441-43; Fiorenza, "Missionaries, Apostles, Coworkers," 425-26; Jewett, "Paul, Phoebe, and the Spanish Mission," 148-49). Fourth, it is worth noting that the initial deacons chosen in the early church were "seven men of good repute" (Acts 6:3) even when the disciples could have easily chosen some women. One could argue, perhaps cynically so, that this particular selection in Acts 6 reflected the patriarchal baggage of the original apostles. Still, one could also view it as an implicit echo of what Paul states in 2:11-12.

Moo offers a very helpful insight in considering this debate. Speaking of Rom 16:1, he writes (*Romans*, 914): "But the qualification of *diakonos* by 'of the church' suggests, rather, that Phoebe held at Cenchreae the 'office' of 'deacon' as Paul describes it in 1 Tim. 3:8-12 (cf. Phil. 1:1). We put 'office' in quotation marks because it is very likely that regular offices in local Christian churches were still in the process of being established,

of the second microchiasm, Paul addresses the audience in general—both men and women together (2:1-2). In the parallel A' element of the second microchiasm, Paul narrows his focus to address men and women—individually but in general, married or unmarried—(2:8-15). In the uninterrupted transition to the A element of the third microchiasm, Paul narrows his focus even further to address married men (3:2).[119] Here, then, in the parallel A' element of the third microchiasm, it would be odd and unfitting for Paul to suddenly disrupt the rhetorical flow of the letter—swimming against his own current, as it were—to address "women" in general—all women, married or unmarried—rather than continue with the funneled movement of the letter to address married women—"wives" (3:11).[120] In the same way, it would be equally odd and unfitting for Paul's audience—who have been listening and are now accustomoned to the flow of the letter—not only to perceive a sudden change in direction by Paul but also to force an understanding in 3:11 that goes against the rhetorical flow that Paul has consistently employed. In sum, when considering the unified progression of the overall macrochiasm—here, the movement of Paul's rhetoric across the parallel A and A' elements of both the second and third microchiasms—the

---

as people who regularly ministered in a certain way were gradually recognized officially by the congregation and given a regular title." He adds (ibid., 914, n. 11): "at a later date, when the office was officially recognized, the feminine term διακόνισσα was used of 'female deacons'... But διάκονος is used of female officeholders in the early church...; in this period, it was clearly used of both men and women." Given that "local Christian churches were still in the process of being established," the difficult question is raised as to how the instructions in 1 Timothy, especially those concerning the offices of overseer and deacon, fit in. Was 1 Timothy seeking to establish "a new norm," particularly in light of the redemptive thrust of the gospel to restore the gender dynamics of creation or was the letter seeking to reaffirm what appear to be the practices of the early church of allowing both men and women to serve officially as deacons? Perhaps the only conclusion is that this discussion will persist in the near future and should be handled at the very least with a modicum of humility. For further reading on the question of women and the office of deacons, see Arichea, "Who was Phoebe?," 401-9; Oberlinner, *Ersten Timotheusbrief*, 141-43; Ollrog, *Paulus und seine Mitarbeiter*, 31; Richardson, "From Apostles to Virgins," 238-39; Towner, *Goal*, 212; Madigan and Osiek, *Ordained Women in the Early Church*, 18-21; Wijngaards, *Ordained Women Deacons*, 12-16; Thatcher, "Deacon in the Pauline Church," 65-66; DeConick, *Holy Misogyny*, 66-67; Stiefel, "Women Deacons in 1 Timothy," 13-29.

119. As noted, where a man's fidelity to his wife is in view, unmarried men would not be excluded. However, the language is clearly speaking specifically to married men.

120. A question may be raised as to whether or not 3:11 marks the beginning of a new movement away from specific terms (e.g., husbands, wives) toward general terms (e.g., all men, all women). This consideration, however, becomes moot in the immediately following verse ("Deacons must be the man of one woman," 3:12), where Paul again refers to married men, thus continuing the rhetorical flow of the second and third microchiasm.

entire congregation—both men and women, married and unmarried—would hear "women" (γυναῖκας) in 3:11 as a specific address to "wives"—the wives of the deacons in the A' element.

The term "Likewise" (ὡσαύτως) in the "c" sub-element, therefore, would be understood by the audience in the sense of "Like their husbands." Moreover, the term would also recall its occurrences in the macrochiasm to indicate similarities between distinct roles.[121] In 2:9 of the second microchiasm, "likewise" (ὡσαύτως) identified that, like men in the congregation, women are to participate in the missional calling of the church, yet in distinct roles. In 3:8 of the third microchiasm, "likewise" (ὡσαύτως) identified that, like overseers, deacons are to be qualified to preserve the sound teaching and promote godliness in the missional household of God, yet in a distinct role. Here, then, in 3:11 of the third microchiasm, the sense of "Likewise" (ὡσαύτως) is that, like their deacon husbands, the wives of deacons are to be qualified to missionally preserve the teaching and truth of the gospel and promote godliness, yet in a distinct role from their husbands.[122] Specifically, Paul indicates that like their husbands and thus like an aspiring overseer, these women are to be "respectable, not devilishly-slanderous, temperate, faithful in all" (3:11). The overall similarities between the deacons and their wives is apparent: not only is "respectable" (σεμνάς) in 3:11 an obvious echo of the opening description of qualified deacons in 3:8 as "respectable" (σεμνούς), but also the audience hear a nearly matching sequences of qualities listed for wives—"not devilishly-slanderous, temperate, faithful in all" (3:11)—and the deacons—"not double-worded, not holding-toward much wine, not avaricious" (3:8). The impression on the audience is that deacons and their wives should mirror each other, especially as a way of concretely embodying what a household of godliness looks like and—perhaps more to the point—evidencing the deacons's ability to lead and care for their own wives.[123]

---

121. Knight, *PE*, 132: "the similarity that ὡσαύτως speaks of in the PE in relation to groups of people... is that the groups in view are to be 'like' those mentioned before in having certain qualifications, though not necessarily the same qualifications and activities. In each of these cases the emphasis is on 'similarity' rather than 'sameness.'"

122. Barcley agrees that "the word 'likewise'... indicates that these women are to be seen as distinct from the deacons" (*1 & 2 Tim*, 114); however, he concludes that these women are not wives but rather "are those who assist the deacons in their work" (ibid., 115). Arguably, there is no reason that the wives of deacons—women who share the same concern for truth and godliness as their husbands—would not want to provide assistance; a separate official role is not in view. This implication is drawn out by the mirroring qualities of deacon husbands and their wives in the "c" sub-element, below. Contra Thatcher, "Deacon in the Pauline Church," 66.

123. Krause aptly comments: "1 Timothy 3:11 refers to the wives of deacons who

In the "c" sub-element, the first quality that describes the wives of qualified deacons is "respectable." As with overseers who are to be "irreproachable" (3:2) and deacons who are to be "respectable" (3:8), Paul uses the umbrella term "respectable" to summarize the overall view that the audience are to have of the wives of qualified deacons. Noticeably, where the deacons and their wives mirror one another as "respectable," the implication is that the deacons have upheld their creational roles to protect, care for, and lead their wives in truth and godliness, much like the aspiring overseers in 3:2 of the parallel A element.[124] Paul then proceeds to list three qualifications of what it means for deacons's wives to be respectable: "not devilishly-slanderous, temperate, faithful in all."

Aurally and conceptually similar to the way that deacons must "not" (μή) be "double-worded" (διλόγους, 3:8), so too it is necessary for their wives "not" (μή) to engage in speech that is "devilishly-slanderous" (διαβόλους). Moreover, where the term "devilishly-slanderous" (διαβόλους) in 3:11 of the A' element recalls the cognate occurrence of "devil" (διαβόλου) in 3:6 and 3:7 of the B and B' elements, two connotations would carry forward. On the one hand, the sense of "not devilishly-slanderous" is that the words of deacons's wives—unlike the devil who deceives the people of God to fall into his condemnation and snare (3:6, 7)—must not have a hidden, harming agenda but rather must be open, trustworthy, and motivated by an alignment with the truth of the sound teaching—the gospel. On the other hand, it is clear that the wives's speech is not to be characterized as being-puffed-up (3:6). Such a focus on humble speech would be reminiscent of Paul's instructions in the second microchiasm for the women to cosmetic themselves with modesty and self-control, not in braids and gold or pearls or rich attire (2:9). In effect, in the same way that the women's godliness was intended to attract many to Christ in the second microchiasm, so too would a woman's humble speech in the third microchiasm. Still, given the sustained polemic of the

---

like their husbands were expected to behave decorously and suitably within church and society" (*1 Tim*, 69). Knight, *PE*, 172: "If it is wives that are in view, then the verse fits here as another qualification necessary for one who would be a deacon and who would conduct his ministry with his wife's assistance. Thus the wife's qualifications are part and parcel of his qualifications for the office of δίκονος." Wall with Steele, *1 & 2 Tim*, 107: "Their spouses must be similarly qualified to serve others as well (v. 11), since caring for members of the household is their principal responsibility."

It is worth noting that Krause, *1 Tim*, 69–70, presents the case that women were deacons in other of Paul's letters (e.g., Phoebe in Rom 16:1) but were not allowed such positions in the PE churches.

124. To be sure, Paul is not indicating that women are not respectable without husbands. Much rather, given that 3:11 has a marriage relationship in view, the audience understand that men who are qualified to be deacons are leading their wives commendably as Christ intends. See above regarding 3:2 in relation to Ephesians 5:25–26.

macrochiasm, "not devilishly-slanderous" would likely be heard as a rebuke, not merely to the deacons's wives but also—and more so—to the unqualified deacons who, being "double-worded," have effectively led their wives to be "devilishly-slanderous." Here in 3:11, Paul again calls the audience to consider whether or not men are qualified to serve-as-deacons—the measure being the conduct of their wives.

The quality of being "temperate" (νηφαλίους) recalls its earlier occurrence in 3:2 of the A element concerning aspiring overseers who are to be "temperate" (νηφάλιον), that is, gospel-thinking in all aspects of life. Thus, "temperate" connotes having in view God's desire for all humans to be-saved (2:4) by coming to have-faith upon Christ Jesus (1:16), the one mediator of God and humans (2:5b) who came into the world (1:15) and gave himself as a ransom on behalf of all (2:6). At the same time, given the correlation between the deacons's wives and the qualities expected of their husbands— "not holding-toward much wine" (3:8)—the term "temperate" in 3:11 likely has in view temperance with respect to drinking. Thus in full, the term connotes a purposefulness and soberness in life—perhaps expressed by missional, humble speech—as part of their role to preserve the sound teaching and promote godliness within God's household and, therefore, to welcome those-outside. That the quality of being "temperate" is repeated again in this microchiasm—occurring in the parallel A and A' elements—underscores to the audience that even though specific men and women must be qualified to model godliness for the entire congregation, the apostle viewed deliberate, intentional living as an essential quality of all those who are "in faith."

The final quality concerning the wives of deacons is to be "faithful in all." The phrase recalls two important themes thoughout the macrochiasm. First, "faithful" (πιστάς, 3:11) would be understood by the audience as a reference to the realm "in faith" (ἐν πίστει, 1:2, 4; 2:7, 15), that is, the mode of existence that humans enter by coming "to have-faith" (πιστεύειν) upon Christ (1:16). More specifically, the term recalls for the audience that Christ considered Paul "faithful" (πιστόν) in the first microchiasm (1:12). Thus in the third microchiasm, Paul seems to be emphasizing that deacons's wives must be fully aligned with Paul, the authoritative apostolic teacher. Moreover, the term "all" (πᾶσιν) in 3:11 of the third microchiasm recalls God's missional concern in the second microchiasm for the salvation of "all" (πάντων, 2:1, 2, 6; πάντας, 2:4a) humans. In short, the audience understand that deacons's wives are to model a missional lifestyle that shares the Savior God's desire for all humans to be-saved (2:3–4a).

Still, the linguistic similarity between the entire phrase "faithful in all" (πιστὰς ἐν πᾶσιν) in 3:11 and the earlier phrase "Faithful (πιστός) is the word and worthy of all (πάσης) acceptance" in 1:15 highlights an essential quality that is necessary for deacons's wives. Though the connection would substantiate that deacons's wives must be aligned with the sound teaching of Paul (1:10b) and the word that he considers "faithful" (1:15; 3:1), more significantly it would also indicate that the wives themselves have proven their loyalty to Paul as their teacher "in faith" and truth (2:7) and, therefore, are worthy of acceptance as models of godliness. Thus in the same way that qualified deacons in the "a" sub-element are holding "the mystery of the faith (πίστεως)" (3:9), so too their wives in the "c" sub-element are "faithful" (πιστάς) with the mystery—the sound teaching, the gospel.[125] Indeed, the audience understand that deacons and their wives not only mirror each other but also equally reflect the gospel to others. Significantly, then, such mirroring indicates whether or not men are qualified to serve-as-deacons: men who are holding the mystery of the faith and lead their wives to be faithful in the same way are certainly qualified to preserve the sound teaching and promote godliness within God's missional household.

1 Timothy 3:12: Deacons, Leaders of Their Own Households

("c'" sub-element)

The "c'" sub-element of the minichiasm begins a movement to enhance the audience's understanding of the preceding "c," "b," and "a" sub-elements: "Deacons must be the man of one woman" (3:12a).[126] The imperative that deacons "must be" (ἔστωσαν) recalls the earlier imperatives that deacons "must be-tested (δοκιμαζέσθωσαν) first; then they must serve-as-deacons (διακονείτωσαν)" (3:8). In 3:12 of the "c'" sub-element, then, the audience hear Paul again emphasizing that what follows is not optional but should be received as a command. Furthermore, the phrase "man of one

---

125. Similarly, though suggesting that wives are not in view, Towner suggests: "It is not necessary, however, to separate this quality [of trustworthiness] from the woman deacon's faith; it is her adherence to the gospel (3:9) that produces her 'trustworthiness' in carrying out whatever tasks she is set" (*Letters*, 267).

126. As a reference to married men and women, 3:12 affirms for the audience that Paul is sustaining the rhetorical movement of the macrochiasm—from general terms to specific terms—from the second to the third microchiasm. In this way, not only would the audience understand that 3:11 refers to the wives of deacons, but it would also convey, therefore, that 3:12 is part of Paul's uninterrupted discussion that began in 3:8 pertaining to qualifications for men to be deacons. As such, it is most unlikely that the audience would consider that Paul had ended his discussion of deacons in 3:10 and is suddenly returning to his discussion on deacons as if he had forgotten to include the significant qualities listed in 3:12 (contra Marshall, *PE*, 494).

woman" (μιᾶς γυναικὸς ἄνδρες) here in 3:12 of the A' element recalls the phrase "man of one woman" (μιᾶς γυναικὸς ἄνδρα) in 3:2 of the parallel A element. The force of the parallel occurrence further emphasizes to the audience that all qualified leaders in God's household must consist of men who are faithful and devoted to their wives.[127] As with overseers in the A element, then, Paul is clearly grounding men's qualification to serve-as-deacons in the A' element by their fidelity to their wives. Furthermore, given that the wives of qualified deacons mirror their husbands (3:8–11), Paul is not only directing the audience to consult the wives's assessments of their husbands—as in the A element—but also to observe the lifestyle of the wives. In short, if the men's wives are not qualified to exemplify godliness, then neither are their husbands whose fidelity includes nurturing and nourishing their wives in sacrificial love that results in godliness. As with overseers, then, Paul's concern for deacons has in view the household-law of God: deacons must be men who exemplify to all men in the audience that Christ Jesus loves, cherishes, and is ever-faithful to the church, his bride (Eph 5:25–32), thus leading all men in the audience to love, cherish, and be ever-faithful to their own wives.

Within the phrase "man of one woman," the audience hear the specific term "woman" (γυναικός), which certainly recalls "women" (γυναῖκας) in 3:11 of the immediately preceding parallel "c" sub-element. Here, then, the rhetorical effect of the minichiasm upon the audience is significant: framed within Paul's discussion on the qualification of deacons, the paired arrangement of "women" (3:11) and "woman" (3:12) in the parallel "c" and "c'" sub-elements indicates for the audience that Paul has in view the same pair of women, namely the wives of deacons.[128] What is more, the parallel relationship between the "c" and "c'" sub-elements within Paul's discussion on deacons affirms the importance of deacons's wives: not only do they have

---

127. Knight, *PE*, 171: "Another consideration that favors the understanding 'wives' in v. 11 is the omission of any reference to their marital status and fidelity (i.e., 'the wife of one husband') . . . this qualification is always mentioned in the PE where positions of ministry or service are in view." See Krause, *1 Tim*, 69–70. Contra Payne, *Man and Woman*, 445–46. Though maritial fidelity is in view rather than marital status (see Thatcher, "Deacon in the Pauline Church," 64), as in 3:2 Paul clearly is addressing married men.

128. Here, it may be helpful to visualize the arrangement of the minichiasm, indicated by the linguistic parallels:
"a". "mystery" (μυστήριον, 3:9);
  "b". "serve-as-deacons" (διακονείτωσαν, 3:10);
    "c". "women" (γυναῖκας, 3:11);
    "c'". "woman" (γυναικός, 3:12);
  "b'". "serve-as-deacons" (διακονήσαντες, 3:13);
"a'". "mystery" (μυστήριον, 3:16).

a fundamental importance in their husbands's lives but also in the audience's consideration of their husbands's qualifications as a deacon. Therefore, due to the connotations established in the progression of the 3:8–16 minichiasm—the A' element of the third microchiasm—the repetition of the phrase "man of one woman" between the parallel A and A' elements is not merely to be understood as a restatement that deacons are held to the same standard as overseers. Rather, in light of the A' element, the audience hear that the qualifying standard "man of one woman" for leaders in the church in both the A and A' elements is to some degree measurable through the godliness of their respective wives.[129]

Paul concludes the "c'" sub-element of the minichiasm within the A' element by stating that deacons must be "leading children commendably and their own households" (3:12b). The phrase recalls the A element, where it was necessary for an aspiring overseer to be "leading his own household commendably, holding children in submissiveness" (3:4) and to know how "to lead his own household" (3:5).[130] Each of the parallel terms in the A and A' elements—"leading" (προϊστάμενον, 3:4; προστῆναι, 3:5; προϊστάμενοι, 3:12), "own households" (τοῦ ἰδίου οἴκου, 3:4; τοῦ ἰδίου οἴκου, 3:5; τῶν ἰδίων οἴκων, 3:12), "children" (τέκνα, 3:4; τέκνων, 3:12), and "commendably"

---

129. Though the apostle makes no specification for the overseer's wives, most likely the audience would have understood that overseer's wives must also "be respectable, not devilishly-slanderous, temperate, faithful in all." Also, we should take seriously Witherington's exhortation: "One must bear in mind that Timothy knew quite well Paul's teaching and leadership principles, and so some things could be omitted and some only intimated because this is part of an ongoing relationship and an ongoing conversation, and not an opening salvo" (*Letters*, 244).

130. It may be worth noting the juxtaposition of "household" and "children" between 3:4 and 3:12 in the A and A' elements:
3:4a: "leading his own household commendably";
3:4b: "holding children in submissiveness";
3:12a: "leading children commendably";
3:12b: "and their own households."
Commentators suggest that this change in order is significant. Marshall, *PE*, 495: "The placing of τῶν ἰδίων οἴκων after τέκνων implies that the reference is to servants/slaves and suggests that the prospective church leaders are people of some standing." Towner, *Letters*, 267: "The order, 'let them manage their children and households well,' distinguishes between offspring and slaves, suggesting that the deacons, like the overseers, were (generally) householders, people of means and position in the social structure." Compare to Trebilco's comments: "Since it is thought that only the well-to-do owned household slaves, it is suggested that the fact that deacons owned slaves shows that they are relatively wealthy and of relatively high social standing. However . . . that a householder owns a slave indicates little about the householder's socio-economic status . . . the fact that leaders are assumed to be 'householders' and so to have 'houses' (see 1 Tim 3:4–5 with regard to overseers) also does not mean that they are wealthy" (*Early Christians in Ephesus*, 408).

(καλῶς, 3:4; καλῶς, 3:12)—signifies for the audience an advancement of the third microchiasm that carries forward the connotations for each term from the A element into the A' element. Yet, as with the parallel phrase "man of one woman" in the A and A' elements, each term within the parallel phrases has been enhanced by the movement of the microchiasm and, therefore, is to be understood according to the cumulative progression of the minichiasm within the A' element. In this way, the occurrence of each parallel term in the A' element is not merely a restatement of qualifications from the A element but is a corroboration of the measures by which men in the audience are to be qualified for leadership in the Ephesian church. On the one hand, Paul is certainly calling upon the audience to consult a man's children and household—relatives, slaves, and significant relationships—to discern whether or not he is leading them commendably. On the other hand, Paul is clearly insisting that his audience observe the daily lifestyle of a man's children and household—relatives, slaves, and significant relationship—to discern whether or not he is leading them commendably. In short, the lives of those living under a man's leadership at home are the tangible measure of his qualification to lead in the church—as deacon or overseer. Where a man's wife, children, relatives, and slaves both validate his leadership with their words and demonstrate the positive result of his leadership by their own actions, Paul assures the first-century Ephesian audience that such a man is qualified to lead in the church. Indeed, such men who know how to lead their own household to this degree will know how to care for the church of God as deacons or overseers.[131]

Still, as noted in the B' element, the purpose of the qualifications for men to lead the household of God was not merely to promote internal godliness for its own sake. Rather, the purpose of the church having qualified men to lead the congregation in godliness was fundamentally missional.[132]

---

131. Regarding the repeated quality of "leading" for deacons and overseers, Towner makes an interesting proposition concerning the possible church structure during this period (*Letters*, 267): "The concern for this management ability suggests that deacons carried out significant leadership duties in service to the overseers, or perhaps (if overseers supervised a cluster of house churches in a locality) on a par with overseers but in a more limited sphere (the house church . . .)." Witherington, however, asserts (*Letters*, 243): "Nothing is said about the relationship between overseers and deacons. Furthermore, we can only guess at the scope of the work of each group, since what we have is primarily character descriptions rather than job descriptions . . . Rhetorically speaking, what Paul is doing here is providing a character sketch far more than a job description, and its main function is to explain *how* a leader should behave, not *what* the leader's full job description should look like."

132. Bassler, *1 & 2 Tim*, 71: "The goal of this was in large part apologetic: these church leaders represent the church to an unbelieving society and through their exemplary lives they could deflect the hostility that new cults often faced. In particular, the

In this way, given the progression of the third microchiasm—particularly of the 3:8–16 minichiasm within the A' element—a twofold purpose for the high qualifications of church leaders is again confirmed for the audience. On the one hand, the lifestyles of godliness by qualified deacons and overseers in God's household welcomes and attracts those-outside, thus having a direct missional impact. On the other hand, as a result of the example of godliness set by the deacons and overseers, the subsequently observable lifestyles of godliness on the part of their wives, children, relatives, slaves, as well as all those under their leadership within the church would be viewed as respectable, welcoming, and attractive to those-outside, thus having an indirect missional impact. In short, the audience understand that Paul's discussion on the qualifications for overseers and deacons is driven fundamentally by his concern in the second microchiasm for God's household to fulfill its missional purpose.

1 Timothy 3:13–15: Those Who Serve-As-Deacons, the Household of God

("b'" sub-element)

The "b'" sub-element (3:13–15) of the minichiasm both concludes Paul's discussion on the qualifications of deacons and begins to enhance the audience's understanding of the household of God. In the first half of verse 3:13 the audience hear: "For those who serve-as-deacons commendably acquire for themselves a commendable standing." Several observations are worth noting. First, just as the audience heard "For" (γάρ) in 2:13 of the second microchiasm as marking the basis for the preceding 2:12 verse, so too the audience understand that the conjuction "For" (γάρ) in 3:13 of the third microchiasm marks the basis for deacons's fidelity to their wives and leadership in their household in the preceding 3:12 verse.[133] That is, given that the fundamental purpose of church leaders's godliness is missional—both directly and indirectly—the basis of such leadership in 3:12 is undoubtedly missional in 3:13. As such, the phrase "those who serve-as-deacons commendably (καλῶς) acquire for themselves a commendable (καλόν) standing" (3:13) recalls the missional basis for overseers holding "a

---

stable households of these men [and women] not only stood as testimony to their leadership skills but also silenced any suspicion among outsiders that the new cult would undermine family structure and thus threaten the social foundation of the orderly and stable empire."

133. Contra Knight, who suggests, "γάρ points forward to the second half of the verse, which gives the reason for the good service described in the first half" (*PE*, 173).

commendable (καλῶς) testimony from those-outside" (3:7). Thus the missional force of the microchiasm is further emphasized and clearly applied to both deacons and overseers.

Second, similar to 3:1b of the A element where Paul encouraged qualified men to aspire to the "commendable (καλοῦ) work" of an overseer, Paul's discussion in the A' element would likely be heard as an encouragement for qualified men to "serve-as-deacons commendably (καλῶς)" and thus "acquire for themselves a commendable (καλόν) standing."[134] Though such "commendable standing" is fundamentally missional, the audience understand that Paul is calling upon those within God's missional household to respect their leaders who are in positions of high "standing" (βαθμόν).[135] In this way, the juxtaposition of the adverb "commendably" and adjective "commendable" in 3:13 reflects God's justice: each person will reap what they sow—here, "those who serve-as-deacons commendably" will reap "a commendable standing."[136] Specifically, those who, according to the "b" subelement, have been tested and called to "serve-as-deacons" (διακονείτωσαν; 3:10) and, subsequently, do "serve-as-deacons" (διακονήσαντες; 3:13) in a commendable manner acquire a position of "standing" (βαθμόν) and of respectability among all who are "in faith."[137] As if to doubly emphasize this point, the audience hear Paul's use of both the middle verb and dative pronoun "acquire ... for themselves" (ἑαυτοῖς ... περιποιοῦνται);[138] in effect,

---

134. Marshall, *PE*, 495: "γάρ gives the wider ground rather than the reason for the instructions; it may serve the same purpose as 3.1."

135. See Kelly, *PE*, 85; Towner, *Letters*, 268. For discussion of various but unlikely proposals on the meaning of "standing," see Knight, *PE*, 174; Marshall, *PE*, 495–96; Oberlinner, *Ersten Timotheusbrief*, 144; Nauck, "Probleme des frühchristlichen Amtsverständnisses," 200–220; Witherington, *Letters*, 242. These proposals include advancement from the office of deacon to the office of overseer; special spiritual insight; or elevated enlightenment and spiritual status.

136. Thatcher, "Deacon in the Pauline Church," 67: "God will recognize and reward their efforts ... the 'fringe benefits' of the work make it well worth the effort."

137. Although it is clear that the verb διακονήσαντες refers specifically to the role of deacons, the principle that "those who serve-as-deacons commendably acquire for themselves a commendable standing" among the audience holds equally true for overseers who serve commendably. In addition to the clear conceptual parallels between the two roles in the church, the adverb καλῶς in 3:13 recalls not only its earlier occurrence in 3:12 of the A' element but also 3:4 of the A element that focuses on the role of an overseer. Given the parallel standards of excellence expected of both offices, there is no reason the audience would not have assumed that 3:13 secondarily implies, in effect, that "those who commendably serve—in general—acquire for themselves a commendable standing."

138. The phrase is literally translated "for themselves (ἑαυτοῖς) ... acquire for themselves (περιποιοῦνται)." The inclusion of the dative pronoun "for themselves" (ἑαυτοῖς) is grammatically unnecessary and, therefore, would be heard as intentional emphasis.

Paul's point seems to be that "rewards are linked to and commensurate with the deacons's initiative and performance."[139] Paul's purpose here is undoubtedly to motivate future deacons and encourage those who currently serve-as-deacons to do so commendably within the household of God.

Third and lastly, the participle "serve-as-deacons" (διακονήσαντες) here in 3:13 the "b'" sub-element recalls the imperative "they must serve-as-deacons" (διακοδείτωσαν) in 3:10 of the parallel "b" sub-element. Given the movement of the minichiasm, the audience are thus to understand that Paul's command for qualified men to serve-as-deacons in 3:10 is not an enlistment to a joyless task but rather a summons to work that is rewarding in itself—both in its missional impact and the respect it acquire from those within God's household (3:13).

In the second half of 3:13, Paul states that those who serve-as-deacons commendably acquire "much confidence in faith that is in Christ Jesus." The term "confidence" (παρρησίαν) usually refers to assurance and freedom in public speaking.[140] Furthermore, given that deacons acquire "much (πολλήν)" confidence, Paul's point is clear: beyond any doubt, qualified men who serve-as-deacons will indeed benefit from their work. The term "much (πολλήν)" in 3:13 recalls for the audience the phrase "not holding-toward much (πολλῷ) wine" in 3:8. The stark contrast would likely be polemical, pitting the unqualified men associated with the false teachers—"much wine"—against the qualified men who must serve-as-deacons—"much confidence."

Notably, such confidence is tied to the phrase "in faith" (ἐν πίστει), which the audience have heard repeatedly throughout the progression of the macrochiasm (1:2, 4; 2:7, 15). Here in the third microchiasm, the mode of existence "in faith" carries with it the entire cumulative effect of its occurrences throughout the overall macrochiasm: it is the familial realm (1:2) of God's household-law (1:4) in which Paul is a teacher of truth (2:7) and where women actively bring in more people (2:15). Thus the confidence that qualified deacons acquire "in faith" pertains to their family ties with those in God's household, their acceptance of the sound teaching—the gospel—and their collaborative missional effort to invite more people into God's household. Also, where qualified deacons are holding "the mystery of the faith" (3:9)—living in a way that preserves the sound teaching and promotes godliness—the implication is that such men become more confident about their lifestyle "in faith," that is, become less likely to hold-toward something different (cf. 1:4, 10b). Such men, then, acquire much confidence to

---

139. Towner, *Letters*, 267.
140. See Quinn and Wacker, *Letters*, 277–78; Knight, *PE*, 174.

serve-as-deacons, influencing those in God's household to live according to their common existence "in faith."

Still, much confidence "in faith (πίστει)" undoubtedly has in view both the deaconss's act of faith and the object of their faith, namely Christ Jesus. In 1:16 of the A' element within the first microchiasm, the audience understood that by coming "to have-faith (πιστεύειν)"—the act of trusting—upon Christ Jesus—the object of trust—sinners like Paul enter into the realm "in faith," where Christ Jesus is "our Lord" in 1:2 of the parallel A element. Here in the third microchiasm, then, the audience understand that those who serve-as-deacons commendably not only acquire greater confidence in their faith—their act of trusting upon Christ Jesus—but also greater confidence with the Lord of the realm in which they live—Christ Jesus himself. To be sure, this latter sense is affirmed when Paul specifies that the confidence acquired is "in faith that is in Christ Jesus."[141]

The phrase "that is in Christ Jesus" (τῇ ἐν Χριστῷ Ἰησοῦ) in 3:13 recalls its earlier occurrence in 1:14 of the first microchiasm: "that are in Christ Jesus" (τῆς ἐν Χριστῷ Ἰησοῦ). Significantly, where Paul directly linked the values associated with the realm "in faith"—"the faith (πίστεως) and love" (1:14)—to their source "in Christ Jesus (ἐν Χριστῷ Ἰησοῦ)" in 1:14, the audience already understood that to be "in faith" (ἐν πίστει, 1:2, 4) is to be "in Christ Jesus" (ἐν Χριστῷ Ἰησοῦ, 1:14). Here in 3:13, then, Paul explicitly reiterates and emphasizes the connection for his audience: to be sure, the realm "in faith" (ἐν πίστει, 3:13) is synonymous with the realm "in Christ Jesus" (ἐν Χριστῷ Ἰησοῦ, 3:13). In this way, those who serve-as-deacons commendably in God's household—the realm "in faith"—acquire much confidence in their relationship with the Lord of God's household, Christ Jesus (1:2, 12).[142] At the same time, such confidence with Christ Jesus—the one mediator who came into the world and gave himself as a ransom to save sinners (1:15; 2:6)—would certainly deepen their awareness that Christ Jesus came into the world because of their own sin. Thus "much confidence in faith that is in Christ Jesus" conveys a multifaceted, interconnected benefit: as deacons acquire much confidence in their relationship with Christ Jesus, they acquire much confidence in the fact of their own sin, thus acquiring

---

141. Towner, *Letters*, 268: "'In faith' here means the deacons' active believing/trusting . . . with the subsequent phrase, 'in Christ Jesus,' indicating both the object of faith and the relationship that this believing sustains."

142. Marshall, *PE*, 497: "The thought is of the relationship with Christ which is characterised by faith . . . the point of the promise is that faithful service brings a greater sense of confidence in God and assurance of salvation." Towner, *Letters*, 268: "faithful service will deepen the deacon's faith and further strengthen the relationship with God and Christ."

much confidence about their need for a relationship with Christ Jesus, and thus acquiring much confidence in their act of faith upon Christ Jesus for their salvation from sin. In effect, with Paul's concluding statement on deacons in 3:13 of the "b'" sub-element, the audience themselves may have much confidence: the men who are qualified to serve-as-deacons will lead the entire congregation—those living "in faith that is in Christ"—to acquire much confidence for themselves. Ultimately, the men who are qualified to serve-as-deacons may be confident during their work to preserve the sound teaching and promote godliness within God's missional household "in faith" because they themselves have confidence with their personal connection to God "in Christ Jesus."

Having completed his qualifications for overseers and deacons, Paul continues the "b'" sub-element of the 3:8–16 minichiasm: "These-things to you I write, hoping to come to you in quickness" (3:14). It is possible that the audience hear the term "These-things" (ταῦτά) in reference to the qualifications of overseers and deacons in the immediate third microchiasm, or to both the second and third microchiasms, or perhaps to the beginning of the letter.[143] The specification "to you" (σοι) recalls for the audience "to you (σοι), child Timothy" in 1:18 of the first microchiasm, wherein Paul highlighted his familial bond "in faith" with Timothy (1:2) and their common charge (1:3, 5, 18) to preserve the the sound teaching against "some" who teach-different (1:3), namely some-thing different that lies-opposed to the sound teaching (1:10b). Here in the third microchiasm, then, the audience understand that Paul intends the same: "These-things"—at the very least, his discussion on qualified overseers and deacons—are "to you"—Timothy—for the purpose of safeguarding God's household against "some" who teach-different, that is, the false-teaching overseers in the Ephesian church who bring-about controversial-speculations rather than the household-law of God in faith (1:3–4). The polemical force of the statement would call upon the audience's allegiance to Paul through their allegiance to his

---

143. Most commentators are in general agreement that the term here refers to the second and third microchiasms (2:1–15 and 3:1–16). Knight, *PE*, 178: "From the other occurrences of ταῦτα in 1 Timothy, it would appear that the reference is to that which precedes... Since chapter 2 and 3 both relate to conduct in God's house, the reference probably includes chapter 2 as well as chapter 3." Towner, *Letters*, 272 n. 6: "the present demonstrative pronoun ταῦτα reaches only as far back as the similar summarizing conclusion in 1:18, where the last occurrence of a second person singule (σοι, "you" = Timothy), accompanied by a summarizing anaphoric ταύτην, appears." Marshall, *PE*, 505: "The precise reference of ταῦτα is uncertain... The function here is to reach back and summarise the connected instructions about church life in 2.1–3.13, just as in 1.18 ταύτην τὴν παραγγελίαν refers back to 1.3–17." Cf. Ngewa, *1 & 2 Tim*, 79, who suggests that the reference is to the whole letter.

representative Timothy over and against "some" who are currently leading as young-plants and being-puffed-up (3:6). Moreover, the audience again are reminded that just as Paul's authority is "according to the command of God our Savior and Christ Jesus our hope" (1:1), so too does Timothy represent an extension of Paul's own authority, thus God and Christ Jesus's authority. In short, as Timothy implements Paul's instructions and qualifications in regard to overseers and deacons in Ephesus, the audience's response to Timothy carries deep significance—certainly demonstrating their allegiance to Paul who entrusted Timothy (1:18) and ultimately to God and Christ Jesus who both commanded and appointed Paul (1:1, 12; 2:7).

The verb "I write" (γράφω) further emphasizes to the audience that Paul's apostolic authority is in view. The letter itself represents an authoritative substitute for Paul's presence;[144] in effect, as the audience hear and observe its performance by the letter carrier, they are reminded that Paul himself is speaking these words directly to them.[145] The audience understand that Paul's expecatation is that they are to receive "These-things" not only as his words but as the faithful words concerning Christ Jesus and salvation (1:15; 3:1), which Paul was appointed to publically teach with the authority of an apostle according to the command of God and Christ Jesus (1:1; 2:7). Adherence to the letter, that which Paul has written (3:14), thus signifies the audience's faithful adherence to the commands of God and Christ Jesus.

The phrase "hoping to come to you in quickness" expresses urgency—the disruption created by the false teachers has become seriousness enough that it necessitates Paul's quick return.[146] Here, rather than the earlier celebration of the factivite truth that Christ Jesus is "our hope" (ἐλπίδος, 1:1) who "came (ἦλθεν) into the world to save sinners" (1:15) and of the Savior God's desire for all humans "to come" (ἐλθεῖν) to a knowing-embrace of truth (2:4b), the audience understand that the opposition by "some" against the truth concerning Christ Jesus has caused a tense, tentative situation in

---

144. Regarding the function of the letter as an authoritative presence of the apostle Paul, see volume 1, chapter 1.

145. Rather than Paul's involvement in writing the letter, the emphasis of "I write" (γράφω) would convey his direct connection to the contents of the letter—his direct apostolic authority—during its performance to the Ephesian audience. Regarding the process of letter writing in first-century Pauline practice, see volume 1, chapter 1.

146. Referencing Collins (*1 & 2 Tim*, 99–100), Witherington, *Letters*, 245 n. 264, highlights that this passing comment in 3:14 evidences that Paul himself was in fact the author of this letter: "the mention of a delay in coming as a reason for sending a letter is definitely not a stock item in ancient letters, nor is it a known device in pseudepigrapha. Here is another small piece of evidence that must count against the idea that someone is trying for verisimilitude here. It is much more natural to take this as reflecting a real situation involving Paul." Contra Long, *1 & 2 Tim*, 98.

which Paul is "hoping (ἐλπίζων) to come (ἐλθεῖν)" (3:14) to bring-about the household-law of God in faith (1:4), that is, to preserve the truth of Christ and the sound teaching concerning him. Along with Paul and Timothy, then, implied is that the audience are to consider the gravity of the situation and their obligation to help Paul and Timothy address the problem of the false teachers "in quickness." Indeed, the very fact of the letter—specifically its polemical concern—emphasizes this urgency.

Although Paul hopes to come to assist Timothy in Ephesus, the audience again hear Paul's main point in sending the letter: "but if I am delayed, that you might know how it is necessary to behave in the household of God, which is the church of the living God" (3:15). The phase "but if I am delayed" further highlights Timothy's authority; the possibility of being "delayed" (βραδύνω) is not merely informative but rather communicates to the audience that, in the apostle Paul's absence, Timothy stands as his representative. That is, the audience understand that their alignment with Paul—moreover, with Christ Jesus whom Paul directly represents (1:1)—demands their alignment with Timothy. Furthermore, the phrase "that you might know (εἰδῇς) how it is necessary to behave in the household (οἴκῳ) of God, which is the church of God (ἐκκλησία θεοῦ)" highlights the forward movement of the macrochiasm. As Paul's "genuine child in faith" (1:2), the audience understand that Timothy has been raised with Paul's teaching and instructions to "bring-about the household-law of God in faith" (1:4) and is thus able to lead and care for the church in Ephesus.[147] Indeed, given that Paul and Timothy had done missionary work together for nearly twenty years by the time that Paul sent the 1 Timothy letter to the Ephesian church, the audience would clearly understand that Timothy already knows "how it is necessary to behave in the household of God" (3:14).[148] Thus whereas in 3:5 of the A element Paul rhetorically states a problem—"if someone does not know (οἶδεν) how to lead his own household (οἴκου), how (πῶς) will he care for the church of God?"—in 3:15 of the parallel A' element Paul provides its definitive resolution: even if Paul is delayed, Timothy will "know how (εἰδῇς πῶς) it is necessary to behave in the household (οἴκῳ) of God." Here, again, Paul progresses the significance of Timothy's authority: the au-

---

147. Paul's statement in 3:15 does not imply that Timothy himself was acting inappropriately (3:5) and therefore needed a reminder of how to behave in God's household. Barcley, *1 & 2 Tim*, 120: Paul "writes specifically to Timothy ('to you', singular), but certainly Timothy is to pass these instructions on to the church. No doubt Timothy already knows what Paul has been telling him. But Paul's sending these instructions through Timothy to the church both validate Timothy's work as a teacher of apostolic doctrine and strengthen his authority to the church."

148. See discussion in volume 1, chapter 1 regarding the historical setting of the 1 Timothy letter.

dience are not only to rely upon Timothy as the model for conduct in God's household but also to adhere to his instructions as Paul's representative in God's household. The conceptual relationship between 3:5 and 3:15 thus functions to underscore the polemic of the letter: Timothy represents the antithesis of the person in view in 3:5.[149] To be sure, Paul's statement in 3:15 does not imply that Timothy himself was acting inappropriately in 3:5 nor that he needed a reminder of how to behave in God's household. Rather, in stark contrast to "someone" in 3:5, the audience are to receive Timothy as a reliable guide for knowing how to lead the church and for demonstrating what behavior is fitting for those who profess godliness.

The verb "it is necessary" (δεῖ) recalls its prior occurrences in 3:2 and 3:7, thus carrying forward the urgency, structure, and missional nature of God's household to welcome and bring in those-outside. Moreover, the phrase "in the household of God" (ἐν οἴκῳ θεοῦ) recalls for the audience "the household-law of God in faith" (οἰκονομίαν θεοῦ τὴν ἐν πίστει) in 1:4 of the first microchiasm. This connection is significant, making explicit to the audience that their existence "in (ἐν) the household of God" is synonymous with their existence "in (ἐν) faith." Certainly, the familial aspect "in faith" (1:2, 4, 18) would be emphasized by being "in the household of God" (3:15).[150] Furthermore, the audience understand that it is necessary for the lifestyle in both spheres of existence to be one and the same: "the household-law of God in faith" (1:4)—the household rules of God the Father (1:2)—are clearly to be observed by those living "in the household of God" (3:15). In this way, the infinitive verb "to behave" (ἀναστρέφεσθαι) would not only be understood as an expression of the audience's love and reverence for God—the Father of the household in which they live (1:2, 4; 3:15)—but also as part of their missional participation with God—the Savior (1:1; 2:3)—to bring those-outside into God's household.[151] Still, the

---

149. In passing, the linguistic and aural similarities between 3:5 and 3:15 may be worth noting:
3:5: "εἰ δέ τις τοῦ ἰδίου οἴκου προστῆναι οὐκ οἶδεν, πῶς ἐκκλησίας θεοῦ ἐπιμελήσεται";
3:15: "ἐὰν δὲ βραδύνω, ἵνα εἰδῇς πῶς δεῖ ἐν οἴκῳ θεοῦ ἀναστρέφεσθαι."

150. Patterson and Kelley, "1 Tim," 670: "By using the term 'household' Paul emphasized the fact that the church was much more than its weekly gathering of believers in the worship assembly. This metaphor uses the 'family,' in which God is the Father, believers are sisters and brothers, and the apostles are the household managers."

151. Witherington, *Letters*, 245: "We should not make the mistake that Paul is talking only about behavior 'in church' here. Paul is also quite concerned about the effect of Christian misbehavior on non-Christians who observe this bad witness."

The translation "to behave" could be misleading; indeed, a full-orbed lifestyle is in view. Towner aptly notes: "Paul uses the term [ἀναστρέφεσθαι] . . . referring to a prescribed manner of living (i.e., Christian living) in which 'conduct' is to assume a specific shape because of theological realities: it occurs here in the typical combination of the

overall force of the phrase "how it is necessary to behave in the household of God" is undoubtedly on the audience's new identity as a result of entering into a new sphere of existence—the realm "*in* faith"—which is described here in terms of being "*in* the household of God." Here, then, Paul is reiterating to the audience that they have entered into a new mode of existence—their attitude toward Paul and Timothy, therefore, ought to correspond. Previously, on account of their sin, they were like Paul "in unfaithfulness" (1:13)—outside of God's household—but now, through the beyond-abounding grace of Christ Jesus (1:14), they have been freed from imprisonment to their sin by Christ's ransom payment (2:6) and now belong to the familial household of God according to Paul's teaching "in faith and truth" (2:7). In short, the audience understand a dual implication in Paul's statement. On the one hand, they are to adhere to Paul and Timothy's leadership and authority to bring-about the household-law of God in faith (1:4), as is necessary for those who live in God's household (3:15). On the other hand, by doing so, they will tangibly demonstrate their own existence with Paul and Timothy "in faith" (1:2), thus that they belong to a common family with God as the Father (1:2), and therefore their own concern as family members to preserve the sound teaching and promote godliness in the missional household of God in which they live.

Concluding 3:15, Paul qualifies the household of God by the relative clause "which is the church of the living God, a pillar and foundation of the truth." The term "which" (ἥτις) recalls the aural similarities to "someone" (τις) in 3:1 and 3:5 of the third microchiasm. Here, the polemical concern of the letter would likely be heard as the contrast between the false teachers's inability to care-for the church of God (3:5) and Timothy's entrustment to lead the church of God. Such is affirmed by the phrase "the church of . . . God" (ἐκκλησία θεοῦ), which recalls "the church of God" (ἐκκλησίας θεοῦ) in the polemical statement of 3:5 in the A element, thus making clear the contrast between the false teachers and Timothy. Furthermore, Paul's statement in 3:15 further emphasizes the force of 3:5, namely that the audience are to understand the church as a household: as "the church"—those called-out by God—they have been brought together "in faith," that is, into "the household of God" (3:15) to be a whole family.[152]

---

verb and a prepositional phrase that more nearly defines in some way the scope of such conduct" (*Letters*, 273). Karris, *PE*, 79: "'The image of the household of God' says that you are welcome to join the group, but we do have some regulations for the members of our household." See also Lips, *Glaube*, 122.

152. Kynes makes the following observation: "This model of the church also suggests the nature of the church's composition. It is to reflect a generational diversity as much as possible. A family has young and old" ("Church," 32). More than likely, this

The specification that the church is of the "living God" (θεοῦ ζῶντος) would likely be heard as the full articulation of the earlier, simpler phrase in 3:5: "the church of God." Goodwin suggests that the phrase connotes God's presence and pervasiveness among his people who comprise the church.[153] This interpretation certainly aligns with the repeated instructions by Paul to pursue godliness, now explicitly in view of God's presence within his own household, his church. Still, the phrase "living (ζῶντος) God" in 3:15 recalls the cognate term "life (ζωήν) eternal" in 1:16 of the first microchiasm, suggesting that the "living God" is the one God who gives "life eternal" to those who come to have-faith upon Christ Jesus. This understanding would echo OT contrasts between God as the giver of life and counterfeit "gods" of pagan religions who could not give life because they themselves were dead.[154] The Ephesisan audience, then, are to understand that they live in and belong to God's church by God's own doing; as the gathered assembly of God's people—a family—they have been called-out to share together in God's missional desire for all humans to be-saved and to come to a knowing-embrace of truth (2:4).[155] Indeed, they are to do so by preserving such truth that is conveyed in the sound teaching, namely by promoting a knowing-embrace thereof through a life of godliness.

The concern to preserve the sound teaching and promote godliness as the missional household of God is reiterated in the appositional phrase that concludes 3:15, describing the household of God—the church—as "a pillar and foundation of truth." "Pillar and foundation" are architectural terms rich with biblical significance. The term "pillar" (στῦλος) highlights for the audience God's continued guiding and protecting presence with his people as the "pillar" (στῦλος) of cloud and fire in the OT.[156] Thus God's presence is not only implied by the phrase "the church of the living God" but also is emphasized by the term "pillar." Still, the fact that "the church" is "a pillar" may also function as a subtle reminder to the audience of their

---

sheds light on the diverse composition of the Ephesisan church.

153. Goodwin, "The Pauline Background," 65–85.

154. See, e.g., LXX Deut 5:26; Josh 3:10; 1 Sam 17:36; 1 Kgs 18:27. Knight, *PE*, 181: "That God is living (and true) contrasts with the deadness (and falseness) of idols."

155. Barcley underscores the essential nature of the church and salvation: "The eternal God exists in community, one God in three persons. It is only in community that God's people grow and flourish . . . He did not add them to the church without saving them. But neither did he save them without adding them to the church. Christ builds his church. And the church is the primary means by which Christ works in the world to extend his kingdom" ("1 Tim," 375).

156. See, e.g., LXX Exod 13:21–22; 14:19, 24; 19:9.

1 TIMOTHY 3:1–16: GODLY LEADERSHIP IN GOD'S HOUSEHOLD   77

missional calling.¹⁵⁷ The juxtaposition of "pillar" with the term "foundation" (ἑδραίωμα) does appear to bring a certain emphasis on the church's calling to be a buttress and reinforcement.¹⁵⁸ Furthermore, given that God's church is to be a pillar and foundation "of truth" (τῆς ἀληθείας), the audience clearly understand the missional implication of their existence in the church. The term recalls the second microchiasm, wherein God's missional desire was for all humans "to come to a knowing-embrace of truth (ἀληθείας)" (2:4) and Paul speaks "the truth" (ἀλήθειαν) as a missional "teacher of the Gentiles in faith and truth (ἀληθείᾳ)" (2:7). Here in the third microchiasm, then, the noun "truth" (ἀληθείας) is referring specifically to salvific-truth (2:4), which Paul has uniquely been appointed to publically make known (2:7). Thus the advancement of the macrochiasm punctuates the significant missional role of the entire congregation: against "some" who teach some-thing different (1:3, 10b) and demonstrably do not know how to behave in God's household (3:5, 15), the audience must help Paul to guard the truth in order for outsiders to come to a knowing-embrace of it, that is, to be-saved.¹⁵⁹ Combined with a lifestyle that is necessary for an existence in the household of God (3:15a), the audience—"the church"—understand that the twofold description "pillar and foundation" is a dual call of a single entity: as God's missional household, their purpose is to preserve the truth of the sound teaching and promote godliness.

1 Timothy 3:16: Confessedly Great is the Mystery of Godliness

("a'" sub-element)

The concluding "a'" sub-element (3:16) of the 3:8–16 minichiasm—the final verse in the concluding A' element of the third microchiasm—moves the audience toward a climactic statement of the truth that God's church is to uphold. Building up to the culmination of the third microchiasm, Paul does not merely state the content but exclaims: "And confessedly great is the mystery of godliness" (3:16a). Within the arrangement of the entire macrochiastic structure, both Paul's exclamation and the truth that follows

157. See Roloff, *Der Erste Brief an Timotheus*, 200–201.
158. Ngewa, *1 & 2 Tim*, 82: "the church's function is to support the truth and prevent it from being distorted . . . This interpretation seems to fit the Ephesian context best. In modern times, we might speak of the church as being a watchman guarding the truth."
159. Muddiman and Barton aptly summarize the protective disposition to which Paul is calling his audience: "The use of the word 'household' summarizes the whole section from 2:1 to 3:13 . . . [and] presents a picture of a solid establishment, run by responsible figures. Any assailant will have a difficult task" ("The PE," 252).

in 3:16b mark the pivot point of the entire letter, which shifts immediately after 3:16 to the second half of the overall macrochiasm.[160] To be sure, Paul's statement in 3:16a does not function as a sort of vapid conclusion. Rather, it summons the audience to view their calling as the missional household of God in light of the greatness of God's mystery that they are to preserve. The term "confessedly" (ὁμολογουμένως) would be heard as an invitation of agreement—literally, "same-wordedly."[161] Together, with Paul and Timothy, then, the audience are to exclaim that the truth they uphold as a pillar and foundation (3:15) is "confessedly (ὁμολογουμένως) great" (3:16). Paul's implication, therefore, is likely that the ability and fervor with which Timothy and the audience fulfill their missional calling correspond directly with their grasp of the greatness of the truth of the gospel.

Still, Paul's rhetorical use (see *italics*) of the adverb "confessedly" (ὁμολογουμένως)—literally, "same-*wordedly*"—would recall its cognate terms throughout the macrochiasm to convey a particular point. In stark contrast to "useless-*words*" (ματαιολογίαν, 1:6) and "double-*worded*" (διλόγους, 3:8), the term "confessedly" (ὁμολογουμένως) in 3:16 would point to and uphold Paul's salvific statement in 1:15: "Faithful is the *word* (λόγος) and worthy of all acceptance, that Christ Jesus came into the world to save sinners." Undoubtedly, then, the rhetorical impact upon the audience would be clear: that which is "confessedly" great (3:16) is the "word" that is worthy of all acceptance, namely that which concerns the person of Christ Jesus. In effect, Paul is inviting and reminding his audience to share in the same acceptance of the "confessedly" great "word" concerning Christ Jesus.

---

160. Towner, *Letters*, 276: "The Christ hymn (v. 16b) now introduced is the rhetorical and Christological high point of the letter." Ngewa, *1 & 2 Tim*, 82: "in 3:16 he [Paul] links the church's role as guardian of truth with the truth about the nature and person of Christ . . . to bring this section of the letter to a climactic conclusion. Wall with Steele also indicate "its placement at the letter's pivot point" (*1 & 2 Tim*, 115).

161. The adverb "confessedly" (ὁμολογουμένως) is comprised of the terms "same" (ὅμοιος) and the root noun "word" (λόγος). Although the wooden translation "same-wordedly" hinders readability in English, it more precisely conveys the sense of Paul's invitation in 3:16, namely that he intends for the Ephesian church to join him in exclaiming the "same-words."

Towner, *Letters*, 276: "The opening word ["confessedly"] . . . serves as a call for affirmation. In this context of church-related teaching (2:1—3:15), the liturgical tone of a call to confession should be retained. All in Ephesus are called to acknowledge the truth of the confession." Witherington, *Letters*, 245 n. 266: "Here, *homologoumenōs* actually means 'by common consent, expressing unanimity' (see 4 Maccabees 6:31; 7:16; 1:1)." Wall with Steele, *1 & 2 Timothy*, 114: "The formula 'great is the mystery of holy living . . .' introduces an agreed-on confession of the pious." See also Collins, *1 & 2 Tim*, 106–7; Quinn and Wacker, *Letters*, 316.

Significantly also, a further implication would likely be heard. Throughout the macrochiasm, Paul has been highlighting the contrast between himself and "some." Paul is an authorized representative of Christ Jesus and was personally appointed by the command of God and Christ Jesus as a teacher in truth (1:1, 12; 2:7), for which reason he was considered-faithful with the sound teaching that exhibits God's radiance and results in blessing him (1:10b–11). The false teachers in the Ephesian church, however, are "some" who teach-different (1:3), namely some-thing different that lies-opposed to the sound teaching with which Paul was divinely considered-faithful (1:10–11). To be sure, here in 3:16, the audience would hear the contrast being emphasized by Paul's rhetorical word-play (see *italics*): whereas "some" "teach-*different*" (ἑτεροδιδασκαλεῖ, 1:3), that is, some-thing "*different*" (ἕτερον, 1:10), Paul exclaims that which is "confessedly" (ὁμολογουμένως, 3:16)—literally, "*same*-wordedly"[162]—upheld and shared by God's household, which is the church of the living God, a pillar and foundation of the truth (3:15).[163] Undoubtedly, then, Paul is making clear that the false teachers do not share the *same* truth that is guided, protected, and reinforced by the family members in God's household; rather, the false-teaching of "some" is plainly *different* and—worse still—is actively hostile to the sound teaching of Paul (1:10).

Still, here in 3:16—the pivot of the macrochiasm—not only do the audience hear a sustained contrast, but they also hear an intended turning point—a call for restoration, an invitation. That is, by highlighting the homogeneous confession of the church—"confessedly" (3:16)—Paul is summoning the entire audience—including "some"—to join him in the *same*—not *different*—exclamation regarding that which is "confessedly" (ὁμολογουμένως) great: "the mystery of godliness" (3:16). In short, here at the pivot point of the letter, Paul is hinging everything not only upon the preservation of the teaching—"confessedly"—but he is also, therefore, exemplifying its result: missional godliness. Indeed, along with the Savior God who desires all humans—even "some"—to be-saved and to come to a knowing-embrace of truth (2:3–4), Paul is welcoming the false teachers to join in the church's common confession of truth (3:15–16) and thus to be-saved.

162. The adverb "confessedly" (ὁμολογουμένως) is comprised of the terms "same" (ὅμοιος) and "word" (λόγος).

163. Beale and Gladd, *Hidden But Now Revealed*, 241: "This adverb [*homologoumenōs*] contains both positive and negative elements. On the one hand, it refers to an agreement reached by all parties. On the other hand, the adverb contains a negative nuance by referring to something that is undeniable. In other words, the word denotes something that is unquestionably truthful or certain." It is in this latter sense that Paul's statement "confessedly great" (3:16) would function as a polemical contrast over and against "some" who "teach-different" (1:3).

Furthermore, where the adjective "great" indicates the inherent eminence of the truth they are about to exclaim, the audience understand that their participation involves a full embrace of it. Still, taken together with the adverb "undeniably," the term "great" (μέγα) may represent a subversive response to the panegyric declared by the Ephesian cult of Artemis: "Great (μεγάλη) is Artemis" (Acts 19:28, 34).[164] Thus by calling the audience to confess the surpassing greatness of the truth, Paul is not only calling for their full embrace but also reminding them of their own narratives—how their lives have radically changed in light of the gospel of the glory of the blessed God, that Christ Jesus came into the world to save them (1:11, 15). Formerly, like those in Ephesus currently outside of God's household, many in the audience had joined in the anthem of singing praise to Artemis. Now, however, their allegiance and worship have definitively shifted to Christ Jesus. In effect, here in 3:16 of the third microchiasm, the progression of the macrochiasm advances the full scope of the gospel that displays God's radiance and results in blessing toward God (1:11). In the concluding A' element of the first microchiasm, Paul's personal reception of God's grace and mercy (1:13, 14, 16) led him to bless God and invite the audience to do the same (1:17). So, too, now in the concluding A' element of the third microchiasm does the reminder of the Ephesian audience's personal reception of God's grace and mercy (3:16) intend to lead them to bless God. In short, as a counter-voice to the counterfeit god Artemis, the audience are to embrace their existence "in faith," that is, "in Christ"—the force of the statement being, "confessedly great is Christ Jesus."[165]

The term "the mystery" (τὸ ... μυστήριον) in 3:16 of the "a'" sub-element recalls "the mystery (τὸ μυστήριον) of faith" in 3:9 of the parallel "a" sub-element.[166] Thus just as qualified deacons are holding "the mystery," so too are the entire audience—the household of God, the church of the living God (3:15)—to exclaim its greatness. Furthermore, the connotation of the

---

164. See discussion in volume 1, chapter 1. See also MacLeod, "Christology in Six Lines," 335–36; Knight, PE, 182; Heil, Letters of Paul, 165. Witherington (Letters, 246) adds: "Supporting this line of thinking, we may also compare a saying about Zeus that actually uses both *megistos* and *homologoumenōs*: 'Zeus, the greatest of gods, there is no denying it' [Athenaeus Deipn. 6239b]."

165. Marshall further notes the possible polemic against the false teachers: "by placing Christ at the centre this text may well be calling attention back from the profitless 'myths and genealogies' and other speculations which were diverting people's attention from the Saviour" (PE, 499).

166. As in 3:9, it may be worth noting the apparent association (uniqueness of the article τό) between τὸ ... μυστήριον ("the mystery," 3:16) and τὸ εὐαγγέλιον ("the gospel," 1:11) and τὸ μαρτύριον ("the testimony," 2:6). Where a linguistic connection is intended, it is likely that they are to be heard as interrelated terms.

term "the mystery" implies that which is hidden. Yet, given the movement of the minichiasm, the audience clearly understand that "the mystery" is no longer hidden but has been revealed, namely in the gospel, the sound teaching (1:10b-11a), to which Paul was appointed as a teacher in faith and truth (2:7). For the audience to exclaim the greatness of "the mystery," therefore, they are to exclaim the greatness of the testimony concerning Christ Jesus who came into the world and gave himself as a ransom to save sinners (1:15; 2:6), that is, the greatness of God's missional desire for all humans to be saved (2:4). Moreover, that the mystery is "of godliness" is significant. The term "godliness" (εὐσεβείας) recalls the force of the second microchiasm, wherein the audience's lifestyles were to be in accord with their salvific-existence "in faith" through "godliness" (εὐσεβείᾳ, 2:3; θεοσέβειαν, 2:10). Here in the third microchiasm, the combination of "godliness" with "the mystery" further emphasizes that the greatness of God's initiative to save sinners and bring them into his household undergirds the audience's communal pursuit of "godliness." Indeed, where "the mystery" directly concerns the person of Christ Jesus, the audience understand that "godliness" finds its source in him. In summary, the "mystery of godliness" (3:16) refers to the plan of salvation that climaxes in the person and work of Christ Jesus and provides the framework for living "in all godliness and respectability" (2:2).[167] More than likely, then, the description "confessedly great" would be understood by the audience in reference to "the mystery" rather than to "godliness," though the two are obviously tied together. The implied response by the audience to the confessedly great mystery is godliness, that is, to collectively uphold the truth of the gospel, not only by exclaiming it but by supporting Timothy to stop and correct "some" who directly oppose the sound teaching that upholds the church's confession concerning Christ. That is, godliness on the audience's part includes the preservation of truth and the teaching.

In the second half of the concluding "a'" sub-element, the content of "the mystery" is poetically summarized in six stanzas concerning Christ Jesus, each beginning with a passive verb and ending in a prepositional phrase— "in" (ἐν), with the exception of the third stanza.[168] Especially noteworthy

---

167. See MacLeod, "Christology in Six Lines," 336-37. Belleville, "Christology, Greco-Roman," 227: "The epitome of εὐσέβια is Christ himself (1 Tim 3:16)."

168. Despite the scholarly attention this "hymn" has received, there is no agreement on its origins and structures. For helpful summaries of the legion of material, see Marshall, *PE*, 497-504; Mounce, *PE*, 21-27; Towner, *Letters*, 277; Witherington, *Letters*, 245-48. A sampling of literature includes Deppe, *All Roads Lead to the Text*, 28-29; Resseguie, *Narrative Criticism*, 60; Barrett, *PE*, 66; Deichgräber, *Gotteshymnus und Christushymnus*; Fee, *God's Empowering Presence*, 767-68; Gundry, "The Form, Meaning and Background," 203-22; Jeremias, *Timotheus*, 27-29; Kelly, *PE*, 92; Stenger, *Der Christushymnus*; Martin, "1 Tim 3:16," 108-120; Yarbrough, *Paul's Utilization of*

is the relative pronoun "he" (ὅς) that initiates this hymnlike poem. Given the preceding phrase "mystery of godliness," the audience would likely have expected to hear the corresponding relative pronoun "it" (ὅ) in reference to "the mystery." Thus the somewhat abrupt shift to the masculine relative pronoun not only signals to the audience that "he" (ὅς)—a person—is the content of the mystery but that "he" (ὅς)—Christ Jesus—is the climax of the mystery and the focus of the poem that is to follow.[169] Specifically, given that 3:16 is the pivot of the entire macrochiasm, the A, B, and C units of the macrochiasm—the first, second, and third microchiasms—would be expected to carry forward and flow into this central hinge point.[170] Thus where Christ Jesus himself is the hinge point of the letter, it is likely that Paul would intend for his audience to hear each stanza in terms of the christological statements made throughout the macrochiasm, particularly in 1:12–16 of the macrochiastic A unit (the first microchiasm) and 2:3–7 of the macrochiastic B unit (the second microchiasm).[171] That is, Paul has already moved the audience to understand the truth of salvation history—namely that Christ Jesus came into the world (1:15) at his own times (2:6)—and its subsequent demand of a lifestyle of godliness upon those who have been brought into the household of God (1:4; 3:15)—the realm "in faith," that is, "in Christ Jesus" (1:14; 3:13). Here in 3:16, then, as both the climax of the A' element of the C macrochiastic unit and the central pivot point for the letter, it is only fitting that the person of Christ Jesus—"he" (ὅς)—is held up for the audience as the confessedly great mystery of godliness:

Preformed Traditions, 95-102. Given the tenuous quality inherent in any proposal, Towner correctly asserts (*Letters*, 278): "In the end we are left with the unsatisfying conclusion that while clearly being a poetic piece, in its present state the organization of its six lines cannot be reduced to either of the most popular schemes. But this need not hinder an effective reading of the hymn. The interests in salvation history, mission, and gospel are all detectable no matter how the lines are arranged."

169. See BDF §296 for notes on the shift in pronoun.

170. For the macrochiastic structure of 1 Timothy, see volume 1, chapter 2.

171. For the purposes of our analysis, it is most helpful to treat each stanza separately and according to Paul's previous christological statements. Adopting a layout that resembles more of a list than a narrative progression of events under the umbrella of salvation history is not intended to deny that there does appear to be some chronological progression within the poetic structure. Perhap's Barrett's proposal here is most helpful (*PE*, 65–66): line 1: incarnation; line 2: resurrection; line 3: ascension; line 4: gospel proclamation; line 5: response of faith and obedience; line 6: climactic victory of Christ. While persuasive in many respects, even this proposal does appear to impose a refined scheme that is not fully supported by the text. For example, the final line seems to focus on Christ's ascension rather than his eschatological victory in the second coming. In the end, it is helpful, on the one hand, to admit a degree of chronological progression, on the other hand, to feel free from having to fit the six stanzas into a clean structure.

"was manifested in flesh,	(ἐφανερώθη ἐν σαρκί)
was declared-just in Spirit,	(ἐδικαιώθη ἐν πνεύματι)
was seen by angels,	(ὤφθη ἀγγέλοις)
was proclaimed in the Gentiles,	(ἐκηρύχθη ἐν ἔθνεσιν)
was counted-faithful in the world,	(ἐπιστεύθη ἐν κόσμῳ)
was taken-up in glory."	(ἀνελήμφθη ἐν δόξῃ.)

First, "he was manifested in flesh" is a reference to Christ's incarnation. The passive verb "was manifested" (ἐφανερώθη) not only brings attention to God as the divine actor but also reiterates the eschatological character of Christ's first coming (1:15) in relation to Paul who "was appointed" a proclaimer, apostle, and teacher, namely of the testimony concerning Christ's first coming (2:6).[172] Furthermore, the passive verb connotes a similar sense to "the mystery," that is, the verb underscores something previously hidden but now revealed. Thus, on the one hand, "the mystery" affirms the christological implication of Christ's pre-existence in 1:15—Christ Jesus, previously hidden, came into the world and revealed himself.[173] On the other hand, "the mystery" also emphasizes that the manifestation of Christ Jesus in flesh—his divine entrance into the world—is that which reveals the radiant glory of God (1:11) from whom grace and mercy flow (1:14, 16) to bring salvation (1:15) to those who sin against God (1:9–10, 13).[174] The similarity in meaning between the verb "was manifested" and noun "the mystery" suggests to the audience that the truth concerning the entrance of Christ Jesus into the world—the revealing of God's glory—significantly and directly impacts how they are to pursue godliness: given the eschatological nature of Christ's advent, the audience are to pursue a lifestyle that

172. Ridderbos, *Paul*, 46–47: "The qualification of this event as the 'revelation of the mystery' . . . is also indicative of this eschatological character of the redemptive dispensation that has dawned in Christ and of its proclamation by Paul . . . the corresponding word 'reveal' not only means the divulging of a specific truth or the giving of information as to certain events or facts, but the appearance itself, the becoming historical reality of that which until now did not exist as such, but was kept by God, hidden, held back. As such, namely, as the realized redemptive plan of God, this mystery is consequently the object of Paul's proclamation . . . From the way in which this expression . . . is used, the eschatological nature of the content of his preaching is apparent once again."

173. Knight, *PE*, 184: "the implication is that he who is revealed previously existed but was unknown." Matera, *God's Saving Grace*, 73: "the preexistent Christ was manifested in the flesh when he became human." See Ngewa, *1 & 2 Tim*, 83.

174. Marshall, *PE*, 523: "The connection here with 'the mystery' establishes that the author intends to interpret God's saving activity as taking place in the historical appearance of Christ." See further Bockmuehl, "Das Verb φανερόω im Neuen Testament," 87–99.

is bracketed by the first and second coming of Christ.¹⁷⁵ More specifically, the audience understand that the inseparable character of Christ's first coming—to save them (1:15)—and his second coming—to bring them fully home, to heaven—demands their missional lifestyle to bring all humans into God's household—the church—before Christ's certain return.¹⁷⁶

It is possible that the prepositional phrase "in flesh" may have been understood by the audience in a variety of ways.¹⁷⁷ Yet, most likely the audience would have understood the declaration "in flesh" in view of Christ's manifestation into the world in the A and B units of the macrochiasm—Paul's teaching, the gospel, the testimony that the human Christ Jesus came into the world and gave himself as a ransom to save sinners (1:15; 2:6). Neither christological statement focuses on simply Christ's entrance but more broadly on the salvific purpose of his incarnation: he came in flesh into the sphere of flesh to save the fleshly.¹⁷⁸ In this way, the first line not only summarizes Paul's previous christological statements but also advances the audience's call to promote godliness: just as Christ Jesus lived missionally in the sphere of flesh to bring sinners into the sphere "in faith," so too are the audience. In sum, the audience understand that "he" (ὅς), Christ Jesus, is the reason why those "in Christ Jesus" exclaim that he is confessedly great—Christ Jesus enables sinners to bless God (1:17; 3:16) as the result of God's mission for all humans to be-saved (2:3–4a).

The second stanza, he "was declared-just in Spirit," would be heard to complement the first. Towner correctly asserts: "It is a response in that within this salvation-historical profile of the Christ-event and the gospel, it portrays Jesus' vindication . . . the affirmation of line two completes the portrait of Christ's existence by depicting its second stage."¹⁷⁹ The passive

---

175. Presumably Paul's audience was not only familiar with Christ's second coming in the Gospels (e.g., Mark 14:62) but also with Paul's teaching. Regarding Christ's second coming, see discussion in volume 3, chapter 3 regarding 1 Timothy 6:14. Also, Titus 2:11–14 explicates this deliberate kind of living in view of Christ's first and second coming: "For the grace of God has manifested (ἐπεφάνη), saving all humans, training us so that by denying ungodliness and worldly desires we might live self-controllably and justly and godly in the present age, awaiting the blessed hope, the manifestation (ἐπιφάνειαν) of the glory of our great God and Savior Jesus Christ." See my discussion in *To Exhort and Reprove*, 78–83.

176. Gaffin, *By Faith*, 61–72, summarizes the elliptical quality of Paul's eschatology.

177. Various interpretations include: Christ's mode of existence as a human (see e.g., Dunn, "Jesus—Flesh and Spirit," 62–64); the arena in which he ministered (see e.g., Kelly, *PE*, 90); a specific period in his earthly ministry (see e.g., Collins, *Tim*, 108–9; Dupont, "Σὺν Χριστῷ," 108–10); his weakness and demise (see e.g., Stanley, *Christ's Resurrection*, 237).

178. See further Gundry, "The Form, Meaning and Background," 210.

179. Towner, *Letters*, 280.

verb "was declared-just" (ἐδικαιώθη) would not merely express God's declaration of Christ's innocence,[180] nor would it be understood as an affirmation of Christ's messianic mission.[181] Instead, the verb would be heard with the propositional phrase "in Spirit" (ἐν πνεύματι) to describe a new mode of existence into which Christ Jesus, the human, entered after he gave himself as a ransom, namely by his resurrection from death. To be sure, "in Spirit" would indicate for the audience that Paul has the activity of the Holy Spirit in view; however, given its immediate placement after line one—Christ's existence "in flesh"—it is clear that Paul is now emphasizing Christ's existence "in Spirit."[182] Moreover, heard together with the first stanza, the declaration "was declared-just in Spirit" underscores the second and final mode of existence that Christ has entered as a human[183]—the realm of existence, namely "life eternal," into which those who would-inevitably-come to have-faith upon him will enter (1:16) and those among the audience who are "in Christ Jesus" (1:14; 3:13) will join.[184] Undoubtedly, it is for this reason that

180. Contra e.g., Dibelius and Conzelmann, *PE*, 62.

181 Contra e.g., Wall with Steele, *1 & 2 Tim*, 116.

182. The emphasis on Christ's mode of existence "in Spirit" is not to minimize the vital role of the Spirit both in Jesus's earthly ministry and particularly in his resurrection (see e.g., Jeremias, *Timotheus*, 29). However, the Spirit's involvement in Christ's resurrection in line two of 3:16 does not mandate that the preposition "in" (ἐν) would be understood as "by" (contra Knight, *PE*, 185). Marshall, *PE*, 525-26: "The phrase may refer to the means or agent of vindication, i.e., the Holy Spirit . . . if vindication and resurrection are identical. However, the frequent antithesis of flesh and spirit in the NT with its OT background, suggests that the contrast is between the human mode (or sphere) and the supernatural mode of Jesus' two-stage existence as characterised by the activity of the Holy Spirit."

183. Matera, *God's Saving Grace*, 73: "the one who made his appearance in the realm of the flesh now lives in the realm of God."

184. Few have articulated the meaning and significance of the flesh-Spirit contrast better than Ridderbos. Quoting at length (*Paul*, 66–67): "It is Christ's being revealed in the flesh . . . that is the specific significance of Christ's life before his resurrection . . . But the new creation is that of Christ's resurrection. For this reason the death of Christ is a turning point in the mode of existence of the old aeon . . . Transition takes place, namely, from the existence of the old to that of the new, from the old aeon to the new creation. By dying Christ has thus snatched his people away from the present aeon (Gal. 1:4). From this moment on faith no longer 'knows,' that is to say, judges 'after the flesh' (2 Cor. 5:16). It regards all things from another point of view, namely, that the aeon of the sole dominion of the flesh is done away with and the mode of existence of the Spirit has been entered upon . . . 'flesh' and 'Spirit' represent two modes of existence, on the one hand that of the old aeon which is characterized and determined by the flesh, on the other that of the new creation which is of the Spirit of God. It is in this sense that the difference is also to be taken between the first Adam as 'living soul,' i.e., flesh, and the second as life-giving Spirit. The contrast is therefore of a redemptive-historical nature . . . It is within this redemptive-historical contrast of flesh and Spirit as the mode of

Paul boldly declares in the first microchiasm "Christ Jesus our hope" (1:1). Here, then, in the pivot of the letter, the certain hope of resurrection from death to a new mode of existence—"life eternal" (1:16) in the realm "in faith that is in Christ" (3:13)—is climactically emphasized for the audience. Indeed, a knowing-embrace of such truth in everyday life would be a confessedly great foundation of hope, attracting those-outside to Christ Jesus and the household of God.

To be sure, it is this twofold mode of existence in the first and second stanza—Christ-in-flesh and Christ-in-Spirit—that comprises "the mystery of godliness" and elicits the audience to exclaim that it is "confessedly great." By becoming a human (2:6) to save humans (1:15) from the effects of humanity's sin (2:14), Christ not only experienced the effect of humanity's sin while remaining sinless but also gave himself in death as a ransom to pay the full price on behalf of sinners's emancipation. His human resurrection declares his innocence from humanity's sin and—even more—indicates that Christ has overcome human death by entering into a new mode of Spirit-existence. Indeed, it is confessedly great that by coming to have-faith upon the life of one human, the mediator Christ Jesus, all such humans will eventually share in his new mode of Spirit-existence, namely life eternal (1:16; 2:5; 3:16). As such, here at the climax of the third microchiasm and the pivot of the letter, the audience are moved toward a full understanding of Paul's earlier statement in 1:9 of the first microchiasm: where the law is not for the "just" (δικαίῳ)—those "in faith"—it is because they have been "declared-just (ἐδικαιώθη) in Spirit"—declared righteous through their existence "in Christ Jesus" (1:14; 3:13). In a word, the audience are no longer under the law but under the Spirit as those joined to Christ by faith.[185] In this way, the audience understand that their pursuit of godliness should not be driven by a desire to become "just" but rather by the conviction that they are already "declared-just in Spirit"—free from the just judgment of the law upon sinners, having experienced a simultaneous release from one realm of existence—"in unfaithfulness" (1:13)—and entrance into another, the realm "in Christ"—"in faith" (1:2, 4; 2:7, 15; 3:13). As those in God's household, the godliness to which the audience are called is nothing other than "eschatological living"—a participation in the new, final mode of

---

existence of the old and new creation that Paul now views the life of Christ before and after his resurrection." Similarly, see Dalton, *Christ's Proclamation*, 127–32; Fee, *God's Empowering Presence*, 765–66; Fowl, *Story of Christ*, 159–62.

185. Ridderbos, *Paul*, 67: "the church is no longer 'in the flesh,' i.e., subject to the regime of the first aeon and the evil powers reigning in it, but 'in the Spirit,' brought under the dominion of freedom in Christ ... All the facets of the contrast of flesh and Spirit ... become transparent and luminous out of this basic eschatological structure ..."

existence that Christ Jesus secured for all humans who come to have-faith upon his manifestation in flesh and justification in Spirit. Such is the confessedly great mystery that the audience are to uphold as both a wonderful truth that must be preserved against the threats of the false teachers and an empowering narrative that compels missional godliness.

Third, he "was seen by angels."[186] It is possible that the passive verb "was seen" (ὤφθη) would be heard with an active sense—he "appeared to" angels.[187] Yet, given the passive sense in the first two lines, it would be more natural for the audience to understand Paul's statement according to the passive sense of the verb—"was seen" or "was gazed upon." The specification that Christ was seen by "angels" may have carried two nuances for the audience. On the one hand, the noun "angels" (ἀγγέλοις) is sometimes used in the NT to describe humans as "messengers" (e.g., Luke 7:24; Jas 5:21), and so it is certainly possible that the audience hear Paul's statement as a reference to Christ's post-resurrection appearances—that he was seen by various individuals.[188] On the other hand, however, it is unlikely that the audience understand the term "angels" in reference to humans;[189] rather, given the sequential movement of the preceding lines from Christ-in-flesh (incarnation) to Christ-in-Spirit (resurrection), it is more likely that the audience would perceive a natural movement to Christ's ascension—the sense being that Christ-in-glory was seen by angels in heaven.[190] To be sure, it is for this

186. As noted, the third line of 3:16 does not contain "in" (ἐν). Knight, *PE*, 185: "ἐν is not used here apparently because it does not quite give the right sense, and the dative by itself can express the idea more clearly."

187. The basis for this interpretation is the verb's use in the LXX (e.g., Gen 12:7; Exod 3:2) and the NT (e.g., Matt 17:3; Luke 1:11); see e.g., Towner, *Letters*, 281; Marshall, *PE*, 526.

188. Knight, *PE*, 185: "All other NT occurrences of ὤφθη used with reference to Jesus refer to his resurrection appearances (Lk. 24:31; Acts 13:31; 1 Cor. 15:5, 6, 7, 8; cf. ὤφθην in Acts 26:16). Probably, therefore, the word refers here to the resurrection appearances rather than to the ascension only, although the ascension need not be ruled out." See Johnson, *Letters*, 233; Seeberg, *Der Katechismus der Urchristenheit*, 119–20.

189. Knight, *PE*, 185: "The NT nearly always uses ἄγγελοι of supernatural powers (angels) rather than humans." See Belleville, "Christology, Greco-Roman," 238.

190. Towner, *Letters*, 282: "In continuing the theme of vindication (implicitly), line 3 extends the thought of line 2 by displaying the meaning of resurrection for the heavenly powers. It may even be regarded as continuing the historical sequence of salvation-historical moments (human life/death; resurrection; manifestation to angelic powers)." Wall with Steele, *1 & 2 Tim*, 116: "In the Pauline canon a happy note is sounded: an angelic host welcomes the risen Son of God Messiah back into its heavenly embrace (Phil 2:9–11; cf. Rev 12:5–12); and I suspect that the creed links the first two parallelisms by maintaining the resurrection subtext of the previous line. That is, 'seen by angels' affirms the gospel's witness to the angelic pronouncement of the Lord's resurrection (Matt 28:5–7) and is the assumed predicate of the apostolic proclamation of the risen Lord

reason that the audience are to understand why Christ Jesus is "our Lord" (1:2, 12)—the one who reigns from heaven into the eternities.

Fourth, he "was proclaimed in the Gentiles." Undoubtedly, both the passive verb "was proclaimed" (ἐκηρύχθη) and the noun "the Gentiles" (ἔθνεσιν) recall for the audience 2:7 of the second microchiasm, wherein Paul "was appointed proclaimer (κῆρυξ) . . . of the Gentiles (ἐθνῶν)." The linguistic connection is significant. Given the movement of each line in 3:16, it is clear to the audience that Christ "was proclaimed" in light of his incarnation (line one), resurrection (line two), and ascension (line three). In the same way, therefore, it is clear to the audience that the movement of the macrochiasm to the pivot of the letter advances the scope of and qualifies Paul's appointment as "proclaimer." That is, the audience understand that the content of Paul's proclamation in 2:7 is not only founded on the testimony that Christ Jesus came into the world and gave himself as a ransom to save sinners (1:15; 2:6) but also on the climactic exclamation of the truth in 3:16. Thus in view of lines one, two, and three, the audience hear in full each of Paul's prior statements in the macrochiasm concerning Christ Jesus. It is confessedly great that the pre-existent Christ "was manifested in flesh" (line one): for this reason Paul states that he is the "one mediator of God and humans, the human Christ Jesus" (2:5b). It is confessedly great that Christ "was declared-just in Spirit" (line two): for this reason Paul states that he is "Christ Jesus our hope" (1:1). It is confessedly great that Christ Jesus "was seen by angels" (line three): for this reason Paul states that he is "Christ Jesus our Lord" (1:2, 12). In short, here the audience understand that when Christ Jesus is proclaimed by Paul, all of Christ's saving activity must be in view.

Still, the audience likely understand that "was proclaimed" not only recalls the activity of Paul the "proclaimer"; rather, given its placement in the third microchiasm, Paul intends to uphold the activity of the entire church. Given the polemic of the third microchiasm, the audience understand that their calling entails the preservation of proclaiming the full truth about Christ Jesus against those who teach-different. Specifically, therefore, Paul is calling upon the audience to appoint qualified overseers to teach and govern and qualified deacons to hold the mystery of the faith—both leaders working together so that the fullness of Christ Jesus is proclaimed.

Where the prepositional phrase "in the Gentiles" (ἐν ἔθνεσιν) recalls for the audience Paul's authoritative appointment as a teacher of "the Gentiles" (ἐθνῶν) in 2:7 of the second microchiasm, the audience understand

---

among the nations (Matt 28:6–20)." Akin, "Mystery of Godliness is Great," 140: "Resurrected and exalted as 'Lord,' the angels were privileged to celebrate his victory . . ."

Compare to the proposal in Gundry, "Form, Meaning and Background, 203–10. Witherington in particular asserts that "this is a reference to what we also find in several other places in the New Testament: the appearance of Christ, on the way to heaven, to the fallen angels kept in Tartarus (cf. Jude 6; 2 Pet 2:4; 1 Pet 3:19)" (*Letters*, 247).

that Paul has in view the universal scope of God's missional desire for all humans to be-saved (2:4), which climaxes in the inclusion of non-Jewish humans, Gentiles. Yet, here in 3:16, the audience understand that Paul is not referring exclusively to his own missional impact. Rather, given its immediate placement in the A' element of third microchiasm, the Ephesian audience not only understand that they themselves are in view—a church comprised of many Gentiles converts—but also that Paul has in view their calling to be "a pillar and foundation of the truth" (3:15). In this way, the audience are to live with a sense of mission, actively preserving the sound teaching of the gospel and promoting godliness to bring all humans into the household of God. Again, given the movement of the third microchiasm, such activity would likely be directed toward appointing qualified men to lead them in teaching and godliness.

Fifth, he "was counted-faithful in the world." The passive verb "was counted-faithful" (ἐπιστεύθη) recalls for the audience 1:11 of the first microchiasm, wherein Paul "was counted-faithful" (ἐπιστεύθην) with the gospel, that is, the sound teaching (1:10b). In this way, then, the audience understand Paul's statement in 3:16 as a reference to Christ's faithfulness in fulfilling the gospel mission that exhibits God's radiance, wherein he is the mediator who enables humans to give proper blessings toward God. At the same time, the entirety of the phrase "was counted-faithful (ἐπιστεύθη) in the world (κόσμῳ)" in 3:16 also recalls Christ Jesus himself who came into "the world" (τὸν κόσμον) (1:15) so that sinners could be-saved by coming "to have-faith" (πιστεύειν) upon him (1:16). Heard in this way, then, the audience are to understand the phrase in 3:16 as a statement that Christ Jesus is the object of their faith.[191] Still, while the preceding statement "was proclaimed in the Gentiles" in line four would indicate that Paul has in view the Gentiles's faith upon Christ Jesus—the person and work of Christ being the object of their faith—certainly without Christ's own faithfulness to voluntarily give himself as a ransom on behalf of sinners (2:6), no Gentile in the world could come to have-faith upon him.

Furthermore, given that Christ "was seen by angels" in heaven (line three), the prepositional phrase "in the world" (ἐν κόσμῳ) in line five articulates the full spectrum of Christ's saving activity in 3:16: no being—angelic or human—is intended to go without knowing the truth concerning Christ Jesus and coming to a knowing-embrace of it.[192] In this way, here at the climax of the third microchiasm, the audience hear an emphatic

---

191. In the passive, the verb ἐπιστεύθη expresses placing trust in a person or object (BDF §312).

192. Though Schreiner's interpretive translation of line five differs, he aptly notes that "*world* here denotes all [people] without distinction and not all without exception" (*Paul*, 186.) That is, all "in the world" are intended to embrace the truth concerning Christ Jesus, yet not all without exception actually do embrace it.

missional statement in line five regarding the spread of the gospel in the world: as the audience exclaim the confessedly great truth concerning Christ Jesus—the mediator, hope, and Lord of humanity (3:16, lines one to three)—more and more humans who were once outsiders—Gentiles (3:16, line four), even more, all humans in the world (3:16, line five)—are to come to a knowing-embrace of the confessedly great truth, that is, come to have-faith upon Christ Jesus.[193] In sum, as those who live in the household of God—the realm "in faith," that is, "in Christ Jesus"—the audience are to be a pillar and foundation of the truth concerning the full scope of Christ's salvific mission. That is, they must preserve the truth of the gospel—as taught by the apostle Paul according to the command of God (1:1)—by living according to their godly existence "in Christ Jesus."[194] In this way, the audience understands that their exclamation of the confessedly great truth will promote faith in Christ Jesus in the world.

In the climactic, concluding statement of the "a'" sub-element in the 3:8–16 minichiasm, of the A' element in the third microchiasm, and of the C unit in the entire macrochiasm, the audience hear that he "was taken-up in glory." The passive verb "was taken-up" (ἀνελήμφθη) is found elsewhere in the NT to describe Christ's ascension (e.g., Luke 24:51).[195] Yet, given its combination with the phrase "in glory," the fuller implication would not merely convey his post-resurrection ascension to heaven but also— and more significantly—the new and abiding mode of existence in which Christ now dwells, namely "in" (ἐν) the sphere of "glory."[196] The term "glory" (δόξῃ) recalls its earlier two occurrences in the first microchiasm to describe the gospel that exhibits God's visible radiance—"glory" (δόξης,

---

193. See Witherington, *Letters*, 247.

194. Frame observes the relationship between preserving the truth of the gospel and pursuing godliness: "theology occurs in the *lives* of people, in their behavior, as well as in their speech. Behavior consists of a series of human decisions, and in those decisions believers seek to follow Scripture . . . Example is an important form of teaching. Imitating godly people is an important form of Christian learning, and the behavior of those people is often a revelation to us of God's intentions for us (1 Cor. 11:1). Their application of the Word in their behavior may be called theology. So theology is not merely a means of teaching people how to live; it is life itself" (*Systematic Theology*, 7).

195. See Lohfink, *Die Himmelfahrt Jesu*, 213; Oberlinner, *Ersten Timotheusbrief*, 169.

196. Towner, *Letters*, 284: "Marshall (525 n. 99) points out that the preposition εἰς would be expected to express the destination of a verb of motion (cf. Heb 2:10); following the action of the verb (ἀνελήμφθη ἐν δόξῃ; 'taken up in glory'), the sense of the prepositional phrase may correspond to its use in 1 Cor 15:43 (ἐγείρεται ἐν δόξῃ; 'raised in glory'), where a quality or character of status (i.e., 'glorification'), rather than a destination, seems indicated." Cf. Kelly, *PE*, 92; Witherington, *Letters*, 247, who suggest that line six focuses on Jesus's destination at the right hand of God the Father. Cf. Belleville, "Christology, Greco-Roman," 238, who suggests that line six refers to a manner of being taken up in glory rather than a status in glory.

1:11)—and in the doxological statement to give "honor and glory (δόξα)" back to God as a result receiving the glory revealed in the gospel (1:17). Its occurrence here is not meant to express that Christ, who came into the world as the revelation of God's radiance, did not possess the quality of glory before his incarnation. Rather it highlights that Christ Jesus—the pre-existent person who "was manifested in flesh" as a human—was conferred a new status "in glory," now as the fully divine and fully human mediator between God and humans.

To be sure, the hymn does not follow a clean sequential pattern of Christ's incarnation, life, death, resurrection, glorification, and second coming; its original purpose was not to provide a nicely arranged set of dogmatic statements.[197] Rather, this hymn, which has at its center Christ Jesus, comprises "the mystery of godliness" that the audience are to preserve as constituents of "the church of the living God, a pillar and foundation of the truth" (3:15), are to rejoice in and exclaim as "confessedly great" (3:16), and are to apply as the framework for pursuing and promoting missional godliness. It is noteworthy that in line five, the active agents are those in the world who have and will place their faith upon Christ Jesus. Line six, then, does not refer solely to Christ's glorified status but also magnifies that Christ Jesus, indeed, is the audience's "hope" (1:1): for all those "in Christ" who live in the household of God, they will someday exist with him "in glory."[198] As Paul suggests in 1:17, such glory involves participating in God's qualities of eternity, without-perishability; in a word, Christ's exaltation in glory—now with a human nature—guarantees the same outcome for all humans who "would inevitably-come to have-faith upon him," namely, "life eternal" (1:16). In view of the concluding A' element of the third microchiasm, then, the manner in which the audience are "to behave in the household of God" in 3:15 is grounded not only in the fact that Christ "was manifested in flesh" and "was declared-just in Spirit," but also in the guaranteed hope of being "in glory" with Christ. As those who have placed their faith upon him for life eternal (1:16)—irrespective of how blasphemous, persecuting, or hubristic their prior lives were (1:13)—the audience understand the paradigm through which they are to view all of life: life "in flesh" will be filled with sorrow and pain, as signified by Christ's own incarnation (3:16, line one), but ultimately life "in Spirit" and "in glory" will be filled with joy and praises, as

---

197. Though, as some have suggested, we may here see "the purpose to what would later become the Symbol, the Apostles' Creed" (Witherington, *Letters*, 247). Not a few commentators regard the hymn in 1 Timothy as the citation of an early Christian creed; see Oden, *First and Second Tim*, 45; Barclay, *1 & 2 Tim*, 122; Ngewa, *1 & 2 Tim*, 83; Knight, *PE*, 182.

198. Wall with Steele, *1 & 2 Tim*, 117: "The accent is Pauline and expresses Jesus' heavenly exaltation as creation's Lord and thus the utter logic of the church's trust in him and proclamation of him in the world."

signified by Christ's justification and exaltation. With this climactic framework in view, along with Paul and Timothy, the audience are able to war the commendable war (1:18), pray on behalf of all humans (2:1-2), pursue godliness in their distinct roles as men and women (2:8-16), and serve faithfully as overseers and deacons (3:1-13) knowing that Christ Jesus, indeed, is "our hope": he will not fail.[199]

The concluding hymn is a fitting ending to the third microchiasm and a climactic turning point in the overall macrochiasm—the 1 Timothy letter itself. It underscores for the audience that Paul's discussion of overseers and deacons in the C unit, missional lifestyles in the B unit, and the gospel in the A unit must all be understood within the backdrop of their calling as God's missional household to preserve the sound teaching and promote godliness. What is more, the hymn highlights the dual movement of the macrochiasm toward its pivot. On the one hand, the advancement of "the gospel" (1:11) in the A unit, to "the testimony" (2:6) in the B unit, to "the mystery" (3:9, 16) in the C unit comprises the confessedly great truth that the Savior God desires all humans to knowingly-embrace through the mission of his household, the church (2:1-4). On the other hand, the advancement of "some" who teach-different in the A unit, to falsifying and ungodliness in the B unit, to a litany of disqualifying attributes in the C unit comprises the false teachers, who have, in effect, denied the truth—the gospel, the testimony, the mystery—and turned-aside for useless-words (1:6).

In sum, at the hinge-point of the entire letter, the audience understand that the preservation of the sound teaching and the confessedly great truth thereof requires the accumulation of the entire macrochiastic movement: it requires the faithfulness of Timothy in the A unit, who has been directly charged by Paul to stop the false teachers; the support of the audience in general in the B unit, who have been exhorted to follow Paul's teaching; and the partnership of the audience in particular in the C unit, namely the qualified men who are able to teach and to govern as overseers and the deacons who are able to hold the mystery of the faith.

---

199. Towner, *Letters*, 285: "These lines fully implicate human beings in the salvation plan of God, not just as undeserving recipients of God's grace (line 5), but first of all as messengers who announce the truth en-fleshed in the Messiah . . . The hymn establishes a balance that rightly begins with the fundamental Christ-event. But the central place of human response and responsibility in mission is essential to the salvation plan of God . . . At present, the church is to identify with the experience of Christ in suffering and witness (lines 1, 4), its hope made sure and purpose for doing so grounded in the fact of his resurrection, vindication, and glorious exaltation." See also Fee, *1 & 2 Tim*, 57; Quinn and Wacker, *Letters*, 346-47.

3

1 Timothy 4:1–16: Preserving the Teaching and Promoting Godliness amidst Apostasy

(C' Unit)

This chapter examines the C' unit of the macrochiasm—the fourth of six microchiasms within the 1 Timothy letter.[1] Within this fourth microchiasm (4:1–16), three minichiasms are heard (4:1–6; 4:9–12; 4:13–16).

The Fourth Microchiasm

The 4:1–16 microchiasm is composed carefully of four elements (A-B-B'-A'); linguistic parallels identifying chiastic arrangements are indicated by the Greek text:

> A. ⁴:¹ But the Spirit explicitly says that in later times some will apostasy from the faith (πίστεως), holding-toward (προσέχοντες) deceitful spirits and teachings (διδασκαλίαις) of demons, ² in the hypocrisy of false-worders, who have become-seared in their own conscience, ³ forbidding to marry, to avoid foods, which God created for reception with thanksgiving by the faithful (πιστοῖς) and those who have knowingly-embraced the truth. ⁴ Because all creation of God is commendable and nothing is to be-rejected, being received with thanksgiving; ⁵ for it is made-holy consistent-with the word of God and intercession. ⁶ Instructing these-things

---

1. For the establishment of 1 Timothy as a macrochiasm, clarifications of terminology, and an explanation of my translation methodology, see volume 1, chapter 2.

to the brothers you will be a commendable deacon of Christ Jesus, being-nourished in the words (λόγοις) of the faith (πίστεως) and of the commendable teaching (διδασκαλίας) that you have followed;

> B. ⁷ but the vile and silly myths reject. But train yourself toward (πρός) godliness (εὐσέβειαν); ⁸ᵃ for bodily training is toward (πρός) little profitability (ὠφέλιμος),
>
> B'. ⁸ᵇ but godliness (εὐσέβεια) is toward (πρός) all profitability (ὠφέλιμός) holding the promise of life for the present and for the inevitable-coming.

A'. ⁹ Faithful (πιστός) is the word (λόγος) and worthy of all acceptance; ¹⁰ for to this we toil and agonize, because we have hoped upon the living God, who is the Savior of all humans, especially of the faithful (πιστῶν). ¹¹ Charge these-things and teach (δίδασκε). ¹² None must look-down-on your youth; rather be an example of those of the faithful (πιστῶν) in word, in behavior, in love, in faith (πίστει), in purity. ¹³ Until I come hold-toward (πρόσεχε) the reading, to the exhorting, to the teaching (διδασκαλίᾳ). ¹⁴ Do not be without-concern with the gift that is in you, which was given to you consistent-with prophecy with the-laying of hands of the presbytery. ¹⁵ These-things be concerned with; be in them, that your progress might be manifested to all. ¹⁶ Strongly-hold yourself and the teaching (διδασκαλίᾳ), strongly-remain in them; for doing this you will save yourself and those who hear you.

1 Timothy 4:1–6: Teachings of Demons Versus The Teaching

(A Element)

Within the introductory A element of the fourth microchiasm (4:1–6), the audience hear one minichiasm (4:1–6).

1 Timothy 4:1–6: A Minichiastic Unit

As a minichiasm in itself, verses 4:1–6 of the A element are composed carefully of five sub-elements ("a"-"b"-"c"-"b"-"a"); linguistic parallels identifying chiastic arrangements are indicated by the Greek text:

PRESERVING THE TEACHING AND PROMOTING GODLINESS 95

"a". ¹ But the Spirit explicitly says that in later times some will apostasy from the faith (πίστεως), holding-toward deceitful spirits and teachings (διδασκαλίαις) of demons, ² in the hypocrisy of false-worders, who have become-seared in their own conscience,

"b". ³ forbidding to marry, to avoid foods, which God created for reception (μετάλημψιν) with thanksgiving (μετὰ εὐχαριστίας) by the faithful and those who have knowingly-embraced the truth.

"c". ⁴ᵃ Because all creation of God is commendable and nothing is to be-rejected,

"b'". ⁴ᵇ being-received (λαμβανόμενο) with thanksgiving (μετὰ εὐχαριστίας); ⁵ for it is made-holy consistent-with the word of God and intercession. ⁶ᵃ Instructing these-things to the brothers you will be a commendable deacon of Christ Jesus,

"a'". ⁶ᵇ being-nourished in the words of the faith (πίστεως) and of the commendable teaching (διδασκαλίας) that you have followed;

The first minichiasm of the 4:1–16 microchiasm is framed by contrasting the activities of "some" versus Timothy in regard to the "faith"—particularly of "teachings" versus the "teaching"—in the "a" and "a'" sub-elements. Within this linguistic framework, Paul's concern for "reception" and "thanksgiving" in regard to God's creation is heard in the "b" and "b'" sub-elements. The minichiasm gravitates around the fact that all creation of God is commendable in the pivot "c" sub-element.

1 Timothy 4:1–2a: The Spirit Versus Deceitful Spirits

("a" sub-element)

The introductory "a" sub-element (4:1–2a) begins the fourth microchiasm of the letter on a somber note following the majestic hymn that concluded the third microchiasm: "But the Spirit explicitly says that in later times some will apostasy from the faith" (4:1). The disjunctive "But" (δέ) is jarring. In effect, after the audience "was taken-up in glory" with Christ Jesus at the pivot of the letter (3:16), the audience are now slammed back to earth by the sudden "But" (4:1). Thus as the macrochiasm progresses toward its conclusion, the conjuction would not only link the third and fourth microchiasms but would also communicate a contrasting shift in mood from the note of joyful praise to sober realism.[2]

The term "Spirit" would carry several implications for the audience. First, the audience would hear a seamless movement—via transitional words—from "Spirit" (πνεύματι, 3:16) in the A' element of the third microchiasm to "Spirit" (πνεῦμα, 4:1) in the A element of the fourth microchiasm.[3] Thus, despite the shift in mood, the confessedly great truth concerning Christ Jesus is carried forward into the fourth microchiasm. Second, where Paul's declaration that Christ "was declared-just in Spirit (πνεύματι)" in 3:16 of the third microchiasm alluded to the activity of the Holy Spirit to usher Christ Jesus to the sphere of existence "in Spirit," the audience understand that the same person—the "Spirit" (πνεῦμα)—is in view here in 4:1 of the fourth microchiasm. Third, therefore, given the connection of "Spirit" in 3:16 and 4:1, not only is the person of "the Spirit" (4:1) in view but also the sphere of existence "in Spirit" (3:16) is in view—the second and final mode of existence that Christ has entered as a human. Thus the audience understand that from the outset of the A element of the fourth microchiasm, Paul is concerned with both the person of and the realm into which "the Spirit" brings humans, namely the realm "in faith" (1:2, 4; 2:7, 15; 3:13), that is, "in Christ Jesus" (1:14; 3:13), that is, "in Spirit" (3:16).

Given the Spirit's involvement with the undeniable truth about Christ Jesus in 3:16, the phrase "the Spirit explicitly says" in 4:1 would grab the audience's attention in several ways. First, whatever the Spirit is about to say, the audience understand that it will be concerned with the final mode of existence "in Spirit," that is, it will have an eschatological connotation. Second, the phrase "the Spirit . . . says (λέγει)" would be reminiscent of the very common, formulaic OT statement, "Thus says the Lord (λέγει κύριος)" (e.g., LXX Isa 30:1).[4] More than likely, then, the audience understand that Paul intends for them to receive the words that follow not as the words of one human to another—Paul to the audience—but as the very words of God speaking through an apostle whom he appointed—the Spirit speaking through Paul.[5] It is God speaking to his church, his

---

2. See Wall with Steele, *1 & 2 Tim*, 117. Contra Marshall who suggests that rather than introducing a point of contrast, "on the whole a fresh start seems to be indicated" (*PE*, 536).

3. Regarding the function of *transitional words*, see volume 1, chapter 2.

4. Further linguistic and thematic similarities between 1 Timothy 4:1 and LXX Isaiah 30:1 will be noted below.

5. Paul does not specify any other source of this prophetic utterance. For various proposals see Dunn, *Jesus and the Spirit*, 453; Fee, *God's Empowering Presence*, 769; Towner, *Goal*, 58. Regardless the source, the rhetorical purpose of the phrase is to

household—the Ephesian audience. Thus the phrase "the Spirit . . . says" would not only identify "the Spirit" with the God of the OT but also emphasize Paul's unique role as an apostle: his teaching is authoritative because he is privy to the words of God.

Third, given that "the Spirit" is directly associated with Christ Jesus who was manifested "in flesh" (3:16, line one) but now exists "in Spirit" (3:16, line two), that is, in heaven (3:16, line three), that is, "in glory" (3:16, line six), the audience understand that their access to Christ Jesus in heaven, "in glory," is at least in part possible through the person who put him there, namely "the Spirit" (3:16; 4:1). Thus upon hearing the phrase "the Spirit . . . says," the audience are prepared not only to hear God's words to them but possibly also Christ Jesus's words to them—the sense being that "the Spirit" (4:1) might actually relay from heaven the very words of the resurrected Christ Jesus (3:16)—"in Spirit"—to Christ Jesus's very own personal respresentative and messenger—Paul (1:1)—and thus to the humans whom Christ Jesus came to save (1:15)—the Ephesian audience. Indeed, it would be fitting for Christ Jesus, the Lord of those "in faith" (1:2), to communicate with those who are in God's household (3:15), that is, "in faith" (1:4; 3:13), that is, "in Christ Jesus" (1:14; 3:13).

Fourth, therefore, where the phrase "the Spirit . . . says" has both the words of Christ Jesus and God in view, the audience—those in the household of God "in faith"—understand that neither Christ Jesus nor God have left them to figure out for themselves how they are to live in this household. Rather, it is evident that Christ Jesus and God continue to guide the audience through intelligible speech, namely through what "the Spirit . . . says (λέγει)" (4:1);[6] indeed, such is communicated through the truth that Christ's apostle Paul is "saying" (λέγω, 2:7) by the command of God (1:1).[7] Moreover, fifth and finally, in combination with the adverb "explicitly" (ῥητῶς), the audience understand that the Spirit, God, and Christ Jesus's speech to the church is not at all obscure but is clear and obvious.[8]

---

underscore that it is the Spirit who provides the warning that is to follow.

6. The aspect of continual guidance would likely be drawn out for the audience by the present tense of the verb "says" (λέγει).

7. Cf. Marshall, PE, 536: "It is debated whether the message [4:1] is regarded as having come through Christ himself or through a Spirit-inspired prophet (perhaps Paul himself), but the latter is more likely, since elsewhere Christ's teaching is attributed to him personally as 'the Lord.'" Given the connection between Christ Jesus and the Spirit (3:16), however, both Christ and the Spirit would be in view here in relation to Paul's words. For further connections between the Spirit and Christ (e.g., 1 Cor 15:45; 2 Cor 3:17), see Gaffin, "'Life-Giving Spirit,'" 578.

8. BDAG, s.v. Knight, PE, 188: "'expressly, explicitly,' emphasizes that the Spirit has communicated in no uncertain terms." See Marshall, PE, 537.

In sum, the audience hear a twofold nuance at the outset of the fourth microchiasm. On the one hand, the opening word "But" presents a contrast to the high point of glory in the A' element of the third microchiasm. On the other hand, the overall rhetorical force of the opening phrase "the Spirit explicitly says" presents a continuation, immediately reminding the audience of the reason for Paul's letter in 3:15 and the implications of 3:16. That is, ultimately the audience live under the guiding authority of God—the Father of the household "in faith" (1:2; 3:15)—of Christ Jesus—their Lord (1:2, 12, 14)—and of the Spirit—the inaugurator of a new mode of existence (3:16). God, Christ Jesus, and the Spirit have provided clear and continual verbal instruction for how the audience are to behave in God's household, the church (3:15), and thus to live "in flesh" on earth while simultaneously "in Spirit" because they are "in Christ Jesus."

Carrying forward all these connotations, the Spirit says "that in later times some will apostasy from the faith" (4:1). The prepositional phrase "in later times" (ἐν ὑστέροις καιροῖς) recalls for the audience "his own times (καιροῖς)" in 2:6 of the second microchiasm, wherein the testimony concerning Christ Jesus was revealed as a present reality for which Paul was appointed a proclaimer, apostle, and teacher (2:7).[9] Moreover, the connection of the phrases "in later times" and "the Spirit . . . says" would indicate that the audience are to have in view the new, second, final mode of existence "in Spirit"—that which Christ Jesus already exists in distinction to the former mode of existence "in flesh" (3:16). Thus the phrase "in later times" simultaneously has a final eschatological connotation of that which has already happened and is now present. In this way, the phrase indicates for the audience an overlap between two distinct times, namely their present human reality "in flesh" but also their present and final existence "in Spirit," that

---

9. Knight aptly observes: "the NT community used futuristic sounding language to describe the present age. Furthermore, when this word was originally said the phenomenon was in a relative sense future, and thus 'later.' Therefore, Paul is speaking about a present phenomenon using emphatic future language characteristic of prophecy. That he goes on to an argument addressed to a present situation (vv. 3–5) and that he urges Timothy to instruct the church members in this regard here and now (v. 6) substantiate this understanding" (*PE*, 189). Marshall, *PE*, 531: "what is prophesied [apostasy and false teachers] is in fact already happening . . . so that current events are identified as signs of the last days." See Barcley, *1 & 2 Tim*, 128.

It may be worth noting that not a few commentators suggest that the phrase "in later times" indicates impending, apocalyptic trouble that await the audience in the future, particularly before Christ's second advent. Muddiman and Barton, "The PE," 252: "It was a commonplace idea in Jewish and Christian apocalyptic that the end would be preceded by a time of persecution and suffering . . . The sense of urgency and immediacy are absent from the Pastoral Epistles, but there is a lingering feeling that before the end there will be difficult and dangerous times." See also Spicq, *TLNT*, 3:427–31.

is, "in faith that is in Christ" (3:13).[10] Thus viewing themselves as living "in later times"—an eschatological yet clearly present reality—the phrase emphasizes for the audience the impetus of the A' element of the third microchiasm: they are to live in light of the person of Christ Jesus, namely to be a pillar and foundation of the confessedly great truth (3:15–16) against the threats of "some" by missionally exhibiting such truth through proper behavior in God's household (3:15).

The phrase "some will apostasy from the faith" would be understood with several implications. First, the term "some" (τινες) in 4:1 undoubtedly recalls the sustained polemical reference to the false teachers throughout the entire macrochiasm: "some" (τισίν) teach-different (1:3); "some" (τινες) have turned-aside from a without-hypocrisy faith for useless-words (1:5–6); "someone" (τις) does not know the lawful use of the law (1:8b); "some" (τινες) have become-shipwrecked regarding the faith (1:19); and though "someone" (τις) aspires to be an overseer, "someone" (τις) does not know how to lead his own household or care-for the church of God (3:1, 5). In effect, the audience understand the opening statement of 4:1 as, "But the Spirit explicitly says that false teachers will apostasy from the faith."[11] Paul intends for the audience to face the hard reality that "some" will undoubtedly abandon the faith; as such, the commendable war to preserve the sound teaching, the gospel, is to be expected (1:10b, 11, 18). Still, given Paul's repeated call for the audience's allegiance throughout the macrochiasm, Paul does not only have "some" in view but also anyone in the audience

10. This overlap is commonly referred to as the "already-and-not-yet." Gaffin succinctly explains the dual nature of Paul's eschatology, a perspective that helps us understand that the phrase "in later times" (and similar phrases [e.g., "the last days," 1 Pet 1:5]) is not to be understood as a temporal reference but a theological description of living between the first and second coming of Christ: "Part of the recent consensus in Pauline scholarship emerging over the course of the twentieth century . . . is that Paul's eschatology has a dual or elliptical focus. For him eschatology is defined not only in terms of Christ's second coming but also by his first, by what has already taken place in Christ, especially his death and resurrection, as well as what is still future at his return. Paul teaches an eschatology that for the church is, in part, present, already realized" (*By Faith*, 26). Towner writes similarly: "The phrase that opens the prophetic word is temporal in appearance but theological in meaning . . . It identifies the eschatological time of the Spirit and salvation (thus = 'the last days'), but does so here specifically by describing an element of the dark reality of sin, struggle, and danger that coexists with the Spirit in this age of incompleteness" (*Letters*, 288). See also Mounce, *PE*, 234.

11. Fee suggests that τινες refers to those who are being led astray by the false teachers and not to the false teachers themselves (*1 & 2 Tim*, 97). To be sure, Paul is not limiting the scope of the Spirit's declaration to only the false teachers; however, consistent with the entire macrochiasm—particularly the first and third microchiasms—it is most unlikely that Paul is referring simply to those led astray by false teachers. Indeed, the term "some" clearly places the emphasis of the statement upon the false teachers.

who will—if they have not already—be led astray by the false teachings of "some." For Paul's audience, then, the full implication is that the content of the false teaching—that which is "some-thing different" that lies-opposed to the sound teaching with which Paul was counted-faithful (1:10b–11)—is not according to the gospel (1:11a) and thus will lead to apostasy for anyone who subscribes to it.

Second, combined with the connotations of "some" who have already turned-aside from a without-hypocrisy faith (1:5–6) and who—by rejecting faith—have become-shipwrecked regarding the faith (1:19), the verb "will apostasy" (ἀποστήσονταί) would certainly carry the strong sense of abandoning. What is more, the powerfully negative characteristic of the verb "will apostasy" would be enhanced by its OT echoes, such as LXX Daniel 9:5: "We have sinned, done wrong, acted wickedly, and apostatized-from (ἀπέστημεν) and broken your commandments and rules." To be sure, the phrase "some will apostasy" in 4:1 would not be understood as neutral status but rather as an active abandonment and rebellion against God.

Third, combined with the term "the faith" (τῆς πίστεως), the audience would understand "will apostasy" not only as letting go of "the mystery of the faith (τῆς πίστεως)" (3:9) but also as a rejection and shipwrecking of "the faith" (τὴν πίστιν, 1:19). Consequently, given the sustained connection throughout the macrochiasm between existing "in faith" and the subsequent lifestyle of godliness, the audience understand that Paul likely has in mind that "some" and their followers have not only abandoned "the faith" but have also deviated from the lifestyle expected of those who belong to the household of God.

Indeed, fourth and finally, this would be emphasized by the force of the participle "holding-toward" (προσέχοντες), which recalls the rhetorical contrast that has been culminating throughout the macrochiasm. Rather than "holding (ἔχων) faith" (1:19) and "holding (ἔχοντας) the mystery of the faith" (3:9) concerning the confessedly great mystery of godliness Christ Jesus (3:16), it is evident that "some" who teach-different and "hold-toward" (προσέχειν) myths and genealogies without-limit (1:3–4a) are the same group of "some" who will apostasy from the faith and are described as "holding-toward" (προσέχοντες, 4:1). Here, Paul makes clear the devastating connotation of "holding-toward" by directly linking it to "deceitful spirits and teachings of demons" (4:1).

The phrase "deceitful spirits" articulates two contrasts for the audience. First, the term "spirits" (πνεύμασιν) recalls "the Spirit" (τὸ . . . πνεῦμα) in 4:1 and his personal activity toward Christ Jesus who now exists "in Spirit (πνεύματι)" in 3:16. A marked difference would be heard between the singular "Spirit" and the plural "spirits." To be sure, the audience understand that the one "Spirit" is not associated with the other "spirits."[12] Second, given that the multiple spirits are "deceitful" (πλάνοις), that is, acting with duplicity and double-dealing, they are clearly the antithesis of the singular Spirit who "explicitly says" clear, unambiguous words to Paul. It is for this reason that Paul, who is aligned with what the one Spirit says (4:1), may thus declare that he himself is saying the truth (2:7) regarding the one God (2:5a) and the one mediator of God and humans, Christ Jesus (2:5b). Furthermore, just as Christ Jesus and God continue to guide the audience through what "the Spirit . . . says" (4:1), it is evident that Christ Jesus and God continue to defend and protect the audience through "the Spirit" by communicating the threat of deceitful opponents—such is the occasion of Paul's letter. In this sense, the audience understand that just as a complete opposition between Paul and "some" is in view, so too between "the Spirit" and "deceitful spirits."[13] Indeed, the apostle Paul's point is to make explicit for the audience that the present danger regarding "some" who teach-different in the Ephesian church has spiritual sources. The commendable war of Paul, Timothy, and the men and women "in faith" against the false teachers (1:2, 18–20) mirrors the war of God, Christ Jesus, and the Spirit against the encroaching danger of deceitful spirits (4:1).

The phrase "teachings of demons" (διδασκαλίαις δαιμονίων) echoes a clear contrast to the phrase "the sound teaching" (τῇ ὑγιαινούσῃ διδασκαλίᾳ) in 1:10b of the first microchiasm. It is thus evident why "some" who "teach-different" (ἑτεροδιδασκαλεῖν, 1:3) and "some" who are holding-toward "teachings (διδασκαλίαις) of demons" (4:1) are engaged in something different that lies-opposed to "the . . . teaching" (τῇ . . . διδασκαλίᾳ, 1:10b) and thus are not "able-to-teach" (διδακτικόν, 3:2), that is, are unqualified to be overseers in the Ephesian church. Indeed, the implication is clear: rather than aligning with Paul who was appointed by God himself as an authorized "teacher" (διδάσκαλος, 2:7), "some" are holding-toward

---

12. Given the context of apostasy and the contrast between "the Spirit" over and against "spirits," the linguistic and thematic similarities of LXX Isaiah 30:1 may be worth noting:

1 Tim 4:1: "But the Spirit (πνεῦμα) explicitly says (λέγει) that . . . some will apostasy (ἀποστήσονταί) from the faith, holding-toward deceitful spirits (πνεύμασιν)."

LXX Isa 30:1 "'Ah, stubborn (ἀποστάται) children,' says (λέγει) the Lord, 'who carry out a plan, but not mine, and who make an alliance, but not of my Spirit (πνεύματός), that they may add sin to sin.'"

13. The flesh-Spirit contrast in 3:16 of the previous microchiasm seems to prepare the contrast here in 4:1. As the flesh and Spirit distinguish two different modes of existence, so too would allegiance to "deceitful spirits" (πνεύμασιν πλάνοις) be distinguished and opposed to "the Spirit" (πνεῦμα). Such opposition of "spirits" in the last days against the faithfulness of God's people is a common theme in eschatological literature. See, e.g., *Testament of Benjamin* 3:3; *Testament of Dan* 5:5; Rev 16:4; 1QS 3:22.

the opponents of God, namely "demons" (4:1). The difference between "the . . . teaching," which is healthy and singular, versus "teachings" of demons, which are opposed to God and plural, would likely be heard as indicative of the unity, wholesomeness, and superiority of the former over the latter.[14] Furthermore, given that the polemic of the overall macrochiasm against the false teachers—"some"—has progressed into the fourth microchiasm—"some" (τινες, 4:1)—the specification that the teachings are of "demons" would be heard as an indictment. That is, in contrast to Paul's apostolic teaching—which is from the one Spirit (4:1), according to the command of the one God (1:1, 17; 2:5), and representational of the one mediator Christ Jesus who appointed and sent Paul (1:1, 12; 2:5, 7)—the false teaching of "some" is directly from the teachings of multiple "demons" (4:1). In this sense, Paul seems to acknowledge to the audience that both he and the false teachers have in fact received revelation.[15] As such, the audience understand that Paul is emphasizing the explicit danger of the false teachers in direct relation to demons.[16]

The term "demons" (δαιμονίων) itself would remind the audience of the current circumstances of the false teachers and how they arrived there. In the first microchiasm, Paul handed two false teachers to "Satan" (1:20) for the purpose of their restoration to faith since they had already fallen into the condemnation of "the devil" (3:7), that is, into the deceptive snare that "the devil" intentionally set for them (3:7).[17] In this way, the audience understand that as much as "some" are actively "holding-toward teachings of demons"

14. It may be worth noting that the noticeably plural forms of both "deceitful spirits" and "teachings of demons" would suggest that the latter is intended to be a qualification of the former. In this case, within the phrase "deceitful spirits and teachings of demons" (4:1), the audience would likely hear the conjuction "and" (καί) epexegetically as a specifying term. This would be apparent enough, given that the spirits in view are demonic. The sense would be that "some"—namely the false teachers—are "holding-toward deceitful spirits, that is, teachings of demons." In effect, then, where "deceitful spirits" are in contrast to "the Spirit," there seems to be an implied contrast between the "teachings of demons" and the (implicit) "teaching of the Spirit."

15. Johnson forcefully demonstrates that it was not uncommon during this period to associate a person or group of persons with demons in order to discredit them ("Anti-Jewish Slander," 419–41). Paul is obviously doing the same, but this should not be misinterpreted as merely the use of a rhetorical technique. To be sure, Paul viewed Satan, the devil, and demons as not only real (1:20; 3:6–7; 4:1) but as pervasive dangers to those whom he ministered and, therefore, regularly reminded believers to be on guard against an exclusively materialist worldview that does not take into account the reality of deceitful spirits (see esp. Eph 6:12).

16. Barcley, *1 & 2 Tim*, 129: "While demons are the ultimate source of the false teaching, it is mediated through human agents."

17. The use of "deceitful spirits" seems to carry the same implication as "snare of the devil" (3:7). See chapter 2.

(4:1), the audience are equally aware that the "demons" in 4:1—much like the devil in 3:6–7—are actively grasping for anyone who themselves are not actively "holding"—clinging tightly to—the faith (1:19; 3:9).

In sum, given that Paul correlates "apostasy from the faith"—an abandoning, turning-aside, rejecting—with the active efforts of the demonic world, the audience understand that in the midst of the polemic against "some" who are unqualified, false-teaching overseers in Ephesus, Paul is calling upon the audience to tighten their grip and remain "in faith" so that they might not also "apostasy." At the same time, pressed with this reality, the audience must make a choice whether they will follow Paul and Timothy or "some"—more ultimately, whether they will follow the one Spirit, one God, and one mediator Christ Jesus or the deceitful spirits, demons, Satan, and the devil. The force of the opening statement of the fourth microchiasm is clear: the audience are not to live naively, as if holding the faith will be without struggle. The audience are to know that "some" will undoubtedly abandon the faith, and thus—as Paul has alluded to already throughout the letter—conflict is to be expected.[18] Here, then, after pivoting around the Christ-hymn in 3:16 of the C unit, the movement of the macrochiasm magnifies the consequences of being associated with the false teachers in contrast to an association with Paul: aligning with the "apostle" (ἀπόστολος) Paul leads to an existence "in Spirit" and "in glory" (3:16) whereas aligning with "some" who will "apostasy" (ἀποστήσονται) leads to deceit and shipwrecked faith (1:19; 4:1).[19] The audience understand that there is no neutral ground: it is Paul the apostle "in faith" (1:1; 2:7) versus "some" the apostates "from the faith" (4:1).

The "a" sub-element of the minichiasm continues in 4:2: "in the hypocrisy of false-worders, who have become-seared in their own conscience."[20] It is possible that the audience hear the phrase "in the hypocrisy of

---

18. Marshall, PE, 538: "The prophetic form emphasises both the inevitability of what is happening and the fact that it should not take people be surprise." Barcley provides a helpful nuance (1 & 2 Tim, 128): "The false teachers should come as no surprise to the church because 'the Spirit' has already 'explicity' predicted their rise. This fact should give the church confidence and boldness in combating them, because it indicates that this evil is under the sovereign control and foreknowledge of God."

19. The aural similarity between "apostasy" (ἀποστήσονταί, 4:1) and "apostle" (ἀπόστολος, 1:1; 2:7) may be worth noting. The implication—if any—would further emphasize the stark contrast between Paul and the false teachers.

20. Due to the ambiguity of this prepositional phrase—specifically the term "in" (ἐν)—the precise connection between 4:1 and 4:2 is somewhat difficult, as the different translations demonstrate. E.g., compare NIV ("Such teachings come through hypocritical liars") and KJV ("Speaking lies in hypocrisy"). Both interpretations are defensible. Marshall, PE, 539: "The force of ἐν may be instrumental ('through the hypocrisy of . . .') or more general ('in association with' cf. 2 Tim 1.13)."

false-worders" as an indication that "some" who "will apostasy from the faith" in 4:1 are led astray through the hypocrisy of false-worders.[21] Yet, given the polemic of 4:1 directed specifically against the false-teaching overseers, it seems more likely that Paul's audience hear the phrase as an indication that "some will apostasy from the faith" because "some" abide "in hypocrisy" and are "false-worders"—indeed, precisely because "some" teach-different (1:3) by holding-toward teachings of demons (4:1).[22]

For Paul's first-century audience, the term "hypocrisy" (ὑποκρίσει) expressed a gap between the claims of a person (or group of persons) and what in fact was true.[23] To be sure, the sustained polemic of the macrochiasm has already elucidated for the audience the specific gap in view: "some" are teaching some-thing different than the sound teaching of the authoritative apostle Paul (1:3, 10b). That is, even though "someone" is an overseer in the church of God in Ephesus, their teaching and governing lies-opposed to the gospel, the testimony, the mystery concerning Christ Jesus who came into the world, who exhibited God's glory, and who gave himself as a ransom to save sinners so that by coming to have-faith upon him for life eternal, saved sinners would be "in Christ Jesus," thus "in Spirit," thus "in glory," thereby giving honor and glory to the King of the eternities for the eternities of the eternities (1:11, 15, 17; 2:6; 3:16). Indeed, the gap between what is claimed to be true and what is actually true—"hypocrisy"—encapsulates "some" who are desiring to be law-teachers yet are not understanding either what they-are-saying or regarding some-things they-are-insisting (1:7). In this sense, perhaps a more fitting word to describe the false teachers is "specious," for they give the appearance of being teachers like Paul, who is saying the truth (2:7), when in fact they are not like Paul at all. To be sure, the fact that the "some" are "in hypocrisy (ὑποκρίσει)" (4:1) affirms that "some" have turned-aside from "a without-hypocrisy (ἀνυποκρίτου) faith" (1:5–6). The

---

21. E.g., Fee, *God's Empowering Presence*, 768 n. 59. The NIV suggests this interpretation.

22. The KJV suggests this interpretation. Knight, *PE*, 189: "These 'teachings' are mediated (ἐν) 'by means of' . . . human beings as the proximate source." See Towner, *Letters*, 291. It has been suggested that 4:2 is describing the "demons" in 4:1 rather than "some"—the false teachers (see e.g., Fee, *1 & 2 Tim*, 768 n. 59); however, this idea seems altogether unlikely, not only because of the sustained polemic of the letter against "some" but also because the subsequent phrase "who have become-seared in their own conscience" is referring to humans.

23. Marshall, *PE*, 539–40: "The LXX uses it to refer to people who are godless and evil (but not in the sense of being two-faced or 'hypocritical' in the modern sense). However, the word-group came to refer to deception; it is associated with lying and contrasted with truth."

clear implication is that "some" who are "in hypocrisy" (ἐν ὑποκρίσει, 4:1) are "in unfaithfulness" (ἐν ἀπιστίᾳ, 1:13).

Furthermore, that "some" are "false-worders" (ψευδολόγων, 4:2) not only recalls Paul's polemical statement that he is "not falsifying (ψεύδομαι)" (2:7) but also the polemical implication that "some" are "falsifiers" (ψεύσταις) for whom the law is laid (1:10a). Paul's sustained rhetoric is clear: "some" who are "falsifiers" (1:10a), "falsifying" (2:7), and "false-worders" (4:2) are nothing like Paul, who is saying the "truth" as a divinely appointed teacher "in faith and truth" (2:7). Indeed, the fact that "some" are "false-worders" (4:2) demonstrates that they have not come to a knowing-embrace of "truth" (2:4a), that is, "some" are likely yet to be-saved. Still, Paul's intentional use of the term "false-worders" (ψευδολόγων) both recalls that "some" have turned-aside for "useless-words" (ματαιολογίαν, 1:6) and simultaneously underscores that the false teachers's words are qualitatively different than the "Faithful . . . word (λόγος)" concerning Christ Jesus that is worthy of all acceptance (1:15; cf. 3:1). In short, the audience understand that the combination of "in hypocrisy" and "false-worders" emphasizes a complete, antithetical relationship between Paul and the false teachers. At this point in the letter, therefore, it is unlikely that the audience understand that "some" are unintentionally misleading the congregation as a result of being passively led astray by deceitful spirits.[24] Much rather, the polemical force throughout the macrochiasm clearly indicates to the audience that the false teachers are deliberately and actively refusing to adhere to the sound teaching that Paul had given to the Ephesian church at least ten years prior—indeed, "some" are actively "holding-toward" deceitful spirits and teachings of demons (4:1).[25] That is, the audience undoubtedly understand that Paul views "some" as those who have made a conscious decision and stubborn commitment to reject Paul's authority and thus the person whom he represents as an apostle, namely Christ Jesus. In this sense, the fact that the false-teaching overseers are "false-worders" suggests that Paul does not view them as victims of good intentions.[26]

The introductory "a" sub-element of the minichiasm concludes with a further description of "some" who will apostasy from the faith, "who have become-seared in their own conscience." The participial "who have become-seared" (κεκαυστηριασμένων) is succinctly defined in the UBS

24. E.g., Fee, *1 & 2 Tim*, 98; cf. Towner, *Goal*, 155.

25. For discussion regarding Paul's establishment of the Ephesian church, see volume 1, chapter 1.

26. Indeed, Paul has implicitly indicated that the false teachers are ill-driven, hence the corrective qualifications (e.g., "without-affection-of-money," 3:4; "not avaricious," 3:8); see discussion in chapter 2.

as "burn[ed] with a hot iron so as to deaden feeling." The perfect tense is intentional, indicating a state that has both come about and persists.[27] It is possible that the sense of branding is in view, as if the false teachers have been marked to show they belong to Satan.[28] Yet, heard within the combined phrase "who have become-seared in their own conscience" the audience would more likely understand that Paul's point is to highlight a contrast. The term "conscience" (συνείδησιν) recalls for the audience the "good conscience (συνειδήσεως)" associated with "faith" in 1:5, the "good conscience (συνείδησιν)" associated with "faith" in 1:19, and the "pure conscience (συνειδήσει)" associated with "faith" in 3:9. To be sure, where "some" are associated with shipwrecked "faith" (1:20) and apostasy from "faith" (4:1), the audience understand that the false teachers are those "who have become-seared"—deadened—regarding their faith. Furthermore, consistent with its use throughout the macrochiasm, the term "conscience" signifies the human faculty that applies principle truth to real life, that is, the instrument through which a person makes correct decisions. Not only, then, are the false teachers those "who have become-seared" to their faith, but they also "have become-seared" to ethical behavior.[29] Undoubtedly, the two go hand in hand: "some" have become deadened to godliness precisely because they have become deadened to their existence "in faith." Heard in full, the phrase "who have become-seared in their own conscience" is nothing other than a conscience that has been rendered ineffective as a result of apostasy from the faith and turning-aside from the truth of the sound teaching that results in godliness—the gospel. Thus as much as the devil and deceitful spirits were actively attracting the false teachers (3:7; 4:1), it is equally clear to the audience that the deadening of their conscience began with a prior decision and commitment by "some" to willingly refuse the sound teaching—the faithful word—of Christ Jesus's messenger, the apostle Paul. Consequently, "some" have a seared conscience that is unable to discern how to live a life in all godliness (2:2) precisely because it is dead to the truth that enables godliness.

Furthermore, the connection between the statement "who have become-seared in their own conscience" (4:2) and the fact that "some" are

---

27. See also Knight, *PE*, 189; Marshall, *PE*, 540–41.

28. See, e.g., Fee, *1 & 2 Tim*, 98–99; Kelly, *PE*, 94–95.

29. Referencing Spicq, Knight interprets the verb "seared" as "'cauterized,' i.e., made insensible to the distinction between right and wrong" (*PE*, 189). Barclay, *1 & 2 Tim*, 130: "The good conscience, as we have already seen, functions as the person' moral indicator of right and wrong. The seared conscience can no longer make proper distinctions." Marshall, *PE*, 541: "The point is that their conscience was no longer effective in condemning what was morally unacceptable."

"holding-toward deceitful spirits and teachings of demons" (4:1) would likely have reminded the audience of 2:14 in the second microchiasm wherein "Adam was not deceived, but the woman being-deceived in transgression became."[30] In this case, the audience would again hear Paul's rebuke, generally, for the men to stop abdicating their creational roles—thus to begin to protect the women from the teachings of demons—and, specifically, for the qualified men to step forward to teach and govern the church so that deceitful teachings of demons would not gain any foothold in God's household.[31] In the OT and NT the devil is presented as the deceptive one who twists the truth of God into "attractively packaged error."[32] Thus where the false teachers have taken the bait, they are not only "holding-toward . . . teachings of demons" (4:1) but are, therefore, applying falsehood rather than truth to everyday life. Such would be evidenced by the fact that they "have become-seared in their own conscience" (4:2), that is, unable to discern right from wrong. Paul's point, then, suggests that the false teachers are familiar with God's truth, yet are only able to apply it in a twisted, incorrect way.

In sum, the audience are to take seriously the repercussion of failing to preserve the sound teaching of the gospel that Paul has clearly taught (1:10b–11; 2:7) and that they themselves are to uphold as the church of God, a pillar and foundation of truth (3:15). There is a succinct articulation of Paul's rhetoric: godliness is impossible apart from a knowing-embrace of truth, the gospel, that exhibits God's glory. Thus as much as Paul's polemic against the false-teaching overseers escalates after the pivotal turning point in the letter (3:16), so too does his call escalate for the church of the living God to actively preserve the sound teaching—thus to promote godliness—as a missional effort to bring "life eternal" (1:16) to "some" who are deadened regarding the faith (1:19; 4:2).

---

30. Although "deceitful" (πλάνοις, 4:3) and "deceived" (ἠπατήθη, ἐξαπατηθεῖσα, 2:14) are not cognate terms, conceptually they are similar and the connection would be apparent.

31. That Paul considers the men to be responsible, see discussion in volume 1, chapter 4 regarding 1 Timothy 2:13–14.

32. Barcley, *1 & 2 Tim*, 129. See e.g., Gen 3:1–5; Matt 4:1–10.

1 Timothy 4:3: Forbidding God's Creation Versus Receiving With Thanksgiving

("b" sub-element)

The "b" sub-element of the minichiasm begins to detail the precise content of the teachings of demons that is being mediated through the false teachers: "forbidding to marry, to avoid foods."[33] The sense of the first phrase "forbidding to marry" (κωλυόντων γαμεῖν) may have been heard more lightly as "discouraging to marry."[34] The striking contrast would be evident between the false teaching—"forbidding to marry" (4:2)—in the A element of the fourth microchiasm and Paul's teaching regarding qualified leaders in the church—"man of one woman" (3:2, 12)—in A and A' element of the preceding third microchiasm. To be sure, marriage was described as being fundamentally important for leadership in God's missional household (3:2, 11–12), that is, for all who exist "in faith."[35] Furthermore, Paul's sustained perspective throughout the macrochiasm has clearly been a celebration of family as one of the defining features of existing "in faith" (1:2, 4, 18; 2:15; 3:4–5, 12, 15). In short, not only is the very notion of discouraging or forbidding marriage altogether absent in Paul's teaching, but the notion of encouraging and promoting healthy marriages is very present.[36]

---

33. Some commentators suggest that such prohibitions are evidence of Gnostic dualistic tendencies among the false teachers (see e.g., Collins, *1 & 2 Tim*, 114–17; Karris, *PE*, 83–85; Kelly, *PE*, 236). However, Witherington succinctly and correctly notes: "Since asceticism was by no means an exclusive practice of gnostics, one cannot insist that Gnosticism is in view in this prohibition either" (*Letters*, 254). Mihoc, "Final Admonition to Timothy," 151: "Although this last term has a broad meaning, here it is surely not referring to later Gnosticism."

34. See ibid.

35. Note that 3:11 and 3:12 are to be heard together as evidence of man's leadership and faithfulness to his wife; see chapter 2.

36. Gench observes: "It is not hard to understand why ascetic teaching and celibate life had real appeal for many early Christian women as an avenue to freedom—freedom from patriarchal households and the hazards of childbirth, the leading cause of mortality among women in the ancient world" (*Tyrannical Texts*, 10). However, this does not take into account Paul's emphasis throughout the macrochiasm, namely that "child-parenting . . . in faith" (2:15) would be heard missionally and that "household" in the third microchiasm identifies—above all else—that men's sacrificial leadership in their own households is intended specifically to foster and encourage godliness, that is, to benefit, love, and protect the wives of households, just as Christ's sacrificial leadership toward his bride, the church (Eph 5:25–26). Against the notion that abstaining from marriage would be an avenue to freedom for first-century women in the Greco-Roman world, Meeks (referencing Weaver, "Social Mobility") notes that marriage was "one of the most common means for female slaves to gain freedom and improved status" (*First Urban Christians*, 23).

The second phrase "to avoid foods" (ἀπέχεσθαι βρωμάτων) would not be heard in reference to all foods but specific foods that were deemed unclean in OT practice. Certainly the audience would understand why Paul describes the false teaching "to avoid foods (βρωμάτων)" as the teachings of demons: the one who sent Paul to teach—Christ Jesus himself (1:1, 12; 2:7)—teaches that "all foods"—(πάντα τὰ βρώματα, Mark 7:19)—are clean, that is, not to be avoided. Furthermore, the false teaching "to avoid foods"—to not partake in specific foods altogether—would be heard in contrast to Paul's teaching about the qualifications of overseers and deacons—not avoiding wine altogether but rather "not addicted-to-wine" (3:3) and "not holding-toward much wine" (3:8).[37] In other words, the teachings of demons to which the false teachers are "holding-toward" (4:1) is a clear distortion of what is proper for men and women who exist "in faith" and are to avoid excess rather than consumption.[38] Heard together, then, the phrase "forbidding to marry, to avoid foods" would indicate for the audience that the false teachers are totally missing the point of the Christian life. The false teachers are consumed with "myths and genealogies without-limit" (1:4a) and ascetic practices (4:3) whereas the apostolic teacher Paul is consumed with preserving the sound teaching and promoting a corresponding lifestyle of godliness that functions as part of God's missional household to welcome, invite, and attract all humans inside. In short, the false teachers are concerned with themselves; Paul is concerned with Christ Jesus (1:1, 2, 12, 14, 15, 16; 2:5) and, consequently, with bringing others to come to have-faith upon Christ Jesus (1:16).

In regard to "forbidding to marry," the false teachers were likely familiar with the Jesus tradition that commended celibacy for the sake of the kingdom of heaven (e.g., Matt 19:12) and perhaps even with Paul's endorsement of celibacy in particular situations (1 Cor 7:26–36).[39] However, it is evident

37. The phrase "to avoid foods" (ἀπέχεσθαι βρωμάτων) is elliptical, meaning that it is impossible to take it with the participle "forbidding." Various translations demonstrate this (see *italics*): ESV: "who forbid marriage *and require* abstinence from foods"; NIV: "They forbid people to marry *and order* them to abstain from certain foods." Consistent with the NIV proposal, Towner suggests that "the best solution is to supply the matching verbal idea, 'ordering, to order' . . . presumably, the similarly spelled previous participle, 'forbidding,' would have immediately called 'ordering' to mind" (*Letters*, 293). See also BDF §479.2.

38. It may be worth noting that "to avoid foods" would function as a means of earning salvation—note: not a means of health as the result of medical instruction. Indeed, the freedom to eat all types of foods is balanced by a healthy avoidance of excess.

39. The composition of Matthew's Gospel likely occurred around the same time as the composition of 1 Timothy. Carson and Moo, *Introduction*, 79, 572, respectively: "the preponderance of evidence suggests that Matthew was published before 70," and "the letter [1 Timothy] was written somewhere in the middle 60s." While the a manuscript

that "forbidding to marry" misapplies both Jesus's and Paul's teaching to reach an unintended conclusion.[40] In addition, the false teachers might have found external endorsement "to avoid (ἀπέχεσθαι) foods" from the Jerusalem Council itself, which commanded all believers "to avoid (ἀπέχεσθαι) the things polluted by idols, and from sexual immorality, and from what has been strangled, and from blood" (Acts 15:20).[41] Yet, clearly the false teaching "to avoid foods"—possibly also "forbidding to marry"—misapplies the words of James at the Council.[42] In sum, even if the false teachers thought that they were aligning themselves with what Jesus taught, what Paul practiced, and what the Jerusalem Council endorsed, the fact that they "have become-seared in their own conscience" (4:2) had deadened them to the reality that they were advocating some-thing different (1:10b) and were thus asserting themselves over and against Paul. For sure, Paul's audience in the Ephesian church are reminded that the different teaching of "some" who are "forbidding to marry" (4:3) is the direct result of "holding-toward deceitful spirits and teachings of demons" (4:2) and is nothing other than the misinterpretation and misapplication of truth. Indeed, the further polemical message would be clear: anyone in the audience who does not align

---

of Matthew's Gospel might not have arrived in Ephesus, it is more than likely that the oral tradition that preceded its composition was made known to the Ephesian church, at the very least, by Paul.

40. Before and after the disciples's statement "it is better not to marry" in v. 10 of Matthew 19, Jesus upholds the value of marriage from the very beginning of creation (vv. 4-6), and he particularly specifies that "not all" (οὐ πάντες, v. 11) can grasp the concept of celibacy—in other words, clearly not all are intended for celibacy. Regarding 1 Corinthians 7, Knight provides a helpful summary of Paul's teaching about marriage: "Although Paul commended singleness as an estate in which one could give more time and energy directly to serving the Lord (1 Cor 7:32, 35), he always insisted that marriage was not wrong (1 Cor. 7:28) and that God had indeed gifted many to marry (1 Cor. 7:7)" (*PE*, 190).

41. Witherington, *Letters*, 253 n. 308: "Notice that the use of *apechesthai* with the genitive is just like what we find in Acts 15:20, 29, where the Jerusalem decree is referred to . . . This may in fact suggest that the false teachers were claiming that they had the support of the decree for the food restrictions for Gentiles that they were insisting on." See similarly Quinn and Wacker, *Letters*, 358.

42. The James of Acts in 15:13-21 sought to preserve certain religious practice without going beyond what Christ himself required. Wall with Steele *1 & 2 Tim*, 118-19: "The James of Acts . . . corrects Peter's myopic commentary on Cornelius's conversion by arguing that the purity practices (Acts 15:20) that complement a 'purity of the heart by faith' (15:9) are the *sine qua non* of Christian fellowship . . . James in particular was concerned that the initiation of repentant Gentiles into the Diaspora church . . . might threaten the Jewish legacy of the faith. Appealing to Israel's Scripture, his solution . . . concerns food and sex . . . [At the same time] James follows the pattern of Jesus, who allows for (but does not require) a celibate lifestyle as a property of a disciple's kingdom vocation (Matt 19:12) and considers all foods kosher (Mark 7:19)."

with the sound teaching (1:10b) of Paul, the "teacher . . . in faith and truth" (2:7), is either teaching or subscribing to "some-thing different" (1:10b).[43]

Paul continues the "b" sub-element by stating a stark contrast to what "some" think about marriage and foods: "which God created for reception with thanksgiving by the faithful and those who have knowingly-embraced the truth" (4:3). The phrase "which God created" has several implications. First, it is possible that the relative pronoun "which" (ἄ) was heard in a limited application to "foods, which God created"; yet, it is likely that the audience would understand that marriage itself is something created by God (e.g., Matt. 19:4-6) and thus would, at the very least, be implied in that "which" God created.[44] Second, Paul's main point here is to underscore to the audience that "God created" (ὁ θεὸς ἔκτισεν) the very things that "some" dismiss as implicitly bad. In a word, the false-teaching overseers certainly have a twisted view of marriage and foods.[45] "God created" undoubtedly directs the audience to the LXX Genesis creation narrative, not only to "God made the heavens and the earth" (Gen 1:1) but particularly to God's repeated refrain about his creation: "God saw that it was commendable (καλόν)" (LXX Gen 1:4, 10, 12, 18, 21, 25, 31).[46] Thus where God created all things—including marriage and foods—and considered them to be commendable,

---

43. The sustained explicit and implicit emphasis throughout the macrochiasm on Paul's apostolic authority provides the only strong clue in 1 Timothy for how such false teaching may have come about, namely the rejection of his apostolic authority, that is, his sound teaching—the gospel. Still, Towner proposes—perhaps correctly so—that the misunderstanding and misapplication of God's truth by the false teachers arose from an incorrect hermeneutic: "for some reason in the Ephesus of 1 Timothy a system of OT interpretation, which Paul terms 'myths and genealogies', appears to play a central role in arriving at certain dualistic conclusions about piety and the present life that stressed avoidance of certain elements proper to creation. What spiritual insights the Corinthians may have been relying on the Spirit for directly . . . are sought by the Ephesian opponents through 'spiritual' exegesis of certain OT stories about creation and early history" (*Letters*, 295).

44 Knight, *PE*, 190: "ἄ agrees with the nearest possible antecedent, βρωμάτων, but it may also include γαμεῖν indirectly if not directly." Contra Marshall, *PE*, 542: "The rel. pron. ἄ manifestly has βρώματα as its antecedent. An extension of the reference to cover both foods and marriage is very difficult, if not impossible, syntactically."

45. At least in part, the incorrect view of "some" may have compelled Paul's specific emphasis on the importance of marriage in regard to an overseer; see chapter 2 regarding 1 Timothy 3:2.

46. Although the verbs "created" (ἔκτισεν) in 1 Timothy 4:3 and "made" (ἐποίησεν) in LXX Genesis 1:1 are different, conceptually they would be understood to be similar in meaning. That God's creation was "commendable" (καλόν) in Genesis would be reminiscent of the theme of "commendable" throughout the 1 Timothy macrochiasm (1:8, 18; 2:3; 3:1, 4, 7, 12, 13); this connection to "commendable" in Genesis is made explicit in 4:4, see below.

the audience clearly understand that the false teachers have an assessment radically different from that of God. Moreover, for the false teachers standing among the audience, Paul's statement would be corrective—making them aware of their error—and perhaps even restorative—in effect, calling upon the false teachers to apostasy from deceitful spirits and teachings of demons (cf. 4:1) and thus to be holding the faith instead (cf. 1:9; 3:9).

Paul specifies the purpose "for" (εἰς) which "God created" marriage and foods, namely "reception with thanksgiving."[47] Noticeably, then, Paul identifies that those in God's household are to respond in a way that entirely differs from that of the false teachers. Rather than forbidding marriage and avoiding foods, the audience are to share God's assessment of his creation—that all is commendable (LXX Gen 1:31)—by receiving God's creation and thanking him for it. The term "reception" (μετάλημψιν) carries the nuance of "participation" or "sharing," indicating not a mere acceptance but also—and much more—a joyful use of God's creation, sharing its goodness with others (3:3).[48] The phrase "with thanksgiving" indicates for the audience an attitude of gratitude, humbly acknowledging that all goodness in creation comes from God and is to be received as such.[49] Furthermore, the term "thanksgiving" (εὐχαριστίας) recalls Paul's exhortation in regard to the lead activity of the church, namely that "supplications, prayers, intercessions, thanksgivings (εὐχαριστίας)" be-done on behalf of all humans in 2:1 of the second microchiasm. Thus as much as "thanksgiving" connotes an attitude for receiving God's creation, the audience understand that it also conveys a leading action, namely to thank God "for reception" of that which he created—including marriage and foods. Significantly, then, not only are the false teachers refusing to receive God's creation but they are failing to give thanks to God for it.

Furthermore, the fact that God's creation is actually received with thanksgiving "by the faithful and those who have knowingly-embraced the truth" would punctuate Paul's polemic against the false teachers. The term "the faithful" undoubtedly recalls for the audience the sustained theme of "faith" throughout the macrochiasm (1:2, 4, 5, 11, 12, 13, 14, 15, 16, 19;

---

47. See Knight, *PE*, 190–91.

48. Witherington, *Letters*, 255: "The relative clause here states that God created food to be received and indeed to be enjoyed (*eis metalēmpsin* suggests not just reception, but fruitful use)."

It may be worth noting that an aural repetition would be heard in the phrase μετάλημψιν μετά ("reception with"). The rhetorical effect upon the audience would likely emphasize the positive reception of God's creation.

49. See Knight, *PE*, 191. Witherington, *Letters*, 255: "Eating while recognizing the source of our nourishment not only sanctifies or hallows the act of eating, but also honors God the creator." See also Kelly, *PE*, 97.

2:7, 15; 3:9, 11, 13, 16). Specifically, "the faithful" (τοῖς πιστοῖς, 4:3) would be understood as a reference to those who are "in faith" (ἐν πίστει, 1:2, 4; 2:7, 15; 3:13). In this way, the term would function polemically against "some" who "apostasy from the faith" (τῆς πίστεως, 4:1), who "regarding the faith (τὴν πίστιν) have become-shipwrecked" (1:19), and who are currently operating in the sphere "in unfaithfulness" (ἐν ἀπιστίᾳ) as Paul was formerly (1:13). Moreover, in combination with the participal phrase "those who have knowingly-embraced the truth" (ἐπεγνωκόσι τὴν ἀλήθειαν), it is evident that "the faithful"—those "in faith"—are the direct recipients of the Savior God's desire for "all humans to be-saved and to come to a knowing-embrace of truth (ἐπίγνωσιν ἀληθείας)" (2:3–4).[50] Significantly, where the open possibility and invitation for salvation is extended "to those who would-inevitably-come to have-faith upon [Christ Jesus]" (1:16) so that they would "come to a knowing-embrace of truth" (2:4), Paul indicates that the possibility is a reality: "the faithful . . . have"—now, already, currently—"knowingly-embraced the truth" (4:3b).[51] The particular connection affirms that "truth," "faith," and salvation are completely intertwined and inseparable. To be sure, such saving "truth" (ἀληθείας, 2:4b; ἀλήθειαν, 4:3) is none other than the "truth" (ἀλήθειαν) that Paul is saying (2:7), the "truth" (ἀληθείᾳ) to which Paul was appointed as teacher (2:7), and the "truth" (ἀληθείας) that the church is to uphold as a pillar and foundation (3:15)—it is the truth of the sound teaching (1:10b), the gospel (1:11a), the testimony (2:6), the mystery (3:16) concerning Christ Jesus. Here, then, a twofold implication is reiterated: while a knowing-embrace of the "truth" equates to being "saved," that is, being "in faith," any rejection of the truth is tantamount to not being saved, that is, being "in unfaithfulness." Consequently, where "some" are "false-worders" (4:2), it is clear that they are not "the faithful" (4:3b), that they are not "those who have knowingly-embraced the truth" (4:3b; cf. 2:4b), and thus that they are yet to be-saved (cf. 2:4a). Yet, given the definite proof that a knowing-embrace of the truth is attainable, as evidenced by "the faithful" in the Ephesian church (4:3b), the missional implication of Paul's statement would not go unnoticed: even for "some" who are currently "holding-toward deceitful spirits and teachings of

---

50. The conjuction "and" (καί) would be understood epexegetically as a specifying term, the sense being "the faithful, that is, those who have knowingly-embraced the truth." The similar use of the conjunction "and" in both 4:1 and 4:3 may further emphasize the contrast between the false teachers who are, in effect, "holding-toward deceitful spirits, that is, teachings of demons."

51. The perfect participle "have knowingly-embraced" (ἐπεγνωκόσιν) conveys a present and continuing aspect. Knight, *PE*, 191: "the perfect active participle is probably used to emphasize the abiding awareness believers have of the truth."

demons" (4:1), are "false-worders" (4:2), and consequently have not knowingly-embraced the truth, it is clear that salvation is a tangible, obtainable reality. In short, Paul's missional intention for the restoration of the false teachers "to be-disciplined not to blaspheme" (1:20) is carried forward here in the fourth microchiasm. Indeed, even the false-teaching overseers who are "forbidding to marry, to avoid foods" (4:3a) may become "the faithful . . . who have knowingly-embraced the truth" (4:3b) by agreeing with the sound teaching of Paul—the gospel (1:10b, 1:11).

The explicit connection between "the faithful . . . who have knowingly-embraced the truth" (4:3b) and "reception with thanksgiving" (4:3a) would indicate the lifestyle of godliness that corresponds to existing "in faith." The audience's call to receive and give thanks for marriage and foods accords with their call to preserve the truth of the sound teaching and promote godliness in God's missional household.[52] Moreover, that the faithful in the audience "have knowingly-embraced" the truth indicates not merely a past reality but a present and persisting lifestyle.[53] The polemical force of Paul's point would be heard: if the false teachers had ever knowingly-embraced the truth, they certainly are not embracing it now. Ironically, a lifestyle "forbidding to marry" and "to avoid foods" as though salvation depended upon such ascetic practices abandons, turns away from, and rejects not only the truth of salvation, which is to have-faith upon Christ (1:16), but also that God created such things "for reception and thanksgiving" (4:3a).[54]

In sum, the audience hear Paul's statements in the "b" sub-element of the minichiasm as an affirmation toward "the faithful" among the audience, a polemic against "some," and simultaneously a missional effort toward "some" who have not knowingly-embraced the truth.

---

52. Marshall, *PE*, 543: "Those who have come to know the gospel should know also that foods were created to be received with thanksgiving."

53. See ibid., n. 51 regarding the perfect participle "those who have knowingly-embraced."

54. Hughes and Chapell, *1–2 Tim*, 106: "Paul considered asceticism a heinous doctrine and emphasized its terribleness in the context of 1 Timothy by attacking it immediately after quoting the creedal hymn that sets forth Christ as 'the mystery of godliness'—the source and origin of true godliness. Asceticism not only slams the Creator, but also the sufficiency of the Son's work."

*1 Timothy 4:4a: God's Creation is Commendable,
Nothing is To Be-Rejected*

("c" sub-element)

The pivot "c" sub-element (4:4a) of the minichiasm advances the thought of the "b" sub-element: "Because all creation of God is commendable and nothing is to be-rejected." The audience hear several important emphases. First, the term "all" (πᾶν) in 4:4a recalls the missional emphasis of the second and third microchiasms. The audience are to pray on behalf of "all" (πάντων, 1:2, 3); the Savior God desires "all" (πάντας, 2:4) humans to be-saved; Christ Jesus gave himself on behalf of "all" (πάντων, 2:6); the men are to pray in "all" (παντί, 2:8) places; women are to learn in "all" (πάσῃ, 2:11) submissiveness, that is, exhibiting a peaceable disposition; and deacons's wives are to be faithful in "all" (πᾶσιν, 3:11), that is, aligned with Paul and God's missional concern. Thus where "all (πᾶν) creation of God" is the concern in 4:4a of the fourth microchiasm, the audience understand that the reception of God's creation with thanksgiving is intended to have a missional impact.

Second, with the statement "Because all creation of God is commendable," the audience would immediately hear two connections. The phrase "all creation (κτίσμα) of God" in 4:4a of the "c" sub-element echoes the verbal cognate "God created (ἔκτισεν)" in 4:3 of the preceding "b" sub-element. In addition, that all creation of God is "commendable" (καλόν) in 4:4a of the "c" sub-element makes Paul's point in the "b" sub-element explicit. That is, where the fact that "God created" in 4:3 implied that God's creation is "commendable" (καλόν, LXX Gen 1:4, 10, 12, 18; καλά, 1:21, 25, 31), here in 4:4a the audience understand that the connection is certain: indeed, "all" (πᾶν) creation—to be sure, marriage and foods—is "commendable" (καλόν) in 4:4a because God said it himself (πάντα . . . καλά, LXX Gen 1:31).[55] In this way, Paul makes it absolutely certain to the audience—and to "some" among them—that the false teaching "forbidding to marry, to avoid foods" in 4:2 is clearly not "of God" (θεοῦ, 4:4a) but is, therefore, "of demons" (δαιμονίων, 4:1). Moreover, the progression of the minichiasm into 4:4a of the "c" sub-element would simultaneously convey a positive emphasis. Where "all creation of God is commendable," the audience understand that the enjoyment of God's creation—reception and

---

55. Knight, *PE*, 191: "Paul asserts of these created things the verdict given by God himself in Gn. 1:31." See Barcley, *1 & 2 Tim*, 132.

A visual comparison between 1 Timothy 4:4a and LXX Genesis 1:31 is helpful (see *italics*):
1 Tim 4:4a: "*πᾶν* κτίσμα θεοῦ *καλόν*";
LXX Gen 1:13: "καὶ εἶδεν ὁ θεὸς τὰ *πάντα* ὅσα ἐποίησεν καὶ ἰδοὺ *καλὰ* λίαν."

thanksgiving for marriage and foods (4:3)—is itself commendable and an activity of godliness.[56] Still, because "some" are holding-toward teachings of demons concerning God's creation, it is clear that Paul intends to warn his audience about the dangers and implications of having a false view of that which God created and deemed to be commendable.

Third, the adjective "commendable" (καλόν) in 4:4a recalls its sustained occurrences throughout the macrochiasm. The law, that is, God's just judgment, is "commendable" (καλός, 1:8) if used lawfully to judge sin; Paul, Timothy, and the audience's war against the false teachers to preserve the the sound teaching is "commendable" (καλήν, 1:18); the missional activities of prayer and godliness are "commendable" (καλόν) because they are in alignment with God's desire for all humans to be-saved (2:3–4a); the work of an overseer to teach and govern the church as a model of irreproachable godliness is "commendable" (καλοῦ, 3:1); leadership in a church leader's own household is to be done "commendably" (καλῶς, 3:4, 12); and those who serve-as-deacons "commendably" (καλῶς, 3:13) acquire a "commendable" (καλόν) standing" (3:13). Significantly, then, the statement "all creation is commendable (καλόν)" here in 4:4a demonstrates an expansive movement in the macrochiasm. Not only are marriage and food commendable because they are "of God," but the audience also understand why the law of God, the war to preserve the truth of God's sound teaching, godliness, overseeing the household of God, leading at home, and serving-as-deacons in the church of the living God are equally commendable: they, too, are equally "of God." Significantly, where "all creation of God is commendable," the audience understand that Paul's earlier reference to creation—"Adam was formed first, then Eve" (2:13), along with its implications for church leadership—is indeed commendable, to be enjoyed, shared, and received with thanksgiving by the faithful, that is, those who have knowingly-embraced the truth (4:3a).

The audience hear the concluding statement of the pivot "c" subelement as an emphatic exclamation point: "and nothing is to be-rejected" (4:4a).[57] Here, the correct disposition toward God's creation is stated

---

56. Johnson, *Contested Issues*, 673: "Paul is sometimes thought of as the most insistent voice against marriage in the New Testament, but . . . In one of the New Testament's most unequivocal statements on the subject, Paul includes marriage with food as among 'all things that God has created as good,' and designates those who forbid marriage as 'liars whose consciences are seared with a hot iron' (1 Tim 4:3)."

In passing, the connection between the "b" and "c" sub-elements—thus that marriage and foods are commendable—is further supported by the conjunction "Because" (ὅτι) in 4:4a, which effectively explains in more explicit detail why the faithful are to receive everything in creation with thanksgiving in 4:3.

57. As in 4:1 and 4:3, the "and" (καί) would be heard epexegetically as a specifying term—"that is"—thus highlighting the necessary conclusion that must follow from

negatively relative to the positive counterpart in the "b" sub-element: indeed, nothing is to be forbidden or avoided because everything is of God and, therefore, inherently commendable.[58] Furthermore, as much as the audience have heard the positive, cumulative impact of the macrochiasm concerning that which is "commendable" in the first half of 4:4a, Paul restates his point negatively for cumulative rhetorical force in the second half of 4:4a: God's law is not to be-rejected, nor the war to preserve the sound teaching against "some" who teach-different, nor lifestyles of godliness, nor the work of an overseer, nor leading at home, nor serving the needs of the church as deacons, nor the creational roles for men and women that God designed precisely because all of these are "commendable." Still, where the polemic of the minichiasm against the false teachers is undoubtedly in view, Paul's Ephesian audience understand the full implication: Paul's teaching on God's creation is not only the truth (2:7) according to the command and appointment of God (1:1; 2:7) and is to be knowingly-embraced (2:4; 4:3), but it is also—and emphatically—not to be-rejected. Rejection of God's creation and his design for it—as evidenced by rejecting the sound teaching of God's appointed teacher, Paul—is none other than a rejection of God. Indeed, the audience understand that "some" who "will apostasy from the faith" (4:1) have done so already.[59] Certainly, that the false teachers have "rejected" (ἀπόβλητον) God's commendable creation (4:4) is indicated by Paul's statements in the first microchiasm: "some—swerving-from [a without-hypocrisy faith]—have turned-aside for useless-words" (1:6); "some—rejecting (αθπωσάμενοι)—regarding the faith have become-shipwrecked" (1:19).[60]

---

the fact that all creation is commendable because it is of God. Contra Marshall, *PE*, 544: "καί introduces a separate clause with οὐδέν ('and none [of them]') as a fresh subject." While possible, this interpretation seems to remove the interconnected movement of Paul's rhetoric.

58. Given the performative aspect of the letter, it may be worth noting the rhythmic flow in the pivot "c" sub-element. When performed aloud, the audience would likely hear the accentuated cadence and coupling of the nominative neuter endings of the adjectives in 4:4:

"πᾶν κτίσμα θεοῦ καλόν";

"καὶ οὐδὲν ἀπόβλητον."

A rough translation that captures the poetic cadence of the language might be "Everything created by God is commendable, that is, nothing is deplorable."

59. Smith, *Pauline Communities*, 91: "Proof of this apostasy could already be seen in Ephesus (4:2–3a)."

60. The terms "rejected" (ἁγιασμῷ) in 4:4 and "rejecting" (ἁγνείᾳ) in 1:19 are not cognates. Yet, conceptually they are similar, and, given the context of apostasy from the faith, the connection would be apparent.

1 Timothy 4:4b–6a: Thanksgiving, the Word
of God, Instructing These-Things

("b'" sub-element)

Progressing around the pivot of the minichiasm, the "b'" sub-element begins with the participle phrase "being-received with thanksgiving" (4:4b). The phrase functions adverbially relative to Paul's previous statement in 4:4a, giving the sense of "nothing is to be-rejected *if* it is received with thanksgiving."[61] In addition, "being-received with thanksgiving" (μετὰ εὐχαριστίας λαμβανόμενον) in 4:4b of the "b'" sub-element recalls "reception with thanksgiving" (μετάλημψιν μετὰ εὐχαριστίας) in 4:3 of the parallel "b" sub-element. Hinging upon the commendable nature of God's creation in the pivot "c" sub-element, then, the parallel framing of the "b" and "b'" sub-elements encapsulate the fact that it is commendable to receive God's creation with thanksgiving.[62] Such air-tight rhetoric leaves no room for false teaching to seep.[63]

Regarding God's commendable creation, in 4:5 of the "b'" sub-element, Paul states, "for it is made-holy consistent-with the word of God and intercession." As in 2:13 of the second microchiasm and 3:13 of the third microchiasm, the audience understand that the conjunction "for" (γάρ) in 4:5 marks the basis for the preceding 4:4 verse. In effect, the audience understand that the reason for receiving all of God's commendable creation with thanksgiving (4:4) is because it "is made-holy consistent-with the word of God and intercession" (4:5).[64] The verb "made-holy" (ἁγιαζεται) recalls for the audience the cognate noun "holiness" (ἁγιασμῷ) in 2:15 of the second microchiasm. In 2:15, the audience understood that to remain

---

61. Knight, *PE*, 191.

62. Here, it may be helpful to visualize the arrangement of the minichiasm, indicated by the linguistic parallels:

"b". "reception with thanksgiving" (μετάλημψιν μετὰ εὐχαριστίας) (4:3b);

"c". "all creation of God is commendable" (πᾶν κτισμα θεοῦ καλόν) (4:4a);

"b'". "being received with thanksgiving" (μετὰ εὐχαριστίας λαμβανόμενον) (4:4b).

The rhetorical accent is on *receiving*. Note the way in which the terminology of the arrangement both begins ("reception"; μετάλημψιν) and concludes ("being received"; λαμβανόμενον). In effect, though "thanksgiving" is undoubtedly in view, Paul is emphasizing the actual reception and acceptance by the faithful—those "in faith"—of God's creation. This undoubtedly intends to highlight a diametrical opposition against the false teachings of "some."

63. Perhaps the force of the arrangement is best articulated by Hughes and Chapell, *1-2 Tim*, 106–7: "God is never properly worshiped by a denial of his gifts."

64. See Knight, *PE*, 192. The implied subject "it" (4:5) would refer to "all creation of God" (4:4).

in the realm of existence "in faith" is to remain "[in] holiness," that is, in the presence of the holy God.[65] Given the progression of the macrochiasm, the audience understand that "made-holy" here in 4:5 certainly pertains to God's holy presence among all of his commendable creation (4:4). Furthermore, that "all creation of God (θεοῦ)" in 4:4a is made-holy "consistent-with the word of God (θεοῦ)" clearly indicates God's activity—not only to create but also to make his creation holy.[66] In effect, where all creation is of a holy God, nothing in creation is inherently defiled or unclean—in fact, it is commendable if received as a gift from the holy God—and thus neither can participation in it defile a person, as seems to be the implication of the false teachers.[67] What is more, that all creation is "of God" (θεοῦ, 4:4a) and is made-holy consistent-with the word "of God" (θεοῦ, 4:5) recalls the church "of God" (θεοῦ, 3:5), the household "of God" (θεοῦ, 3:15), and the church "of . . . God" (θεοῦ, 3:15). Here, then, the audience hear a twofold nuance. On the one hand, just as creation and being made-holy are actions "of God," so too is God's household—the church, those "in faith"—the result of an action "of God."[68] On the other hand, that God is active in creation, in making things holy, and in bringing humans into his household explains why "the faithful and those who have knowingly-embraced the truth" (4:3) are able to understand that anything in creation can be regarded as a part of God's domain of existence, for they themselves exist in God's domain—"in faith" (1:2, 4; 2:7, 15; 3:13), "in holiness" (2:15), "in the household of God" (3:15). In short, the audience understand that all things in God's domain are intended to be a means of edification if received properly and in accordance with the truth.

The phrase "the word of God" may be intended as a further reference to God's words about his creation in LXX Genesis, suggesting that all

---

65. See discussion in volume 1, chapter 4.

66. Perhaps the best articulation of this point is found in Sproul, *Holiness of God*, 55–56: "When the Bible calls God holy it means primarily that God is transcendentally separate. He is so far above and beyond us that He seems almost totally foreign to us. To be holy is to be 'other,' to be different in a special way. The same basic meaning is used when the word *holy* is applied to earthly things . . . None of the [earthly] things . . . is holy in itself. To become holy they must first be consecrated, or 'sanctified' ["made-holy," 4:5] by God. God alone is holy in Himself. Only God can sanctify something else."

67. Similarly, Romans 14:14: "I know and am convinced in the Lord Jesus that nothing is unclean in itself, but it is unclean for anyone who thinks it unclean."

68. Such is implied by the term "church" (ἐκκλησίας, 3:5; ἐκκλησία, 3:15) itself, namely that it is God's activity to "call-out" sinners to come into his household (3:15), that is, to come to have-faith upon Christ Jesus for eternal life (1:17) and thus exist in the place where the holy God is present. See chapter 2 regarding 1 Timothy 3:5.

created things are "made-holy" by God's own assessment.[69] However, it is more likely that the audience hear the phrase according to Paul's sustained theme throughout the macrochiasm. The term "word" (λόγου) recalls its prior two occurrences within the phrase "Faithful is the word (λόγος)" (1:15; 3:1a)—the first of which was specific to Christ Jesus's entrance into the world as a fact that is worthy of all acceptance, the latter alluded to qualified leadership in God's household that would missionally welcome those-outside into God's household (3:7). Thus in 4:4 the audience would hear the progressive impact of the macrochiasm: "the word" not only regards the specific activity of Christ Jesus in regard to sinners and a missional activity to attract those-outside to Christ Jesus, but it also connects both Christ Jesus and sinners to the holy God's activity in 4:5 to make all of his creation holy. That is, because of Christ Jesus, saved sinners are not only able to receive all of creation with thanksgiving toward the holy God but are to do so as act of sharing and participating—reception (4:3)—in the presence of the holy God. Significantly, in reference to Christ Jesus, the audience understand that all of creation is made-holy and fitting to have fellowship with God specifically "consistent-with" the content of the "word" (1:15; 4:5), that is, Christ Jesus.

The preposition "consistent-with" (διά) in 4:5—the sense being "in keeping with"—recalls its prior occurrences in the letter: in 1:16 Paul declared that "consistent-with" (διά) his status as the first, lead of sinners (1:15b, 16a) and the fact that Christ Jesus came to save sinners (1:15a), he was granted-mercy; in 2:10 Paul specified that women are to cosmetic themselves in that which is "consistent-with" (δι') their profession of godliness, namely good works; and in 2:15, Paul stated that women will be-saved "consistent-with" (διά) a missional lifestyle that evidences their existence "in faith" (2:15). In all these instances, Paul's use of "consistent-with" is not only heard within the specific context of salvation—"Christ Jesus came . . . to save sinners . . . consistent-with this, I was granted-mercy" (1:15–16a); "she will be-saved consistent-with . . ." (2:15)—but also in regard to the subsequent lifestyle that is "consistent-with" salvation, namely good works (2:10). Here in 4:5, then, the rhetorical connotation that Paul intends with the term "consistent-with" would clearly convey that God's saving activity in Christ Jesus and the subsequent lifestyle by those who are saved are in view.

Therefore, the cumulative implication is that all creation is "made-holy consistent-with the word of God" in the sense that a knowing-embrace of the truth, that is, of the "word of God" concerning Christ Jesus is what enables sinful humans to not only receive creation as holy but also to use it

---

69. E.g., Kelly, *PE*, 97.

as an act of worship to give thanks to God who is holy. In short, the phrase highlights Christ's role and activity as the one mediator of God and humans (2:5b): "consistent-with" Christ Jesus, nothing in creation is to be-rejected, being-received with thanksgiving (4:4b–5). That is, for the faithful who have knowingly-embraced the truth (2:4; 43), who have already come to have-faith upon Christ Jesus for life eternal (1:16), and who exist in the household of God, which is the church of the living God (3:15), it is their existence in the holy presence of God because of Christ's mediatorial role that enables them to receive and give thanks for God's commendable creation as an act—indeed, a rehearsal—of giving blessing back to the only God for the eternities of the eternities (1:17). It is only "consistent-with the word of God" (4:4)—having faith upon the activity of Christ Jesus (1:15)—by which all creation in 4:4 is made-holy: Christ Jesus is the means by which all creation is made-holy for sinners. Thus, in effect, the rhetorical sense of Paul's statements in 4:3–4 would be heard: "in keeping with faith upon Christ Jesus, nothing is to be-rejected," that is, "in Christ Jesus nothing is unclean." In sum, the audience understand that it is the mediator Christ Jesus—fully Creator and fully created—who connects and makes-holy all creation—especially marriage and foods—for reception with thanksgiving in the domain of God's existence.

Still, given the polemic against the false teachers, Paul's focus on the "word (λόγου) of God" would certainly be heard as a stark contrast. To be sure, "some" who are holding-toward deceitful spirits and teachings of demons (4:1) have turned-aside for "useless-words" (ματαιολογίαν, 1:6) by apostatyzing from the faith (4:1)—precisely in accordance with what the Spirit says (4:1). The false teachers in the Ephesian church have rejected a knowing-embrace of "the word of God" (λόγου θεοῦ, 4:5) concerning the faithful word about Christ Jesus (1:15), who is the mediator of God and humans (2:5). The contrast between spirits and the Spirit (4:1), demons and God, "useless-words" (1:6) and "the word" about Christ (1:15; 4:5) demonstrates why "some" do not accept that "all creation of God is commendable" (4:4a) nor receive it with thanksgiving (4:3; 4:4b). To be sure, without the mediator Christ Jesus to relate the holy God with sinful humans, it is not possible for the false teachers to enjoy, share, or participate with "all creation" in a right relation to God in his holy presence.

Paul states that creation is also made-holy through "intercession" (ἐντεύξεως), recalling Paul's exhortation in 2:1 of the second microchiasm for the congregation's missional prayers, including "intercessions" (ἐντεύξεις).[70]

---

70. The specific nuance of "intercessions" may refer to pleading to a superior—in this case God, who created everything that is to be received. See volume 1, chapter 4 regarding 1 Timothy 2:1.

As in 2:1, "intercession" would be understood as a type of prayer that complements prayers of "thanksgiving" (2:1; 4:3; 4:4b). Here, then, where God himself has provided the means for the faithful to receive God's commendable creation with thanksgiving—namely, God's word concerning Christ Jesus—the audience understand that not only prayers of thanksgiving but also prayers of intercession express a complete dependence on God's provisions. Indeed, coming to God in prayer with faith, that is, dependence upon the mediator Christ Jesus certainly would strengthen those "in faith" to receive all of God's creation as holy in the same way that they received God's greatest provision on their behalf, Christ Jesus. Through intercession the audience acknowledge God as the author of all good things—the commendable creation and their own salvation—and are thus able and reminded that all they can do is receive what God gives with humility and respond with thanksgiving. In short, nothing that God created is to be-rejected as unclean—neither marriage nor foods—since God himself provided it.[71] In contrast to the false teachers who promote an austere, ascetic lifestyle "forbidding to marry, to avoid foods" (4:3a), who hold-toward myths and genealogies without-limit (1:4a), and who are holding toward deceitful spirits and teachings of demons (4:1), the prayerful act of "intercession" in view of "the word of God" concerning Christ Jesus underscores the goodness of creation and the freedom for the faithful who exist "in Christ Jesus" to enjoy all aspects of creation.

The "b'" sub-element continues in 4:6a: "Instructing these-things to the brothers you will be a commendable deacon of Christ Jesus." At the very least, the audience understand that the term "these-things" (ταῦτα) in 4:6a include the specific contents of the minichiasm, namely Paul's apostolic interpretation and application of God's creation, that is, Paul's gospel-hermeneutic in light of Christ Jesus.[72] The participle "Instructing" (ὑποτιθέμενος) is best understood in light of the parallelism between the "b" and "b'" sub-elements.[73] Timothy is not merely to suggest to the audience but to provide authoritative instruction that counters the prohibitions of the false teachers. Specifically, then, in stark contrast "some" who are "forbidding to marry, to avoid foods" (4:3a), Timothy is to encourage the audience to apply the reality of Christ Jesus to their lives by freely partaking in creation, namely in marriage and food. In this way and consistent throughout

---

71. Towner aptly notes that "through prayer . . . believers develop an awareness and conviction of the truth that 'nothing is unclean in itself'" (*Letters*, 299).

72. Knight, *PE*, 193: "ταῦτα, 'these things,' refers primarily, but perhaps not exclusively, to the immediately preceding verses."

73. Different translations account for the participle as "place before" (*ESV*), "point out" (*NIV*), and so forth.

the entire macrochiasm, Paul's concern is not simply to preserve the sound teaching (1:10b)—that salvation is offered to all humans by coming to have-faith upon Christ Jesus (1:16)—but also to promote godliness—that salvation is accompanied by a lifestyle aligning with the profession of godliness (2:10) and faith upon Christ Jesus (1:16). Thus "Instructing" would be to transcend suggestion or even recommendation:[74] Timothy is to call the audience to do the things that Paul teaches, namely by marrying and receiving all aspects of creation with humility and thanksgiving. Indeed, that the participle "Instructing" (ὑποτιθέμενος, 4:6) conveys authority would be clearly understood by the audience, recalling Paul's earlier use of the cognate term "I entrust" (παρατίθεμαί, 1:18), which specifically pertained to the charge to preserve the sound teaching against "some" who teach-different and hold-toward some-thing different that lies-opposed to the sound teaching (1:3, 10b). Here in 4:6, then, such "Instructing" by Timothy would certainly relate to the charge against "some" (1:3; cf. 1:5, 18), particularly "some" who apostasy from the faith and are holding-toward teachings of demons (4:1). Furthermore, that Timothy is to be instructing these-things "to the brothers" (τοῖς ἀδελφοῖς) is significant, highlighting the familial aspect of those "in faith" (1:2), namely "the faithful" (4:3b) over and against the false teachers. The implication is that Timothy's "Instructing" to "the brothers" intends to protect the family in God's household from the present danger of "some." Indeed, rather than the divisive, controversial-speculations by "some," Paul's specification of "the brothers" underscores the unity of God's household as one family that brings-about the household-law of God "in faith" (1:4b). That is, in God's household where God is the Father (1:2; 3:15), the faithful who have knowingly-embraced the truth (4:3b) are "brothers" (4:6).[75]

By instructing the audience to knowingly-embrace the truth of Christ, Paul indicates that Timothy "will be a commendable deacon of Christ Jesus" (4:6a). The verb "you will be" (ἔσῃ) indicates for the audience that Paul is referring specifically to Timothy. Also, that Timothy will be "a commendable deacon of Christ Jesus" (καλὸς . . . διάκονος Χριστοῦ Ἰησοῦ) in the A element of the fourth microchiasm recalls the immediately

---

74. Contra Witherington, *Letters*, 255.

75. It is not unlikely that "brothers" (ἀδελφοῖς) is referring to all of the audience, that is, "brothers and sisters"; see Ellingworth, "'Men and Brethren . . .' (Acts 1.16)," 153–55; Belleville, "1 Tim," 88; Dionson, "1 Tim 4:6–16," 11; Marshall, *PE*, 549 n. 66; Towner, *Letters*, 303. However, in passing it may be worth noting that Paul could have easily said "Instructing these-things to all . . ." It is possible, therefore, that Paul specifies the "brothers" as the object of instruction to reinforce that the men among the audience must lead their individual households as well as the household of God. Though uncertain, such a nuance would fit with Paul's instructions in the second and third microchiasms.

preceding A' element of the third microchiasm wherein "those who serve-as-deacons commendably (καλῶς διακονήσαντες) acquire . . . much confidence in faith that is in Christ Jesus (Χριστῷ Ἰησοῦ)" (3:13). In effect, whereas Hymenaeus and Alexander are named as models of "some" who have become-shipwrecked regarding the faith and whom Paul has given-over to Satan (1:19-20), in stark contrast Timothy is named as the model of "a commendable deacon" who acquires a "commendable" standing and a confident relationship with Christ Jesus (3:13) by holding the mystery of the faith (3:9). To be sure, if "the brothers" want to know how to behave in the household of God, the residence and church of the living God (3:15), then they are to align not only with Timothy's "Instructing" in truth but also his "commendable" lifestyle of godliness (4:6).

Moreover, Paul's identification of Timothy as a "deacon of Christ Jesus" (διάκονος Χριστοῦ Ἰησοῦ) in 4:6a of the fourth microchiasm echoes Paul's identification as an "apostle of Christ Jesus" (ἀπόστολος Χριστοῦ Ἰησοῦ) in 1:1 of the first microchiasm.[76] Clearly, this would strengthen the relationship between Paul and Timothy that has continued throughout the macrochiasm, namely their leadership and relationship with each other "in faith." Indeed, where "Christ Jesus" (Χριστῷ Ἰησοῦ) appointed Paul for "service" (διακονίαν) in 1:12, so too Timothy is to exhibit service as a "deacon" (διάκονος) of "Christ Jesus" (Χριστοῦ Ἰησοῦ) in 4:6. Still, heard in the context of the overall macrochiasm, a further nuance would be observed by the audience. The first half of the letter—the A, B, and C units of the macrochiasm—began by naming Paul as the model authority in association with Christ Jesus: Paul, apostle of Christ Jesus (1:1). Now, after the pivot of the macrochiasm in 3:16, the focus has shifted the audience's attention on Timothy's authority, not only in association with Paul, as in the first half of the letter (1:2, 18; 3:15), but specifically in association with Christ Jesus— Timothy is "deacon of Christ Jesus" (4:6a). As the macrochiasm progresses toward its conclusion, therefore, the audience understand that Timothy is to be front and center as the leader and model among the faithful in Ephesus. Indeed, in the current minichiasm, the audience are to view Timothy as the antitype of "some" who have already apostatized from the faith, namely the false-teaching overseers.

---

76. In the performance of the letter, the nearly identical rhythm, cadence, and vowel-sounds of both phrases would be noticeable and apparent (see *italics*):
1:1: "*ἀπόστολος* Χριστοῦ Ἰησοῦ";
4:6: "*διάκονος* Χριστοῦ Ἰησοῦ."

1 Timothy 4:6b: Being-Nourished in The Commendable Teaching

("a'" sub-element)

In the concluding "a'" sub-element (4:6b) of the minichiasm, Paul connects the fact that Timothy will be a commendable deacon of Christ Jesus (4:6a) to his "being-nourished in the words of the faith and of the commendable teaching." The present participle "being-nourished" (ἐντρεφόμενος) reflects Timothy's continual, present dependence.[77] That Timothy is to depend exclusively on "the words of the faith" is significant. The phrase "the words" (τοῖς λόγοις) recalls for the audience Paul's immediately prior emphasis on "the word (λόγου) of God" in 4:5 concerning the mediator Christ Jesus to enable the faithful to enjoy God's commendable creation in God's holy presence. Moreover, the plural form of "the words" in 4:6b is not referring to variant words—nor an alignment with the plural "myths and genealogies without-limit" (1:4) nor "deceitful spirits and teachings of demons" (4:1). Rather, "the words" of continual nourishment for Timothy are defined by and bound to singular and unified terms: "of the faith and of the commendable teaching." At the same time, therefore, the plural form of "the words" in the combined phrase "the words of the faith" would most likely indicate to the audience that the apostle has in view at least two aspects heard throughout the macrochiasm. Primarily, "the faith" (τῆς πίστεως, 4:6a) in the A element of the fourth microchiasm recalls "the mystery of the faith (τῆς πίστεως)" (3:9) in the A' element of the third microchiasm. As in 3:9, then, the audience understand that Timothy's nourishment "in the words of the faith" undoubtedly refers to his continued existence in the realm "in faith." However, specifically, the connection of "the faith" in 4:6b to "the mystery of the faith" in 3:9 would refer to Timothy's refusal to let go of the confessedly great truth concerning Christ Jesus—the gospel—which is concisely described as the "word" (λόγος) that is "Faithful" (πιστός) (1:15) and poetically summarized as "the mystery" (3:16). Secondarily, therefore, "the faith" in 4:6b would also have the proper lifestyle in view to bring-about the household-law of God in faith (1:4), namely the "word" (λόγος) that is "Faithful" (πιστός) (3:1a) concerning the appointment of overseers and deacons (3:1–13) in order that all of the men and women in the missional household of God would attract, welcome, and bring in those-outside (2:1–4, 8–15; 3:7). That is, the audience understand that Timothy will be a commendable deacon of Christ Jesus—a model of the sound teaching and godliness for God's missional household—so long as he himself continues

---

77. See Barcley, *1 & 2 Tim*, 136; Marshall, *PE*, 549.

to be nourished in and adhere to the truth and lifestyle thereof. Still, regarding the immediate minichiasm, unlike the false teachers who "apostasy from the faith (τῆς πίστεως)" in 4:1 of the parallel "a" sub-element, Timothy continues to be nourished "in the words of the faith" (τῆς πίστεως) in 4:6b of the "a'" sub-element. To be sure, Paul is underscoring that Timothy's ability to instruct "the brothers" as a model leader in the church will depend directly upon continually nourishing himself in the truth of the gospel so that he may nourish others.[78]

Furthermore, in the "a'" sub-element, Timothy is to be nourished in the words of the faith "and of the commendable teaching" (4:6b). Similar to its occurrences in 4:1 and 4:3, the conjuction "and" (καί) would likely be heard epexegetically as a specifying term to connect "the faith" specifically to "the commendable teaching." Thus in the same way that Timothy is to adhere to the truth of the gospel and its corresponding lifestyle, he must be nourished in "the commendable teaching." The phrase "the commendable teaching" (τῆς καλῆς διδασκαλίας) in 4:6 recalls Paul's significant reference to "the sound teaching" (τῇ ὑγιαιούσῃ διδασκαλίᾳ) in 1:10b of the first microchiasm. Notably, the descriptors "sound" (1:10b) and "commendable" (4:6) underscore a qualitative category of "the . . teaching" (1:10b; 4:6). For sure, given Paul's statement that "all creation of God is commendable (καλόν)" (4:4), "the commendable (καλῆς) teaching" (4:6) would refer to the correct teaching in regard to creation, namely its reception with thanksgiving consistent-with the word of God, Christ Jesus (4:3a, 4; cf. 1:15). Still, Paul's specific inclusion of the definite article in both instances—"the . . . teaching" (τῇ . . . διδασκαλίᾳ, 1:10b); "the . . . teaching" (τῆς . . . διδασκαλίας, 4:6)—would highlight its uniqueness as a single, recognized teaching by Timothy and the audience, namely that to which Paul was appointed a "teacher" (διδάσκαλος, 2:7). Undoubtedly, therefore, Paul's use of the phrase "the (τῆς) commendable teaching (διδασκαλίας)" here in 4:6b of the "a'" sub-element would be heard in stark contrast to "some" who are holding-toward "teachings (διδασκαλίαις) of demons" in 4:1 of the parallel "a" sub-element. Indeed, Timothy's nourishment in "the (τῆς) commendable teaching (διδασκαλίας)" (4:6b) of Paul the "teacher" (διδάσκαλος, 2:7) specifically delineates an antithesis to "some" who "teach-different" (ἑτεροδιδασκαλεῖν, 1:3), who are desiring to be "law-teachers"

---

78. Belleville aptly observes: "Timothy's second pastoral responsibility was to take care of himself. Self-care is foundational to congregational care" ("1 Tim," 88). Marshall, PE, 549: "The 'goodness' of the teacher depends on the 'goodness' of what he himself has learned and now imparts." In this regard, there seems to be an echo of the rhetorical question in 3:5 regarding the ability of a man to lead the household of God if he is unable to lead his own household.

(νομοδιδάσκαλοι, 1:7), who teach some-thing different that lies-opposed to "the (τῇ) sound teaching (διδασκαλίᾳ)" (1:10b), and who are likely influencing women "to teach" (διδάσκειν) and to govern men in the church (2:12). In short, the polemic of the letter is significantly emphasized in the fourth microchiasm: whereas the sound teaching (1:10b) of Paul (1:11; 2:7) is the commendable teaching (4:6) because it is from God (1:1, 11; 2:7), Christ Jesus (1:1, 12), and the Spirit (4:1), the different teachings of "some" are inherently deceitful because they are revelation from demonic spirits and demons (4:1).

In the concluding statement of the "a'" sub-element and A' element, the audience hear the clause, "that you have followed" (4:6). The verb "have followed" (παρηκολούθηκας) connotes "giving careful attention to," thus a thoughtful commitment. In effect, the audience understand that Timothy has not only resolved to follow "the words of the faith and of the commendable teaching" but also that he continues to do so—"being-nourished" (4:6). Indeed, given that Timothy is Paul's "child in faith" (1:2; cf. 1:18), who not only accompanied Paul on numerous missionary journeys but did so for nearly twenty years as Paul's companion, it would be evident to the audience that Paul's factitive statement "that you have followed" would be highly rhetorical. In effect, Paul is emphasizing to the entire audience that Timothy—more than anyone else in the Ephesian church—knows "the commendable teaching" and is qualilfied to instruct these-things to the brothers (4:6).[79] In sum, therefore, the first minichiasm clearly conveys to the audience that Timothy, in contrast to "some" who are apostate false-teaching overseers, is a worthy leader and is to be followed.

1 Timothy 4:7–8a: Training for Godliness Versus Bodily Training

(B Element)

The B element of the fourth microchiasm launches into an abrupt statement: "but the vile and silly myths reject" (4:7a). The disjunctive "but" (δέ) immediately establishes a contrast from the goodness that was described in 4:6b. The sequence of Paul's statement—the two adjectives "vile and silly" preceding both the object "myths" and the imperative "reject"—would be heard as a strong polemical assessment against the content of the false teaching.[80]

---

79. For Paul's missionary history with Timothy, see volume 1, chapter 1.
80. Grammatically, it is unnecessary to place the adjectives prior to the noun. The

The term "myths" (μύθους) in 4:7a recalls the "myths" (μύθοις) in 1:4 to which "some" hold-toward. As in 1:4, the term here in 4:7a is polemical. Yet, given the progression of the macrochiasm, the term would likely connote a specific contrast—mere unprovable, fanciful stories[81]—in stark contrast to the provable testimony (2:6–7), the observable mystery concerning Christ Jesus who was manifested in flesh (3:16), that is, was seen, touched, heard, and followed by other humans in flesh. In this way, the rhetorical force of Paul's statement is heard: as the false teachers hold-toward unverifiable myths that result in controversial-speculations (1:4), Timothy and the audience are to actively "reject" (παραιτοῦ)—refuse to listen, keep away from— the very things that "some" who apostasy from the faith are trying to teach within the household of God.[82]

The descriptors "vile and silly" further qualify that the false teachers's "myths" are contrary to the words of the faith and the sound teaching. The adjective "vile" (βεβήλους) recalls its earlier occurrence in the first microchiasm: "for the just the law is not laid but for . . . the without-reverence and vile (βέβηλος)" (1:9). Thus by using the term "vile" here in 4:7a, the audience understand that such "myths" (4:7a; cf. 1:4a) are indicative not only of the content of the false teachings but also—and more significantly—that those who are teaching "myths" are indeed the "vile" persons for whom the law is laid (1:9), namely those "in unfaithfulness" (cf. 1:13). Given this connection, the fourth microchiasm undoubtedly corroborates the implication of the first microchiasm: "some" who teach-different are acting "in unfaithfulness" even after having experienced the revelation of God's grace in Christ Jesus; in the Ephesian church, "some" have already apostatized from "the faith" (4:1; cf. 1:5–6, 19).[83] To be sure, Paul is underscoring to the audience the irony that "some" who claim to be leaders in God's household are actually commited to "myths" that are perfectly contrary to the household-law of God in faith.

Furthermore, the second adjective "silly" (γραώδεις) was a pejorative term used among philosophers to disparage opposing perspectives.[84] The

---

rhetorical arrangement of the statement is, therefore, intentional to emphasize the "vile and silly" characteristic of the false teaching.

81. Knight, PE, 195: "μῦθοι . . . fables that are both unhistorical and untruthful."

82. Here, the conceptual juxtaposition between the false teachers who have "rejected" (4:4a) and Timothy who is commanded to "reject" (4:7a) the false teachings would likely be heard as an overall rhetorical statement for Timothy and the audience. The effect may likely have carried the sense, "Correctly accept what 'some' incorrectly reject, and correctly reject what 'some' incorrectly accept."

83. See volume 1, chapter 3 regarding 1 Timothy 1:13.

84. See Collins, *1 & 2 Tim*, 121; Marshall, PE, 550; Wall with Steele, *1 & 2 Tim*, 120.

term expressed a particular kind of foolishness—ungrounded superstitions—the sort that old women were allegedly guilty of propagating in their ignorance and deteriorating mental capacities.[85] Thus the combined phrase "silly myths" would have conveyed a double-emphasis on the unverifiable nature of the content of the different teaching of "some"—certainly a contrast to the commendable teaching that Paul has verified and grounded in the person of Christ Jesus.[86] In sum, the "silly myths" of the false teachers are to be rejected because they have nothing to do with factitive truth of Christ Jesus, and "the vile . . . myths" represent a refusal to receive Christ Jesus as a ransom from God's just judgment (cf. 1:9; 2:6).

Continuing the B element, in 4:7b Paul underscores the positive complement to his commmand to reject vile and silly myths: "But train yourself toward godliness." The disjunctive "but" (δέ) initiates a contrast with the notion of pursuing myths in 4:7a. In effect, the rhetorical force of 4:7a is reiterated: the act of rejecting false teaching must be accompanied by the act of pursuing the commendable teaching of Paul, hence's Paul's command "train yourself toward godliness" (4:7b). The verb "train" (γύμναζε) connotes exercise, discipline, and the adoption of the strict and focused life of an athlete—not only physically but mentally.[87] Furthermore, upon hearing

---

85. Translated as "old wives' tales," Belleville nuances that the expression "is an idiom of the day for an uninformed and unlearned opinion. It reflects the assumption that to not be formally educated is to be ignorant. This was specifically the case for Greek women, whose education typically stopped at the marriageable age of 14 or 15, while the education of Greek men continued well into their thirties" ("1 Tim," 89). However, given the context of the minichiasm, Paul undoubtedly has in view the false teachers, namely men (1:20). That is, Paul's reference to "old wives' tales" would certainly not be a pejorative statement about women (contra Schottroff, *Lydia's Impatient Sisters*, 73) but rather about the false teacher's blatant ignorance despite their knowledge both of the law (1:7–10) and the faith from which they have now apostatized (4:1).

86. It is worth restating Long's comment in regard to 1 Timothy 2:6: "The gospel is not the private narrative of some local Roman deity nor is it the abstract answer to some mystical spiritual puzzle. It is a public event, performed by the human being Jesus—visible, embodied, historical, and universal" (*1 & 2 Tim*, 67).

87. Witherington, *Letters*, 256: "Paul uses his favorite athletic metaphor again, that of an athlete in training. In this case he refers to the *gymnasia*, the physical training that usually took place in a *gymnasium* (whence our same word)." Schreiner and Caneday, *Race Set Before Us*, 107–8: "the figurative words 'train yourself for godliness' . . . compel us to relate spiritual exercise to body training . . . The admonition calls for athletic vigor that pushes the believer to the point of pain in order to attain strength, stamina and endurance for victorious competition." See Wall with Steele, *1 & 2 Tim*, 121.
It may be worth noting that the term likely also connoted intellectual training. Sandelin, *Attraction and Danger of Alien Religion*, 9: "In the Hellenistic cities, boys and young men belonging to the Greek elite were educated in the gymnasia, where they received physical and intellectual training." For further discussion, see Kyle, *Athletics in Ancient Athens*, 65–66.

Paul's command to train "yourself" (σεαυτόν), the audience understand that the onus is on Timothy to have discipline in his own life, to train himself—the implication being that no one else will do it for him. At the same time, in view of the macrochiasm, the audience would likely understand that such training has already been imparted directly by Paul to Timothy: he is Paul's "child in faith" (1:2) who has both known Paul and labored with him for nearly twenty years.[88] It is for this reason that Timothy knows how it is necessary to behave in the household of God (3:15). Thus while Paul is not present in Ephesus to coach, mentor, and guide Timothy, Paul's command "train yourself" would effectively be a summons to continue in the way that Paul had raised him, namely by "being-nourished in the words of the faith and of the commendable teaching that you have followed" (4:6b).

Such a relationship between Paul and Timothy would be reminiscent of Paul's emphasis on the fundamental importance of men leading their own household in the third microchiasm. Where Paul has led his "child" Timothy commendably "in faith," Timothy has been nurtured to be an effective leader himself. Moreover, while the audience are reminded of Timothy's qualification to lead, there is undoubtedly a polemic directed against the false teachers who, not being raised by Paul, do not know how to train themselves properly (4:7a), have not followed the words of the faith nor the commendable teaching (4:6b), and, therefore, do not know how to lead their own households (3:5), nor care-for the church of God, which is God's household (3:5; 3:15), nor behave in God's household (3:15).[89] Still, in light of the qualifications to lead the household of God, the spotlight remains on Timothy: Timothy cannot lead others unless he disciplines himself to be a commendable leader for others. In effect, Paul's words to Timothy—"train yourself"—would likely carry the full sense of "Train yourself in the way that I trained you; lead others in the way that I led you."

The stated purpose of such training is "toward godliness." The noun "godliness" (εὐσέβειαν) recalls its earlier occurrences throughout the macrochiasm. In 2:2 of the second microchiasm, Paul exhorted the entire audience to lead their lives in all "godliness" (εὐσεβείᾳ). To be sure, then, Paul's command to Timothy has the entire audience in view. That Timothy is to be

---

88. See discussion in volume 1, chapter 1.

89. In light of the polemical specification that the false teachers may be those who are "a young-plant" (3:6), it seems likely that the false teachers did not receive training directly from Paul during the founding of the Ephesian church at least ten years prior. Yet, in the case that all or even a few of the false teachers were present to receive Paul's direct apostolic teaching, the fact that they are not "in submissiveness" to Paul's training is indicative that they are not, in fact, his children "in faith." See chapter 2 regarding 1 Timothy 3:4.

"a commendable deacon of Christ Jesus" (4:6a) implies not merely that he is to be a model deacon; rather, Timothy is to be a model to the entire church as one who holds the mystery of the faith (3:9)—the content of Paul's teaching, the truth concerning Christ Jesus—and who lives a godly, respectable life. Thus as Timothy is commanded to train himself "toward godliness," the audience understand that his disciplined training is for their benefit and imitation. Furthermore, given the missional impetus of godliness in the second microchiasm, Timothy's training to be a model for God's household implies that his training is to bring in those-outside (cf. 3:7).

Still, the noun "godliness" was heard at the end of the the third microchiasm and carries forward a more fundamental implication. In 3:16, "godliness" (εὐσεβείας) was defined in terms of the confessedly great mystery concerning Christ Jesus. At least in part, then, Paul's command to "train yourself toward godliness" does not entail a diffuse, generalized purpose but rather a concentrated, specific purpose, namely to train in light of Christ Jesus. Indeed, where the A, B, and C units moved the entire audience toward Christ Jesus as the pivotal hinge of the entire macrochiasm, so Timothy is to train with one person in mind. That is, more than Paul, more than the audience, more than the false teachers in Ephesus, Timothy's full training—all of the discipline, hard work, perseverance, grit, sweat, and tears—is ultimately focused on Christ Jesus, who is "in glory" (3:16). Certainly, the entire reason why Timothy is to obey Paul as a "child" (1:2, 18), why he is to be a leader and model for the entire audience (4:6), and why he is to remain in Ephesus to war against the "some" (1:18–19) is because of one person, the human Christ Jesus, who gave himself as a ransom (2:5–6) on behalf of Timothy, on behalf of Paul, on behalf of "the faithful" (4:3b)—and on behalf of "some" *if* they to come to have-faith upon Christ Jesus and knowingly-embrace the truth (1:16; 2:4b; 4:3b). Moreover, given that to exist "in faith" is to exist "in Christ Jesus" (3:13) and thus is to be with Christ Jesus "in glory," Timothy's training is "toward" the location where Christ Jesus was seen by angels and currently exists "in glory": heaven. Thus Paul's command is heard in full effect: Timothy is not only to train himself for Christ Jesus but also "toward" Christ Jesus—to be with him in heaven. Subsequently, Timothy's training "toward godliness" will lead the entire audience "in faith" to be with them in heaven. Indeed, Timothy's training will have a missional impact in regard to "some" who have apostatized from the faith in the Ephesian church (4:1) and those-outside in the surrounding Ephesian community (3:7), namely by pointing them toward Christ Jesus in heaven.

In view of the present microchiasm, it is also worth noting that Paul's command to "train yourself toward godliness" in the B element likely has in view the immediately preceding A element, which centered on Paul's corrective teaching in regard to the reception of God's creation. In the A element, the audience understood that godliness is impossible apart from having knowingly-embraced the truth (4:3)—the gospel that displays God's glory, namely Christ Jesus (1:11; 2:4-5). Specifically, over and against "some" who have seared consciences—dead to truth and unable to discern how to pursue godliness (see 4:2 above)—Timothy's training for godliness would involve an application of the truth regarding the holy use of all of God's commendable creation because of the mediator Christ Jesus (see 4:5 above). In other words, to not reject anything in creation but rather to receive God's creation—including marriage and foods—with dependent thanksgiving as gracious gifts from the Creator is itself an example of practicing godliness and preserving the sound teaching concerning Christ Jesus. Significantly, then, the command to "train yourself toward godliness" would be understood by the audience to involve the application of the sound teaching—the gospel—into Timothy's daily life so that what he professes is practiced and, therefore, reinforced through praxis. Furthermore, given that Timothy is to be a model for the church, the audience understand that his training—that which he received from Paul—is to be imitated. Thus as much as Paul is concerned with preserving the sound teaching, again he emphasizes his equal concern to promote godliness among the people of God—the tangible, organic product thereof—particularly through the example of church leaders. Moreover, the apostle makes clear that training toward godliness—the application of the gospel—requires intentional and regular participation by all who have knowingly-embraced the truth: divine sovereignty, in the mind of Paul, never precludes human responsibility.

Concluding the B element, Paul explains why Timothy is to train for godliness: "for bodily training is toward little profitability" (4:8a). Consistent with its earlier occurrences throughout the macrochiasm, the conjunction "for" (γάρ) in 4:8a identifies the basis for the preceding statement in 4:7b. That is, Timothy is commanded to train himself for godliness because "bodily training is toward little profitability." The phrase "bodily training (γυμνασία)" (4:8a) recalls the preceding command for Timothy to "train (γύμναζε) yourself" (4:7b) and thus the connotation of discipline. However, rather than having "godliness" in view (4:7b)—heavenly living with Christ Jesus—the specific training in view of 4:8a is "bodily" (σωματική). The contrast here would be straightforward: in view of life eternal —coming to have-faith upon Christ and thus existing "in faith," "in Christ," "in glory" in heaven (1:16; 3:13, 16)—life on earth is temporary and pales in comparison. Thus there is all the more reason for Timothy to train, in effect, for eternity than for temporality.

Still, the occurrence of "bodily training" within the fourth microchiasm would likely convey a further nuance to the audience. In the A element, Paul specifically underscored the ascetic practices of the false teachers—"forbidding to marry, to avoid foods"—who were rejecting God's creation (4:3–4a). Ironically, then, such practices were merely concerned with temporary, earthly things—rejecting creation—rather than eternal, heavenly things—enjoying creation in light of Christ. Thus the "bodily training" in 4:8a may be heard by the audience as a reference to such ascetic practices.[90] In this case, the declaration "bodily training is toward little profitability" may not simply be—positively—a comparison to highlight the significance of training "toward godliness" over and above "bodily training" but rather—negatively—an absolute, polemical statement against the false teachers regarding the futility of such extreme physical discipline, which not only relegates the commendable nature of God's creation but also undermines the truth concerning Christ. Given both positive and negative aspects, the apostle's basic point to the audience is clear: physical discipline "is toward little profitability" (πρὸς ὀλίγον ἐστὶν ὠφέλιμος) because the hope of the gospel is that all who have-faith upon Christ will share in, that is, profit from his glorious and eternal mode of existence (1:16; 3:16). To be sure, in matters of eternity, "bodily training" (4:8a) is limited "toward" earth whereas training "toward godliness" has the expansive scope of life in heaven with Christ Jesus, the fully God and fully human mediator (2:5).

1 Timothy 4:8b: Godliness Holds the Promise of Life

(B′ Element)

In the B′ element (4:8b) of the fourth microchiasm, the emphatic contrast between training toward godliness and the limited profitability of bodily training is stated with no uncertain terms: "but godliness (εὐσέβεια) is toward all profitability (ὠφέλιμός)." As before, the disjunctive "but" (δέ) in the B′ element signifies a contrast; in effect, the clear parallelism with the B element gives the sense of "bodily training is toward little profitability, however indeed godliness is toward all profitability." Furthermore, through the linguistic connection between the parallel B and B′ elements, the stark contrast could not be heard any more strongly: whereas bodily training in 4:8a "is" (ἐστίν) "toward" (πρός) *little* "profitability" (ὠφέλιμός) in the B element, godliness training in 4:8b "is" (ἐστιν) "toward" (πρός) *all* "profitability"

---

90. Kelly, *PE*, 100; Towner, *Goal*, 149–50; see Knight, *PE*, 195.

(ὠφέλιμός).[91] The term "all" (πάντα) recalls its occurrence throughout the macrochiasm, particularly "all (πᾶν) creation of God" (4:4a) in the A element of the immediate microchiasm. The progression of the microchiasm, then, would be heard to advance the earlier notion: godliness is associated with enjoying God's creation. What is more, in light of the missional theme of the macrochiasm, "all" (πᾶν) in 4:8a would recall Paul's exhortation to pray on behalf of "all" (πάντων) humans (2:2) just as the Savior God desires "all" (πάντας) humans to be-saved (2:4a) and as Christ Jesus gave himself as a ransom on behalf of "all" (πάντων) (2:6). Thus here in the fourth microchiasm, training for godliness would have missional profitability. Heard in a straightforward way without any polemic, the contrast between "little profitability" and "all profitability" would certainly indicate for the audience that any personal attention to physical training should be far exceeded by a zeal for growing in godliness and also, therefore, that their zeal for godliness should be motivated by their shared desire with the Savior God who saved them, that is, for all humans to come to a knowing-embrace of the truth—the testimony concerning Christ Jesus (2:3–6).

Still, where the audience heard "bodily training" as a polemical statement against the false teachers in the B element, the polemical force continues here in the B' element. Both types of training are "toward... profitability" (πρὸς ... ὠφέλιμος, 4:8a; πρὸς ... ὠφέλιμός, 4:8b), but only one—"godliness" (εὐσέβεια) training (4:8b)—is ultimately profitable because it is defined by the mystery, the testimony, the gospel that exhibits God's glory and results in blessing toward him, namely the revelation of "godliness" (εὐσεβείας) in the person of Christ Jesus (3:16). To be sure, the audience understand Paul's point: the profitability of bodily training originates in someone's own effort—"forbidding to marry, to avoid foods" (4:3)—but the profitability of godliness originates in the effort of Christ Jesus—who "came into the world to save sinners" (1:15) and "who gave himself as a ransom on behalf of all" (2:6). Thus by way of the contrast between the B and B' elements in the fourth microchiasm, it seems that the audience arrive at a fuller understanding of what it means to "to have-faith upon him" in the first microchiasm (1:16), that is, "to come to a knowing-embrace of truth" in the second microchiasm (2:4b), that is, to be "a pillar and foundation of the truth" in the third microchiasm (3:15): it is to rely upon the godliness of Christ Jesus while simultaneously training oneself toward an existence with Christ Jesus in heaven—even while presently on earth. Over and against bodily training, Christ Jesus is the reason why training for godliness is

---

91. Here, it may be helpful to visualize the linguistic parallels:
B element: "is toward little profitability" (πρὸς ὀλίγον ἐστὶν ὠφέλιμος) (4:8a);
B' element: "is toward all profitability" (πρὸς πάντα ὠφέλιμός ἐστιν) (4:8b).

toward all profitiablity. In sum, the audience understand that "the faithful," that is, "those who have knowingly-embraced the truth" (4:3b) may indeed practice godliness—enjoy and bless God because of Christ Jesus—not only in eternity but also here and now during their training. On earth, those "in faith" may enjoy, participate with, and share in all of God's commendable creation (4:3b–5) while they are training toward heaven.

The implication and precise nature of training for godliness is made explicit to the audience in the concluding participle phrase of the B' element: "holding the promise of life for the present and for the inevitable-coming" (4:8b). The term "promise" (ἐπαγγελίαν) is not abstract but rather connotes a personal aspect—that which a person said that they will do. Thus where training for godliness is toward all profitability, it is because whoever made "the promise" will guarantee "all profitability." The term "holding" (ἔχουσα) recalls its prior occurrences throughout the macrochiasm. Timothy is to war the commendable war against the "some" who teach-different by "holding (ἔχων) faith and a good conscience" (1:19); in the same way, qualified overseers in the church are to be "holding (ἔχοντα) children in submissiveness" by preserving the sound teaching and promoting godliness in their own children (3:4) and are "to hold (ἔχειν) a commendable testimony from those-outside" for the missional purpose of inviting them into God's household (3:7); deacons are qualified by "holding (ἔχοντας) the mystery of the faith" (3:9), that is, by clinging to the truth of concerning Christ Jesus and the life of godliness that corresponds. Notably, therefore, the advancement of the macrochiasm in the fourth microchiasm further qualifies the connotation. That is, in connection with "the promise," "holding" in 4:8b shifts the focus away from human responsibility: the person who made "the promise" is holding it for those who train for godliness—God himself.

Paul states that the promise is "of life for the present and for the inevitable-coming." The term "life" (ζωῆς) in 4:8b recalls both the "life (ζωήν) eternal" that is entered by coming to have-faith upon Christ Jesus (1:16) and the "living (ζῶντος) God" who is eternal (3:15; cf. 1:17), that is, the "living God" who gives "life eternal" to those who have-faith upon Christ. Undoubtedly, then, the audience not only understand that the term "life" (ζωῆς, 4:8b) has eternity in view but also that "the promise of life" is from God himself. What is more, given that "godliness" in 4:8b is associated with both eternity and the promise of life from God, the audience understand that godliness itself functions as an indicator of those who have actually received God's promise of eternal life here and now, namely "the faithful" who "have knowingly-embraced the truth" (4:3b).

Paul goes on to identify a twofold nuance regarding godliness and the promise of its all profitability: "for the present and for the inevitable-coming"

(4:8b). In keeping with the theme of the fourth microchiasm concerning the reception of God's creation with thanksgiving here and now (4:3–5), Paul states that the promise of life is "for the present" (τῆς νῦν, 4:8b). It is most unlikely that the audience would understand "the promise of life for the present" as a suggestion that God rewards godliness with material blessings in this life. Rather, given its placement within the fourth microchiasm, the all-profitable promise by God for "the present" is most certainly to enjoy the benefits of practicing godliness here and now on earth, namely by receiving—sharing and participating in—God's commendable creation in the holy presence of God. To be sure, if the audience want to have a deeper experience of God, they are not only to refrain from the ascetic practices of the false teachers but also to join Timothy in preserving the sound teaching by promoting a life in all godliness, which is both lived in God's presence and toward God's presence.

Still, the promise of life in 4:8b is "for the inevitable-coming" (τῆς μελλούσης), which recalls "those who would-inevitably-come (τῶν μελλόντων) to have-faith upon him for life eternal" (1:16).[92] Certainly, then, the emphasis of God's promise is oriented toward the eternal aspect of godliness. In other words, just as the promise "for the present" is understood in view of the promise "for the inevitable-coming," so too is the profitability of godliness in "the present"—receiving God's creation—to be understood in view of "the inevitable-coming"—thanksgiving to God for eternity.[93]

The movement and interconnectivity of the macrochiasm would still convey further significance. Given that the promise concerning "godliness" (εὐσείβεια) in 4:8b has in view the "godliness" (εὐσέβειαν) in 4:7b and thus the pivotal Christ-hymn concerning the mystery of "godliness" (εὐσεβείας) in 3:16, the audience would understand that the full implication of the genitival phrase "for the present and for the inevitable-coming" is describing the two modes of existence encapsulated by the mediator Christ Jesus—that he was manifested "in flesh" and was declared-just "in Spirit" (3:16). Thus for the faithful (4:3b) in the audience who are "in faith," that is, "in Christ Jesus" (3:13), "the promise of life for the present and for the inevitable-coming" is none other than union with Christ Jesus—sharing the life "in flesh" that he lived, yet also sharing the life "in Spirit" that he now lives (3:16). Indeed, both aspects are in view of the promise to which God is holding (4:8b). In accordance with the Savior God's desire for all humans to be-saved (2:3–4a),

---

92. The connection between 4:8 and 1:16 is apparent by the parallel use of ζωῆς/ζωήν and μελλούσης/μελλόντων, respectively.

93. Perhaps Ridderbos says it best: "in rejecting all manner of ascetic and spiritual heresy, [Paul] writes to Timothy that godliness is profitable for all things, having promise for life for the present as well as for the future (1 Tim. 4:8). The revelation of Christ does not abrogate the order of the natural and present life, but makes it recognized and practiced, from the viewpoint of Christ, exactly in its divine significance" (*Paul*, 315).

Christ Jesus "in flesh" gave himself as a ransom on behalf of the audience who are living in flesh (2:6); as such, Christ Jesus now "in Spirit" issues forth the eternal mode of existence to all who have-faith upon him (1:16). In other words, for the faithful who are living in the present—"in flesh," on earth, among God's commendable creation—yet are simultaneously living in the inevitable-coming—"in Spirit," in heaven, in God's full presence—the overlap between the two modes of existence supplies the fundamental truth that promotes their godliness.[94] Here, then, at the conclusion of the B' element, this full-orbed perspective on the promise of life in relation to Christ Jesus would intend to have a profound impact on Paul's audience: they would be able to exclaim with Paul that godliness is toward all profitability and must be promoted over and against the practices of "some."

1 Timothy 4:9–16: The Teaching, the Leadership of Timothy

(A' Element)

Within the concluding A element of the microchiasm (4:9–16), the audience hear two minichiasms (4:9–12; 4:13–16). In this section, each of the two minichiasms will be examined.

1 Timothy 4:9–12: A Minichiastic Unit

As a minichiasm in itself, verses 4:9–12 of the A' element are composed carefully of five sub-elements ("a"-"b"-"c"-"b'"-"a'"); linguistic parallels identifying chiastic arrangements are indicated by the Greek text:

"a". [9] Faithful is the word (λόγος) and worthy of all acceptance; [10a] for to this we toil and agonize, because we have hoped upon the living God, who is the Savior of all humans,

    "b". [10b] especially of the faithful (πιστῶν).

        "c". [11] Charge these-things and teach.

    "b'". [12a] None must look-down-on your youth; rather be an example of those of the faithful (πιστῶν)

"a'". [12b] in word (λόγῳ), in behavior, in love, in faith, in purity.

---

94. For more on this overlap—the "already-and-not-yet"—see above regarding 1 Timothy 4:1, "later times."

The minichiasm is framed by Paul's concern for the "word" in the "a" and "a'" sub-elements, which has a direct bearing for "the faithful" in the "b" and "b'" sub-elements. The minichiasm hinges upon the imperative for Timothy to "charge" and "teach" in the pivot "c" sub-element.

1 Timothy 4:9–10a: Faithful is the Word, We Have Hoped Upon the Living God

("a" sub-element)

The concluding A' element of the fourth microchiasm and the introductory "a" sub-element of the first minichiasm within it begins: "Faithful is the word and worthy of all acceptance" (4:9). In its exact form, the phrase recalls "Faithful is the word and worthy of all acceptance" in 1:15 of the first microchiasm, wherein Paul highlighted to the audience that Christ Jesus came into the world to save sinners. To be sure, here in 4:9 the audience understand that they are to have not only Christ Jesus in view but also the salvation that he brought. Still, the placement of the phrase in the A' element of the fourth microchiasm would be heard in context of the explicit presence and danger of "some" in the parallel A element. There is, then, undoubtedly a polemical quality in this declaration.

Following the movement of the microchiasm, the sustained polemic is carried forward. In the A element, it was the false teachers who "will apostasy from the faith (πίστεως), holding-toward deceitful spirits and teachings (διδασκαλίαις) of demons" (4:1) versus "the faithful" (πιστοῖς, 4:3b) among the audience and Timothy who is "being-nourished in the words of the faith (πίστεως) and of the commendable teaching (διδασκαλίας)" (4:6b). In the B and B' elements, it was Timothy and the audience rejecting the vile and silly myths and ascetic bodily training of the false teachers while also receiving God's commendable creation in his holy presence as part of their godliness training for heaven. Here, then, in the A' element, the polemical effect of Paul's statement "Faithful is the word and worthy of all acceptance" is clearly that "some" do not accept that the word is faithful. That is, whereas the false teachers do not accept the word concerning Christ Jesus and are thus concerned with rejecting God's creation through bodily training, the audience understand that Paul, Timothy, and the faithful among them have already accepted the faithful word—that Christ Jesus came to save sinners, enabling them to receive and give thanksgiving for all of God's commendable creation in the presence of the holy God, that is, in God's household.

Furthermore, the audience would hear "acceptance" in 4:9 as the positive complement to "reject" the vile and silly myths in 4:7a.

While the polemical effect may indicate that "Faithful is the word" would be heard in view of the overall fourth microchiasm, it may also be heard with a specific reference within the microchiasm.[95] The reminiscence between "Faithful (πιστός) is the word (λόγος)" in 4:9 and "the words (λόγοις) of the faith (πίστεως)" in 4:6 would not go unnoticed. Thus in 4:9 Paul seems to have in view 4:6, "the words of the faith," not only its content—Christ Jesus—but also its connotation—that Timothy and the audience must continue to be nourished by the content. In this sense, the flow of the macrochiasm is observed: 4:9 in the A' element rounds off the encouragement given in 4:6 of the parallel A element. Simply, the audience are to continually nourish themselves in "the words of the faith" (4:6) precisely because "faithful is the word" (4:9). In summary, then, the opening declaration of 4:9 is heard in the context of apostasy and, therefore, calls for the audience to continually accept the word that is faithful, even though "some" in their midst reject it. For sure, those who have already knowingly-embraced that the faithful word is worthy of "all (πάσης) acceptance" must continue to accept all of it; to do so would not only be a practice of godliness but also a continued experience of its "all (πάντα) profitability" (4:8b).

The "a" sub-element continues in 4:10: "for to this we toil and agonize, because we have hoped upon the living God, who is the Savior of all humans." The phrase "to this" (εἰς τοῦτο) would likely be understood as a reference to what precedes it, namely a continual acceptance of the faithful word concerning Christ Jesus and the promise of eternal life that overlaps the present and the inevitable-coming.[96] Indeed, such would be corroborated by the conjunction "for" (γάρ), which the audience have consistently heard (2:13; 3:13; 4:5, 8a) to provide the basis for what precedes it. In effect, not only are the audience to understand 4:10 in light of Christ and eternal life—"to this"—but Paul is providing a strengthened reason—"for"—why Timothy and the audience are to continue accepting the faithful word concerning Christ and eternal life.

The first person plural verbs "[we] toil" and "[we] agonize" communicate that Timothy's war against "some" to preserve the sound teaching, the gospel (1:18), his continual nourishment in the words of the faith and the commendable teaching (4:6b), and his summons to train for godliness (4:7b) is in essence a collaborative effort with the apostle. Even though

95. There is no scholarly consensus about how far back—or forward—the phrase "Faithful is the word" in 4:9 goes (see the list provided by Marshall, *PE*, 554).

96. The assumption is that the conjunction "for" (γάρ) is pointing backward (contra Mounce, *PE*, 254); see Marshall, *PE*, 555; Towner, *Letters*, 309.

Timothy must war, be nourished, and train in Ephesus without Paul, the apostle Paul is inspiring his "child in faith" Timothy (1:2; cf. 1:18) to remember that despite Paul's bodily absence he is not alone; they are both co-laborers of the gospel, the testimony, the mystery concerning Christ Jesus (1:11; 2:6; 3:16), of salvation from sin (1:15), and of life eternal (1:16).[97] Thus as Timothy hears the performance of the letter, he is encouraged to persevere, "to remain in Ephesus" and "charge some not to teach-different" (1:3), namely "some" who have already apostatized from the faith (1:20; 4:1) by holding-toward teachings of demons (4:1). Furthermore, given Paul's call for allegiance throughout the macrochiasm, undoubtedly the audience understand in 4:10a that they are summoned, invited, and encouraged to "toil" and "agonize" together with Paul and Timothy against the false teachers.

The verb "toil" (κοπιῶμεν) expresses exertion to the point of becoming weary. Thus "toil" in the A' element continues the idea that is both implicit in the parallel A element and explicit in the B and B' elements: the audience understand that the work of preserving the teaching and promoting godliness among those within God's missional household in order to reach those-outside is laborious, to say the least. The verb "agonize" (ἀγωνιζόμεθα) connotes an athlete or warrior's commitment to struggle and endure for victory, thus advancing the theme of training from the B and B' elements.[98] Amidst the apostasy in the Ephesian church, therefore, Paul is emphasizing to Timothy and the audience that acceptance of and adherence to the teaching (1:10b; 4:6)—the faithful word (4:9; cf. 1:15; 4:6)—will require discipline and pain in the present life, not very different from the agonies of training that athletes in the first century experienced. Heard together, then, "toil and agonize" in the A' element convey the sense of a long and difficult

---

97. The force of this camaraderie would likely be felt in the performance of the letter itself. That is, where the letter was understood to function as Paul's stand-in presence at Ephesus, Timothy and the audience would effectively hear Paul speaking in exactly the same way as if physically present right then and there. For further discussion of first-century letters and their performances, see volume 1, chapter 1.

98. Knight, *PE*, 202: "ἀγωνίζομαι means generally 'struggle of strive' and may be used more specifically of an athletic contest or of fighting with weapons." See Wall with Steele, *1 & 2 Tim*, 122. Similarly, see Marshall, *PE*, 555–56. Belleville's comments are helpful to summarize the athletic theme: "To be effective in ministry one must also develop self-discipline. 'Train yourself to be godly' is Paul's command (4:7). Pastoral ministry is pictured as a daily work-out in the gymnasium (*gumnaze*) and as training for an athletic contest (*gumnasia*). Body building and weight lifting exercises are in vogue today. The benefits of such activities are not achieved overnight; it takes months of working out to build up the muscles of the body. In much the same way, spiritual hard work (*kopiaō*) and much struggle (*agōnizomai*, 'agony') produce muscles that become an established part of our spiritual physique (4:10)" ("1 Tim," 89).

struggle against "some" in the parallel A element.⁹⁹ In sum, the audience hear a twofold nuance. In general, Paul, Timothy, and the audience are to toil and agonize toward the all profitability of godliness, namely life eternal and its implications here and now. In specific, they are to toil and agonize against the opponents of godliness who train themselves for some-thing different, namely bodily rejection of God's creation and God's promise of life for the present and for the inevitable-coming. Still, given the missional, restorative purpose of Paul's polemic, the audience understand that such a public struggle against the false teachers is not for war in itself but rather is for "some" to come to a knowing-embrace of truth (2:4b; 4:3b) and, in turn, train themselves for godliness (4:7b).

Paul now states the reason why he, Timothy, and "the faithful" among the audience are to toil and agonize to preserve the teaching and promote godliness: "because we have hoped upon the living God, who is the Savior of all humans" (4:10a). Here, then, the audience understand the full implication of the basis—"for" (γάρ, 4:10a)—that they are to continue accepting the faithful word concerning the promise of life from God—"because" (ὅτι). The perfect tense of the verb "we have hoped" connotes a past decision that has abiding significance.¹⁰⁰ Furthermore, "we have hoped" (ἠλπίκαμεν) recalls its cognate occurrence in "Christ Jesus our hope" (ἐλπίδος), the opening statement of the letter (1:1). Given the advancement of the macrochiasm, the audience understand a twofold nuance. On the one hand, Christ Jesus is "our hope" because he was manifiested in the flesh to save sinners, that is, he gave himself as a ransom on their behalf (1:15; 2:6; 3:16). On the other hand, for Paul, Timothy, and the audience, Christ Jesus is "our hope" because he was declared-just in Spirit to secure their life eternal, which was received when they came to have-faith upon him and a knowing-embraced of truth (1:16; 2:4b; 3:16). Thus when Paul says that "we have hoped," the audience understand not only that Christ Jesus is in view but also that salvation and life eternal are in view precisely because Christ Jesus died on their behalf (2:6) and is now living "in glory" (3:16). The rhetorical force of the connection would likely draw attention to a collective camaraderie, something to the effect of "*we* have hoped upon the living God; indeed, Christ Jesus is *our* hope."

Still, "we have hoped" (ἠλπίκαμεν) in 4:10a recalls Paul's "hoping" (ἐλπίζων) in 3:13 to come to Ephesus to preserve the teaching concerning Christ Jesus against the false teachers, to promote godliness, and to

---

99. See Towner, who suggests that the coupling of the terms might be a formulaic way of describing the challenging nature of missionary work (*Letters*, 310).

100. See Knight, *PE*, 202.

bring-about the missional household-law of God in faith. Here, then, given the overall progression of the macrochiasm and the specific polemic against the false teachers in the fourth microchiasm, the audience understand two further nuances for "we have hoped." On the one hand, "we have hoped" (4:10a) certainly entails Paul's defensive "hoping" (3:13) as an urgency to uphold the object of "hope" (1:1), namely Christ Jesus. On the other hand—and simultaneously—"we have hoped" is neither tentative nor a response to dire circumstances; rather it is grounded in the upheld factivite truth of events that already happened: Christ Jesus is "our hope" (1:1) because he came into the world to save sinners, gave himself as a ransom, was declared-just in Spirit, and was seen by angels in heaven when he was taken-up in glory (1:15; 2:6; 3:16).

Still, though the audience understand that "Christ Jesus our hope" is connected to the object upon which "we have hoped," Paul goes on to further specify that the object of their hope is "upon the living God" (4:10a). Where both "Christ Jesus" and "the living God" are at once the object of Paul, Timothy, and the audience's hope, Paul seems to be equating Christ Jesus with the living God. The term "upon" (ἐπί) recalls "those who would-inevitably-come to have-faith upon (ἐπ') him [Christ Jesus] for eternal life" (1:16). The connection between Christ Jesus and the living God would likely be corroborated for the audience. In effect, those who have come "to have-faith upon" Christ Jesus are those who "have hoped upon the living God" (4:10a). Moreover, the phrase "the living God" (θεῷ ζῶντι) in 4:10a recalls "the living God" (θεοῦ ζῶντος) in 3:15 of the parallel C macrochiastic unit. In 3:15, Paul's declaration is in regard to the behavior and function of the God's household—the church of the living God—to be a pillar and foundation of truth. Thus the second occurrence of "the living God" in 4:10a underscores a dual implication. On the one hand, given the presence and influence of "some" in Ephesus who not only teach some-thing different that lies-opposed to the sound teaching but also practice some-thing different than godliness, Timothy and the audience understand that, negatively, toil and agony to defend God's household is inevitable. On the other hand, as those who "have hoped upon the living God" (4:10a) they are, positively, "to behave" as those living "in the household of God, which is the church of the living God" (3:15); such is to be done by aligning with Paul's instructions to bring-about the household-law of God in faith, namely that which regards qualified leadership in the church. In short, in contrast to the apostate false teachers, the audience are reminded that the one upon whom they have hoped is the head of the household in which they live, not only "the living

God" (3:15; 4:10a) but also the Father of those "in faith" (1:2, 4).[101] For this reason, they are to behave as those living in God's presence, in God's household, by training for godliness, that is, for the promise of life according to the faithful word concerning Christ Jesus.

Paul goes on to further identify the living God: "who is the Savior of all humans" (4:10a). The phrase "who (ὅς) is the Savior (σωτήρ) of all humans (πάντων ἀνθρώπων)" here in the fourth microchiasm undoubtedly recalls "our Savior (σωτῆρος) God, who (ὅς) desires all humans (πάντας ἀνθρώπους) to be-saved" in 2:3-4 of the second microchiasm.[102] Thus the missional priority of salvation throughout the macrochiasm is emphasized here in view of training for godliness (4:7b, 4:8b), accepting the faithful words (4:9), toiling and agonizing (4:10a), and having hoped upon the living God (4:10a). Also, therefore, the reiteration that God is the Savior of "all humans" (πάντων ἀνθρώπων, 4:10a) echoes the first, lead activity of the church to pray on behalf of "all humans" (πάντων ἀνθρώπων, 2:1) in accordance with God's missional desire for the salvation of "all humans" (πάντας ἀνθρώπους, 2:4a). Here, then, Paul is reminding the audience not only of

---

101. Here, it may be worth noting the implicit christological significance. In the beginning of the letter, Paul identified that "Christ Jesus our Lord" shares status with "God the Father" as head of the same house, namely the realm "in faith" (see volume 1, chapter 3 regarding 1 Timothy 1:2). As noted above, in 4:10 there are further connections between "Christ Jesus" and "God," whether it be in regard to hope—"Christ Jesus our hope" (1:1); "we have hoped upon the living God"—or in regard to *life*—"faith upon him [Christ Jesus] for eternal life" (1:16); "the promise of life" (4:8b) and "the living God" (4:10). Significantly, while these connections are apparent, they do not blur the distinctions between "God the Father" and "Christ Jesus our Lord" (1:1), between having "faith upon Christ Jesus for eternal life" (1:16) and having "hoped upon the living God" (4:10). Rather, both their distinction and connection articulate that Paul's point is equality: they both share equal authority over one and the same household, that is, over all who are "in faith." Thus both God the Father and Christ Jesus may equally and distinctly be "the King of the eternities" (1:17) and "the living God" (3:15; 4:10).

102. To appreciate the full connection between 4:10 and 2:3-4, a comparison of the similar portions of each phrase in Greek is helpful:
2:3-4: "τοῦ σωτῆρος ἡμῶν θεοῦ, ὅς πάντας ἀνθρώπους";
4:10: "θεῷ ζῶντι, ὅς ἐστιν σωτὴρ πάντων ἀνθρώπων."
In passing, it may also be worth noting the occurrence of the relative pronoun ὅς in relation to both God and Christ Jesus. The audience heard its use by Paul in three places: twice to refer to God as the Savior (ὅς, "who," 2:4; 4:10) and once to refer to Christ Jesus (ὅς, "he," 3:16). In this way, the pronoun may have been a rhetorical strategy to corroborate the christological significance regarding the connection and distinction between Christ Jesus and God. Still, given the connection between "the living God" (4:10) and "the living God" (3:15), it is certainly possible that the advancement of the macrochiasm both qualifies and affirms that "the living God who (ὅς) is the Savior" (4:10) is precisely "the living God . . . who (ὅς) was manifested in flesh" (3:15-16), namely Christ Jesus who came into the word to save sinners (1:16).

God's missional desire as "the Savior of all humans" (4:10a) but also their duty and responsibilitiy as God's church—those whom he has saved—to pray for salvation on behalf of "all humans" (2:1). Negatively, this inclusive, universal scope stands in stark contrast to the apostate false teachers who attempt to exclude salvation to only those who observe their ascetic practices, that is, fail to knowingly-embrace the inclusive truth that "all creation of God is commendable" (4:4a). Positively, the Savior's inclusion of "all humans" provides an essential reason for toiling and agonizing to preserve the teaching of the gospel and to promote godliness among all who belong to the household of God.[103] In sum, the effect on the audience punctuates the overarching theme of the fourth microchiasm. Paul, Timothy, and the audience are in a war not only for the preservation of the truth and promotion of godliness but also, therefore, for the salvation of all humans. The fourth microchiasm is clear: there is a war between the Spirit versus deceitful spirits, the commendable teaching versus the teachings of demons, the faithful versus those who apostasy from the faith, the truth versus myths, and godliness-training that holds the promise of life from God versus ascetic, bodily training that rejects what God has given. Though at times it may appear that their toiling and agonizing is in vain, Paul, Timothy, and the audience are to always have confidence in the midst of the missional war for the salvation of all humans, for they have aligned themselves with the very "Savior of all humans" (4:10a).

1 Timothy 4:10b: Especially of the Faithful

("b" sub-element)

In the "b" sub-element of the minichiasm (4:10b), Paul qualifies his prior statement: "especially of the faithful." While it is possible that Paul's statement was heard in a variety of ways,[104] the audience would understand its clear meaning in the explicit missional context of "all humans" in the fourth and second microchiasms (2:3; 4:10a). The background to 2:3 and 4:10a is the presence of the apostate false teachers who are seeking to delimit salvation. Paul's response in both instances is to underscore the universality of God's salvation in Jesus Christ. That is, the audience understand that

---

103. See Belleville, "1 Tim," 90.

104. The two main interpretations are: (1) to translate the adverb μάλιστα as "that is," which specifies "all people" to just those who believe (e.g., Marshall, PE, 556–57; Knight, PE, 203; Barcley, 1 & 2 Tim, 140); or (2) within "all people," to distinguish between those who receive the gospel and those who reject it (e.g., Kelly, PE, 102–3; Wall with Steele, 1 & 2 Tim, 123).

though there is exclusively one living God in relation to all humans (2:5a; 4:10a), and though there is exclusively one mediator Christ Jesus to relate God and humans (2:5b), indeed this one God inclusively desires all humans to be-saved (2:4a), and for this reason the one mediator Christ Jesus inclusively gave himself as a ransom on behalf of all (2:6). Simply, the one exclusive God is the one inclusive Savior of all humans (4:10a). Paul's point is that salvation is offered to the first, lead of sinners (1:15), to both Jew and Gentile (2:7)—in a word, to all humans (2:4a; 4:10a).[105] Furthermore, given that both statements in 2:4a and 4:10a are coupled with a knowing-embrace of the truth (2:4b; 4:3b), the audience understand that salvation depends directly on preserving the inclusive truth—the faithful word (4:9)—and striving for its universal acceptance. To be sure, then, as the audience have been listening to the performance and movement of the letter—particularly here in the fourth microchiasm—it is certain that Paul has in view the war against the false teachers who exclude humans from salvation on the basis of ascetic self-effort. Paul is thus emphasizing the truth of the gospel: salvation comes by coming to have-faith upon the inclusive effort of Christ Jesus, who actively came into the world to save sinners and gave himself as a ransom on behalf of all (1:15; 2:6).

In this way, the term "especially" (μάλιστα) is heard by the audience as a polemical response to the false teachers who—holding-toward deceitful spirits (4:1)—deceive the audience to accept that salvation comes by abstaining from God's creation, such as marriage and foods (4:3a), rather than by accepting the faithful word (4:9) that salvation comes by Christ Jesus's entrance into creation (1:15). Furthermore, the polemic against "some" is further emphasized for the audience by the term "of the faithful." Placed within the A' element of the fourth microchiasm, "of the faithful" (πιστῶν) recalls the polemical contrast in the parallel A element regarding "the faithful" (πιστοῖς) who have knowingly-embraced the truth (4:3) versus "some" who apostasy from "the faith" (τῆς πίστεως, 4:1) and are false-worders (4:2). Given this contrast, the polemical force of the statement "especially of the faithful" would be heard with a twofold nuance. There is the positive sense, to the effect of "God is the Savior of all humans who allow him to save them." Thus for "of the faithful" (πιστῶν, 4:10b) who have come "to have-faith"

105. Belleville, "1 Tim," 90: "The emphasis is not on the whole of humanity being saved (*pas* without the article) but on salvation's availability to each and every person (*pas* without the article . . .). There are no exclusions. He is savior for 'each and every person' who receives him, whether Jew or non-Jew, circumsized or uncircumsized, barbaric or civilized, slave or free, male or female (Gal 3:28; Col 3:11)." Yarbrough, *Paul's Utilization of Preformed Traditions*, 113: "the poetic presence is not a contrast, but is more synthetic and climactic, completing the previous thought about the function of the living God who is the Savior."

(πιστεύειν) upon Christ Jesus (1:16) by accepting the "faithful" (πιστός) word that Christ Jesus came to save sinners (1:15), undoubtedly the living God is their Savior (4:10a). Negatively, however, the audience hear the sense that "God is not the Savior of all humans who try to save themselves."[106] That is, for "some" who apostasy from the faith, (4:1) are holding-toward teachings of demons (4:1), pursue bodily training that rejects God's creation (4:3a; 4:8a), and do not accept that Christ's mediatorial, bodily manifestation in flesh (2:5; 3:16) is the means by which all of creation is made-holy (4:5), undoubtedly there is no room in their different teaching or practice for Christ Jesus to save them nor for God to be their Savior.

As the introductory "a" sub-element concludes, the audience understand that Paul's statement is not a limitation of salvation but rather an attack on the very idea of limiting it. The qualifying phrase "especially of the faithful" certainly is a public declaration in front of the entire household of God to indict the radical error of the false-teaching overseers, namely that an exclusive salvation fails to account for the inclusive, missional nature of what God's household is and represents: it is the church of the living God (3:15), the living God who is the Savior of all humans (4:10a), the Savior God who desires all humans to be-saved (2:3–4a). Still, for those "of the faithful" in the audience (4:10b)—"the faithful" (4:3b)—Paul's statement would be a call to celebrate and participate in the fact that God is their Savior. The faithful (4:3b, 4:10b) who have knowingly-embraced the truth are free to practice godliness by receiving God's creation with thanksgiving in the present life. At the same time, they do so as part of their training to give thanks to God in the inevitable-coming life (4:8b), that is, for the life eternal that they received from him (1:16). Indeed, unlike "some" in the A element who apostasy from the faith (4:1), the audience understand that those "of the faithful" in the parallel A' element missionally toil and agonize not only against "some" but also for the sake of the salvation of "some"—that they, too, would-inevitably-come to have-faith upon Christ Jesus (1:15), proclaim God as their Savior (2:4a; 4:10a), and thus lead a life of godliness (2:2, 10; 4:7b, 8b) specifically in view of the mystery of godliness, Christ Jesus (3:16).

---

106. Couser, "Sovereign Savior," 119 n. 72: "the very limitation of God's status as savior to believers suggests that, while God may indiscriminately make provision for the salvation of all in Christ, he cannot be claimed as savior by those who do not believe."

1 Timothy 4:11: *Charge These-Things and Teach*
("c" sub-element)

In the pivot "c" sub-element of the minichiasm (4:11), Paul commands Timothy to "Charge these-things and teach." The phrase "Charge (παράγγελλε) these-things and teach (δίδασκε)" in 4:11 recalls Paul's opening exhortation in the first microchiasm for Timothy to "charge (παραγγείλῃς) some not to teach-different (ἑτεροδιδασκαλεῖν)" in 1:3, which was the same "charge" (παραγγελίας) that intended love for "some" who have turned-aside from a without-hypocrisy faith (1:5–6), namely the "charge" (παραγγελίαν) that Paul entrusted to Timothy (1:18) in order to war the commendable war against "some" (1:19).[107] Here in 4:11 of the fourth microchiasm, then, given Paul's sustained polemic against the false teachers—particularly to correct the false teachers's delimited view of salvation in the immediately preceding verse (4:10)—it is evident that the phrase "Charge these-things and teach" is a remedial command with the intention of correcting and counteracting the apostate false teachers.

The verb "charge" (παράγγελλε) reiterates to the audience—and to the false teachers among them—that Timothy possesses authority. Indeed, where the phrase "Charge these-things" (παράγγελλε ταῦτα) nearly verbatim recalls "This charge (ταύτην τὴν παραγγελίαν) I entrust to you, child Timothy" in 1:18 of the first microchiasm, the audience are reminded that just as Paul was appointed by Christ Jesus (1:12), so too Paul has entrusted Timothy (1:18). In short, to not align with Timothy is not only to reject Paul but also Christ Jesus. The emphasis on Timothy's authority would be an encouragement to execute his office with confidence—to toil and agonize with Paul against the false teachers (4:10a) knowing that the word is faithful and worthy of all acceptance (4:9). Even though the apostate "some" will assert themselves, Timothy is not to shy away from the fact that he, in accordance to the prophecies preceding upon him (1:18), is the appointed leader in Ephesus who will instruct the audience in the words of the faith and of the commendable teaching (4:6).

The term "these-things" (ταῦτα) recalls its prior occurrences throughout the macrochiasm and would most likely be heard in reference to what

---

107. It may be worth noting that the first microchiasm is framed by the verb "charge" (παραγγείλῃς) in 1:3 of the A element and by the cognate noun "charge" (παραγγελίαν) in 1:18 of the parallel A' element. Paul's use of the the verb "Charge" (παράγγελλε) here in the fourth microchiasm would, in effect, carry forward and encapsulate the entire force of the first microchiasm, namely the themes of Paul's authority from God and his sound teaching that accords with God's self-disclosure in the gospel. Such would strengthen the rhetorical impact of his command in 4:11.

precedes it.[108] Thus Timothy is to charge "some" in regard to inclusive salvation (4:10), eternal life (4:8b), godliness (4:7b), and the words of the faith, that is, the commendable teaching (4:6).[109] To be sure, the audience understand that the charge is to be heard within the polemical backdrop of "some" who promote ascetic bodily training as part of an exclusive salvation. In this way, the command for Timothy to "teach" in the pivot "c" sub-element of the minichiasm amplifies the corrective function of Paul's command to "Charge." Furthermore, the audience would understand that the content of what Timothy must "teach" (δίδασκε, 4:11) comprises "the (τῆς) commendable teaching (διδασκαλίας)" in which Timothy himself is being-nourished (4:6)—to be sure, "the (τῇ) sound teaching" (διδασκαλίᾳ)" of Paul (1:10b–11), who was divinely appointed as a "teacher" (διδάσκαλος, 2:7). In this way, what Timothy must "teach" (δίδασκε, 4:11) stands in obvious contrast to the "teachings (διδασκαλίαις) of demons" to which "some" are holding-toward (4:1), that is, "some" who "teach-different" (ἑτεροδιδασκαλεῖν, 1:3) and are desiring to be "law-teachers" (νομοδιδάσκολοι, 1:7). In sum, the audience understand that the apostle and "teacher" Paul (2:7) who authoritatively entrusted the "charge" to Timothy (1:18; cf. 1:3, 5) is explicitly validating Timothy's credentials as an authority and teacher to "Charge these-things and teach" in the Ephesian church (4:11).

In sum, Paul's commands in the pivot "c" sub-element for Timothy to "Charge these-things and teach"—specifically in view of "some" (4:1)—has several motivations derived from the fourth microchiasm and the second minichiasm within. First, the influence of "some" makes Timothy's appointment at Ephesus all the more exigent for the sake of the teaching, godliness, and the functioning of God's missional household. Second, in addition to the faithful word, Paul and Timothy's colloborative toiling, agonizing, and established hope upon the Savior of all humans ought to inspire confidence in Timothy as he remains in Ephesus. Third, the missional goal of salvation puts an eternal perspective on the difficult work to which Timothy has been called; indeed, it is for this reason that Timothy is to toil and agonize to

---

108. Knight, *PE*, 204: "the ταῦτα to be taught and prescribed is the section closest at hand. Here the preceding section seems most appropriate, since it consists of general truths for believers, whereas the section following is directed almost exclusively to Timothy."

109. It is likely that "these-things" (ταῦτα) in 4:11 includes Paul's prior statements as far back as the previous "these-things" (ταῦτα) in 4:6 (see e.g., Towner, *Letters*, 272 n.6 in regard to 1 Timothy 3:14). However, given the sustained polemic and connectedness of the microchiasm, it is not unlikely that to "Charge these-things" in 4:11 of the A' element includes the content of "Instructing these-things" in 4:6 of the parallel A element, namely the reception of God's creation—marriage and foods—and the commendable teaching (4:3–6).

preserve the sound teaching—the gospel.[110] Fourth and finally, the emphasis on Timothy's authority is to be clearly heard by the audience; they are summoned to respond in submissiveness to Timothy, the leader of God's household in Ephesus.

1 Timothy 4:12a: None Must Look-Down-On You, Be an Example of the Faithful

("b'" sub-element)

The "b'" sub-element (4:12a) continues Paul's assertion of Timothy's authority to lead the church in Ephesus: "None must look-down-on your youth." Though the pronoun "None" (μηδείς) would refer to anyone among the audience in general, Paul's sustained connotation of its cognate terms would most likely convey a specific polemical allusion toward the false teachers. The term "None" (μηδείς, 4:12) recalls the consistent association of the activities by "some": Timothy is to "charge some not (μή) to teach-different, nor (μηδέ) to hold-toward myths and genealogies without-limit" (1:3-4); "some" are "not (μή) understanding either (μήτε) what they-are-saying or (μήτε) regarding some-things they-are-insisting" (1:7); if "someone" aspires to overseer, it is necessary for him to be "not (μή) addicted-to-wine, not (μή) violent" (3:3), "Not (μή) a young-plant" (3:6), that he might "not (μή) fall into disgrace" (3:7); similarly, qualified deacons are "not (μή) double-worded, not (μή) holding-toward much wine, not (μή) avaricious" (3:8). In this way, and particularly given the sustained polemic against the false teachers in the previous verse (4:11), the rhetorical impact of 4:12a would be heard to the effect of, "None—particularly not some—must look-down-on your youth."[111] The next phrase would literally refer to "the youth of yours" (σου τῆς νεότητος), and combined with the verb "look-down-on" (καταφρονείτω), the audience clearly understand that Timothy's youth is the stated reason for such disregard or contempt, thus "None must look-down-on your youth." Although Timothy was immersed in a culture in which veneration came with age,[112] it is unlikely that the audience understood Paul's command merely as a statement concerning

---

110. Quoting John Chrysostom (*Hom. 1 Tim.* 12), Witherington notes: "But where the salvation of others is concerned, command and interpose with authority. This is not a case for moderation but for authority, lest the common good suffer" (*Letters*, 257).

111. See 1 Cor 16:10-11 for a similar exhortation to the Corinthian church concerning Timothy.

112. Spicq, *Les Épîtres Pastorales*, 511-12.

Timothy's age.[113] Rather, in the fourth microchiasm the audience have not only been listening to an ongoing contrast—a war of truth versus falsehood concerning the salvation of all humans—but also a sustained emphasis on Timothy's qualifications to lead the missional household of God. In this specific context, the audience would understand that Paul intends a polemical contrast against the false teachers to highlight Timothy's authority and leadership.

The term "youth" (νεότητος) in 4:12 recalls Paul's statement regarding "someone" who aspires to an overseer but is "a young plant" (νεόφυτον) in 3:6. The term "young-plant" was associated with the false teachers who did not have deep roots in the faith and thus were entirely unqualified to lead God's household, as evidenced by being-puffed up with pride when presented with their leadership position, thus falling into the condemnation of the devil (3:6). Undoubtedly, given that Timothy has been consistently portrayed as the antithesis of the false teachers, the audience understand that Timothy is no young-plant. Rather, he is Paul's "genuine child in faith" (1:2) who has been deliberately entrusted by Paul to lead the church in Ephesus (1:18; cf. 1:3), was raised by Paul to know how to behave in the missional household of God (3:15), continually nourishes himself in the words of the faith and of the commendable teaching that he has followed (4:6b), toils and agonizes with Paul against some-thing different that lies-opposed to God's universal offer of salvation (4:10; cf. 1:10b), and along with Paul has hoped upon the Savior of all humans (4:10a). In complete irony, where the "young-plant" (νεόφυτον, 3:6) false teachers who have apostatized from the faith are themselves those who look-down-on Timothy's "youth" (νεότητος, 4:12) because they are being-puffed-up with pride, the audience understand Paul's rhetorical implication: everyone in the audience must look-down-on the false teachers. Remedially, the false teachers must look up to Timothy.

In short, Paul has cumulatively built up a strong case for the audience that Timothy—in contrast to the apostate false teachers—is a man proven to have deep roots in the faith and, therefore, is a worthy leader whom "None

---

113. Focusing on Timothy's "youth," many commentators have given various proposals on Timothy's age. Knight suggests that Timothy is "in his thirties (the estimate most would agree on)" (*PE*, 205). Marshall suggests that Timothy "would probably have to be less than 40 years old to be accounted 'young' at this point" (*PE*, 560). See also Collins, *1 & 2 Tim*, 127–28; Jeremias, *Timotheus*, 34; Kelly, *PE*, 102; Simpson, *PE*, 69. Still, several commentators suggest that something to the effect of age discrimination or immaturity are in view; see Wall with Steele, *1 & 2 Tim*, 123; Belleville, "1 Tim," 90. Overall, however, it is generally agreed upon that "youth" does not mean that Timothy was particularly young or "a young-plant," that is, a recent convert. Witherington, *Letters*, 257: "The words 'let no one despise your youth' . . . do not suggest that Timothy is either very young in actual years or a mere babe in the faith."

must look-down-on" but rather must be looked up to and must be followed. Thus while Timothy did not have Paul's apostolic credentials, the audience understand that Timothy is held up as the authoritative representative of Paul in Ephesus who must be heeded over and against the false teachers who were vying to wrest authority both from him and the apostle.[114] Thus, the force of the exhortation "None must look-down-on your youth" is clear, specifically in view of "some" in the parallel A element and Paul's command in the preceding "c" sub-element, the sense being: "Irrespective of what the false teachers say and do, preserve the teaching, promote godliness, and don't let anyone stop you from doing otherwise!"

The second half of the "b'" sub-element enhances Paul's public announcement for Timothy's leadership: "rather be an example of those of the faithful." The force of the statement would be heard by the disjunction "rather" (ἀλλά), as if the apostle were saying, "Instead of stepping down, step up and be an example of those of the faithful." The specific command for Timothy to "be an example of those of the faithful" (τύπος γίνου τῶν πιστῶν) recalls for the audience Paul's earlier statement of how he was granted-mercy as the lead of sinners so that Christ Jesus might display all patience as "an example (ὑποτύπωσιν) to those who would-inevitably come to have-faith (πιστεύειν) upon him for life eternal" (1:16). In other words, just as Paul is an "example" to those who would-inevitably-come to have-faith upon Christ for life eternal, so also Timothy—Paul's child "in faith" (1:2)—is now to be an "example" to those who have already come to have-faith upon Christ, namely "those of the faithful." To be sure, the audience understand that Paul is not only highlighting his connection with Timothy—thus Timothy's authority—but also that Timothy was raised by Paul to be like Paul—thus Timothy's qualification. Still, the participal phrase "those of the faithful" (τῶν πιστῶν) in 4:12 recalls "of the faithful" (πιστῶν) in 4:10b of the present A' element and "the faithful" (τοῖς πιστοῖς) in 4:3b of the parallel A element. In both prior instances, Paul's polemic against the false teachers was view. Thus, as a model of "those of the faithful" (4:12)—"the faithful" who have knowingly-embraced the truth (4:3b) that the living God is the Savior of all humans (4:10)—Timothy is to lead

---

114. Though certainly intended to summon the audience's alignment with Timothy, Paul's repeated encouragements to Timothy throughout the fourth microchiasm suggest that Paul understood the difficult and exhausting task in Ephesus to which he had assigned Timothy, his "child in faith" (1:2). It is possible that Timothy was beginning to fatigue in the ongoing war against the false teachers in Ephesus and, therefore, needed such encouragement. Yet, the overall emphasis of Paul's letter seems to underscore an element of empathy, familial-friendship, and profound longing to come to Timothy's aid (3:14) as a co-laborer (4:10) in the preservation of the teaching and promotion of godliness in God's missional household.

the Ephesian church in exactly the opposite manner as the false teachers, who are false-worders (4:2) and relegate salvation to the rejection of God's creation (4:3a, 8a).[115]

1 Timothy 4:12b: In Word, In Behavior, In Love, In Faith, In Purity

("a'''" sub-element)

In the concluding "a'''" sub-element of the 4:9–12 minichiasm, Paul specifies five ways that Timothy must be an example of those of the faithful: "in word, in behavior, in love, in faith, in purity" (4:12b).[116] The phrase "in word" (λόγῳ) echoes "Faithful is the word (λόγος) and worthy of all acceptance" in 4:9 of the parallel "a" sub-element. In this way, Paul reiterates Timothy's calling to be an example of what it means to accept that the "word" is faithful. It also means, therefore, that Timothy must be an example of "being-nourished in the words (λόγοις) of the faith" over and against the vile and silly myths (4:6b–7). Furthermore, he is to be an example of receiving all of God's creation, which is made-holy consistent-with the "word" (λόγου) of God and intercession (4:5). Undoubtedly, then, Timothy is to be an example "in word" (λόγῳ) particularly due to the influence of "false-worders" (ψευδολόγων, 4:2) who endanger salvation for all humans. In short, the

---

115. Knight, *PE*, 205: "With the definite article (τῶν) it designates the specific believers among whom Timothy lives."

It may be worth noting that the theme of leadership throughout the macrochiasm may have relevance here. Given that Timothy is called to be the archetype deacon in 4:6 who is to instruct "the brothers"—possibly a reference to only the men—"the faithful" for whom Timothy is to be a model in 4:12 may itself refer to a specific group within the church, namely prospective overseers and deacons. Certainly, the fact that the false teachers are attempting to lead and influence the church in Ephesus would demand new leaders who themselves have a model to follow, namely Timothy whose model was Paul.

116. The rhetorical repetition of the preposition "in" (ἐν) functions to underscore the comprehensive way in which Timothy is to set an example of the faithful who belong to God's household. It is possible that the ascetic tendencies of the false teacher, in contrast with the freedom of the gospel to partake in all of creation, might have made Timothy susceptible to the charge of indulgence. For this reason, it would have been all the more urgent for Timothy to serve as a model in a holistic manner.

It may also be worth noting the rhetorical alliteration of the "α" sound in the terms "behavior" (ἀναστροφῇ), "love" (ἀγάπῃ), "purity" (ἁγνείᾳ). Combined with the repetition of "in" (ἐν), the alliteration would likely strengthen the rhetorical force of the entire phrase.

audience understand that for Timothy to be an example of those of the faithful "in word," he is to be the opposite of the false teachers.[117]

Timothy is also to be a model "in behavior" (ἀναστροφῇ)—his manner of life.[118] The term "behavior" (ἀναστροφῇ) in 4:12 recalls its cognate verbal occurrence in 3:15 regarding how it is necessary "to behave" (ἀναστρέφεσθαι) in the household of God. Thus, as an example "in behavior" for the church (4:12), Timothy is to demonstrate how everyone in the church is "to behave" (3:15). To be sure, the juxtaposition of "word" and "behavior" was common in Jewish and Greek moral instruction.[119] However, though a consistent manner of life commanded the respect of others, the audience would understand that the apostle Paul has in view something more than a respectable and moral life. The "b" and "b'" parallel sub-elements in the minichiasm summarized Paul and Timothy's collaborative manner of life and motivation to toil and agonize for the preservation of the teaching regarding God's inclusive offer of salvation to all humans. Consequently, Paul and Timothy's consistent manner of life was understood as purposeful and missional in nature. Thus Paul's command for Timothy to be an example "in behavior" within the household of God would include the dimension of moral living but specifically for the sake of progressing the gospel among all humans. Thus as "some" seek to undermine the truth, Timothy's call to be an example "in behavior" would certainly require him to war the commendable war against "some" who teach-different in Ephesus (1:18).

Such a missional lifestyle is immediately qualified by the triplet "in love, in faith, in purity."[120] Several observations are worth noting. First, the audience would likely hear an echo of Paul's earlier statement in the first microchiasm, wherein the end of the charge to stop the "some" who teach-different is "love (ἀγάπη) from a pure heart and a good conscience and a without-hypocrisy faith (πίστεως)" (1:5). In this way, Timothy is to bear the marks of a pure heart, good conscience, and a without-hypocrisy faith—"love." Yet, the audience also understand that Timothy's efforts to stop the false teachers who limit the scope of salvation would certainly be an

---

117. In this sense, Timothy's calling to be an example "in word" has further implications than the traditional interpretation that the phrase refers to conversation or speech (e.g., Collins, *1 & 2 Tim*; 128; Towner, *Letters*, 315; Barcely, *1 & 2 Tim*, 142).

118. See Barcely, *1 & 2 Tim*, 142.

119. See Towner, *Letters*, 315 n. 17.

120. The terms "in love, in faith" are sometimes viewed as a pair in parallel to the prior two virtues "in word, in behavior." At the very least, certainly "love" is rightly understood as the outworking of "faith."

However, the remaining three virtues may be taken together as a triplet (e.g., Barcley, *1 & 2 Tim*, 142), wherein the last term "purity" provides a concrete example of what the interaction of "faith" and "love" should produce; see below.

example "in love." Second, the phrase "in love (ἀγάπῃ), in faith (πίστει), in purity (ἁγνείᾳ)" in 4:12 recalls their more explicit tandem occurrences both in regard to "the faith (πίστεως) and love (ἀγάπης) that are in Christ Jesus" (1:14) and to the women who will be-saved "if they remain in faith (πίστει) and love (ἀγάπῃ) and holiness with self-control" (2:15). Notably, as in 1:5, Paul in 1:14, 2:15, and 4:12b couples "love" and "faith" together. Hearing the coupling of these terms together for a fourth time, then, the audience clearly understand that the two go hand-in-hand. Yet, where Timothy is to be an example of "those of the faithful" (τῶν πιστῶν, 4:12a; cf. 4:3b, 10b)—namely those "in faith" (ἐν πίστει, 4:12b)—it is equally clear that Timothy is to exemplify what it looks like to exist as "the faithful" in the realm "in faith." To be sure, he is to express "love" that not only has in view the salvation of all humans (4:10a) but also celebrates and equips those "of the faithful" (πιστῶν, 4:10b) to welcome, attract, and invite those-outside into the missional household of God (cf. 3:7). In this sense, the audience understand that Paul's command for Timothy to be an example "in love, in faith" is a summons for Timothy to lead the church to further knowingly-embrace the truth (4:3b) regarding their existence "in Christ Jesus" (3:13). That is, Paul's indication is that the church's existence "in faith" equates to a manner of life "in behavior" that aligns with the implications "in word," namely "in love" (4:12b). Thus as Timothy lives a life of godliness according to his faith upon Christ for life eternal (1:16), which holds the promise of life for the present and for the inevitable-coming (4:8b), so too will the faithful in the Ephesian church. Furthermore, the audience understand that in light of the faithful word concerning Christ Jesus (1:15), Timothy is to be an example of what it looks like to have hoped upon the living God (4:10), and thus to claim Christ Jesus as his hope (1:1). Indeed, where Christ Jesus was manifested in flesh in order to give himself as a ransom on behalf of the fleshly, to save sinners so that they would be declared-just "in Spirit" and be with Christ Jesus "in glory" (1:15; 2:6; 3:16), Timothy is to preserve and promote what such union with Christ looks like for all humans.

Still, Timothy's example "in love, in faith" is also to be "in purity." As noted, this triplet in 4:12b echoes the triplet in 2:15. Significantly, then, where the audience understood that to exist "in faith" and "in love" was inseparable from remaining "in holiness" (ἁγιασμῷ) (2:15), so too Timothy's example "in faith, in love" is inseparable from his example "in purity" (ἁγνείᾳ).[121] Though it is possible that the audience heard "in purity" as a reference to motives, its placement within the fourth microchiasm suggests

---

121. The terms "holiness" (ἁγιασμῷ) and "purity" (ἁγνείᾳ) are not cognates. While conceptually they are similar, their association with each other here in 4:12b is understood by their connection with the phrases "in love" and "in faith."

that the term "purity" was understood to describe sexual virtue.[122] In 4:3 of the parallel A element, Paul identifies that marriage is God's creation and is to be received with thanksgiving by "the faithful" (τοῖς πιστοῖς). Thus to be an example of "those of the faithful" (τῶν πιστῶν) in 4:12, Timothy's reception of marriage would certainly be in view. Furthermore, given Paul's repeated emphasis on church leaders's marital fidelity in the third microchiasm (3:2, 12) and Timothy's call to be a model deacon (4:6), it is clear to the audience that Timothy must be an example of not merely the reception of marriage but the *proper* reception of marriage, namely fidelity—"in purity"—where sexuality is expressed within the boundaries of marriage. In this way, Timothy would be a radical example of what it means to receive the commendable creation of the holy God and give thanks to him. That is, for the faithful who have knowingly-embraced the truth that all creation is made-holy in light of the mediator Christ Jesus, Timothy is to avoid the ascetic extremes of the false teachers who reject God's creation and the promiscuous extremes that reject God's intention for sexuality. To be sure, the audience understand that Timothy is to lead the church to have a proper view of purity, namely to enjoy sex within marriage as a holy act of godliness in the same way that all qualified church leaders must demonstrate fidelity to one wife.

In sum, as the concluding "a'" sub-element moves toward a culminating high point, the audience gain a full understanding of the second minichiasm. Timothy's participation with Paul to toil and agonize against "some" for the preservation and acceptance of the inclusive offer of salvation in the introductory "a" sub-element equates to exemplifying the integrated facets of existing "in Christ," namely "in word, in behavior, in love, in faith, in purity" (4:12b) in the concluding "a'" sub-element.[123] Here again, Paul emphasizes that the preservation of the teaching and the promotion of godliness

---

122. Knight, *PE*, 206: "ἁγνεία . . . means generally 'purity' and more specifically 'chastity.' Here the general meaning, which would include the specific, is probably intended." Marshall, *PE*, 562: "Although it is used of cultic purity in the LXX . . . here it is used of character. It may refer to chastity . . . but it is more likely to refer to purity and integrity in motive."

123. Fiore aptly summarizes the idea: "At 1 Tim 4:12, virtues dominate over teaching as constituents of the desired model (*typos*) to be imitated, the model that the letter advances. As with Paul's example, a negative counterpart is outlined here as well . . . There is a rhetorical strategy at work here in proposing these examples to the readers. If the audience follows the virtuous and authentic example proposed, they will thwart the advance of the rival teachers. Furthermore, adopting the examples into their own lives, the audience will give authenticity to the positive teaching by the blameless lives that it produces . . . This in turn validates the criticism of the other teachers' failings" ("Paul, Exemplification, and Imitation," 245).

are intertwined and rooted in God's missional desire for all humans to come into his household.

1 Timothy 4:13–16: A Minichiastic Unit

As a minichiasm in itself, verses 4:13–16 of the A' element are composed carefully of four sub-elements ("a"-"b"-"b'"-"a'"); linguistic parallels identifying chiastic arrangements are indicated by the Greek text:

> "a". ¹³ Until I come hold-toward to the reading, to the exhorting, to the teaching (τῇ διδασκαλίᾳ).
>
>> "b". ¹⁴ Do not be without-concern (ἀμέλει) with the gift that is in you, which was given to you consistent-with prophecy with the-laying of hands of the presbytery.
>
>> "b'". ¹⁵ These-things be concerned (μελέτα) with; be in them, that your progress might be manifested to all.
>
> "a'". ¹⁶ Strongly-hold yourself and the teaching (τῇ διδασκαλίᾳ), strongly-remain in them; for doing this you will save yourself and those who hear you.

The third minichiasm of the 3:1–16 microchiasm is framed by the importance of "the teaching" in the "a" and "a'" sub-elements. Within this arrangement, the minichiasm gravitates around Paul's command for Timothy to be "concerned" in the "b" and "b'" sub-elements.

1 Timothy 4:13: Hold-Toward to The Reading, to The Exhorting, to The Teaching

("a" sub-element)

The introductory "a" sub-element transitions to specific duties that Timothy must carry out in Paul's absence: "Until I come hold-toward to the reading, to the exhorting, to the teaching" (4:13). The phrase "Until I come" (ἕως ἔρχομαι) would have several effects on Timothy and the audience. First, the shift of attention toward Paul would emphasize that his apostolic authority is not only present in the letter (3:14) and by his entrusted representative Timothy (1:18), but also that Paul's authority will, indeed, be physically present.[124] Second, therefore, the audience would hear a rhetorical movement

---

124. Burton suggests rendering ἕως ἔρχομαι to "as I am coming," which gives a

from the third microchiasm to the fourth microchiasm. That is, though Paul is hoping to come in quickness, even if he is delayed (3:15) the audience understand that Timothy is to maintain full authority and lead the church to behave as it is necessary in the household of God (3:15) until the apostle Paul himself arrives to do the same. Third, undoubtedly Paul's reference to his coming would provide motivation for Timothy to continue to toil and agonize. On the one hand, it would be encouraging to be reminded that Timothy will not be in Ephesus by himself indefinitely. On the other hand, as Paul's "genuine child in faith" (1:2), Timothy is reminded of his filial responsibility to do what Paul commands. Fourth and finally, the audience themselves would be reminded that Paul—"apostle of Christ Jesus according to the command of God our Savior and Christ Jesus our hope" (1:1)—has been calling for their allegiance, and he will soon come to ensure it. That is, even as Paul has already publically identified and remedially given-over Hymenaeus and Alexander for their apostasy—their swerving-from and shipwrecking of faith (1:6, 20)—so too will he identify and discipline those who submit themselves to the different teachings of the apostates (4:1–3a) rather than being in submisivesness to Paul and Timothy's leadership (3:4).[125] In short, the audience understand that their salvation is at stake: their alignment with Timothy and thus Paul ultimately expresses their alignment with Christ Jesus. For Paul to come to Ephesus and find the audience not adhering to Timothy would be their functional declaration that Christ Jesus is not their Lord (cf. 1:2, 12).[126]

The verb "hold-toward" (πρόσεχε) in 4:13 of the A' element recalls its earlier occurrence regarding the apostates who are "holding-toward" (προσέχοντες) in 4:1 of the parallel A element. However, rather than drawing a similarity between Timothy and the false teachers, the audience

---

sense of anticipation versus possibility (*Syntax of Moods and Tenses*, §328). Marshall, *PE*, 562: "The clause here leaves the time of Paul's coming uncertain, but not the fact that he will come."

125. It may be worth recalling that Paul's action toward Hymenaeus and Alexander had a positive outcome in view, namely being restored to faith upon Christ Jesus (see volume 1, chapter 3 regarding 1 Timothy 1:20). Also, in light of the third microchiasm, such restoration to faith would be evidenced by being "in submissiveness" to the leaders who seek to bring-about the household-law of God in faith (see chapter 2 regarding 1 Timothy 3:4).

126. Towner's comments helpfully summarize the import of the phrase "Until I come": "The brief statement is pregnant with possible meaning. Clearly, Timothy does not fully represent Paul in Ephesus; what Timothy is to do, Paul would do himself if he were present. By indicating his forthcoming arrival (the time is uncertain but not the fact), Paul establishes continuity both of his apostolic authority over the church (in spite of his absence) and of his work of proclamation, teaching, and correction" (*Letters*, 316).

clearly understand that Paul is introducing jarring polemical contrast. To be sure, the rhetorical effect was similarly heard in the comparative contrast in 4:12a between Timothy's "youth" (νεότητος) over and against "a young-plant" (νεόφυτον, 3:6). In the same way, Paul's rhetorical comparison here in 4:13 between Timothy and the false teachers is equally forceful: in stark contrast to the apostates who are "holding-toward deceitful spirits and teachings of demons" (4:1) and who "hold-toward" myths and genealogies without-limit (1:4), Timothy is commanded to "hold-toward to the reading, to the exhorting, to the teaching" (4:13)—in effect, the exact opposite.[127] Here, then, Paul is not only distinguishing Timothy from the false teachers but he is calling upon Timothy to further distinguish himself from "some," namely by devoting himself to the activities that were most likely interrupted or disregarded by the false-teaching overseers.[128] Still, the sustained movement throughout the macrochiasm to associate the apostate false teachers with those "hold-toward" (1:4; 3:8) would emphatically call upon the audience to examine if and to what they are themselves "holding-toward." Indeed, if any among the audience "hold-toward" (προσέχειν) myths and genealogies without-limit instead of rejecting them (1:4; 4:7a) or could be described as "holding-toward" (προσέχοντας) much wine" (3:8), Paul's point is clear, in effect: "Stop! Follow Timothy's lead instead." It is very well possible that not a few among the audience had become unconsciously engrossed in the myths and different teachings of the apostates at the expense of attending to the reading of Scripture and to the teaching that Paul had established in the Ephesian church.[129]

Paul commands Timothy to hold-toward three liturgical activities in the church: "to the reading, to the exhorting, to the teaching."[130] The first duty

---

127. Knight, *PE*, 207: "προσέχω . . . means generally 'turn one's mind to' and is used here for the first and only time in the PE in a positive sense with the special nuance (appropriate to the imperative) of 'occupy oneself with, devote or apply oneself to' (BAGD s.v. 1c)."

The full force of the rhetorical comparison between Timothy and the false teachers would be felt as a result of the cumulative dichotomy throughout the macrochiasm: the faithful's *holding* (1:19; 3:4, 7, 9; 4:8) versus the false teachers's *holding-toward* (1:4; 3:8; 4:1).

128. Towner, *Letters*, 316: "These [reading, exhorting, teaching] were certainly not innovations in the worship service, but rather activities that needed to be continued (or possibly resumed) in view of the disruption caused by the false teaching."

129. Marshall suggests that all three activities—reading, exhorting, teaching—"are the activities based on the use of Scripture" (*PE*, 562–63).

130. The repetition of the definite article "the" (τῇ) in 4:13 suggests that each was a regular and recognizable component of the church's liturgy during worship; see Towner, "Public Reading of Scripture," 44–53; Marshall 562. In this way, it is very well possible that at least a portion among the audience had been influenced by the false teachers to

Timothy must attend to is "the reading" (τῇ ἀναγνώσει), which technically refers to the reading aloud of Scripture—a practice taken from the reading of the OT in synagogue worship (e.g., ἀνέγνωσαν ... τῇ ἀναγνώσει, LXX Neh 8:8).[131] Towner's comments on this liturgical duty are insightful, particularly in view of the fourth microchiasm's arrangement, which pits Timothy and the audience against the apostate false teachers. Towner writes:

> It is normally assumed, apparently, that the primary function of the public reading of Scripture in the worship setting was to lay the groundwork for the preaching and teaching to follow ... This is a partial explanation ... Yet the public reading of the Scriptures served a deeper social function as well ... reading/hearing certain significant texts influences the formation, shaping, defining, and redefining of individual and corporate identity. From the perspective of the historical description of the practice as noticed in the OT and NT records ... it may be suggested that the Scriptures were intentionally read as a way of answering the always present and pertinent question: Who are we? ... The public reading of Scripture becomes a point of emphasis at crucial or crisis moments.[132]

Towner's comments are fitting when considering the current opposition against Paul, Timothy, and the members of God's household. While they fight to preserve the truth of the gospel and promote godliness as the missional household of God, the apostates are going astray and seeking to mislead others as well. As noted, the result of the crisis with the false teachers in Ephesus is not only a distortion of truth and proper lifestyle but also, therefore, a hindrance to the progress of the gospel for the salvation of humans. Paul's response to this is intriguing: he calls upon Timothy to lead the church in the reading of Scripture—the word of God (4:5)—thus to remind the audience of their acceptance of the faithful word, their existence "in

---

shift their attention away from these worship activities, thus becoming engrossed in the myths and practices of the apostates.

131. See Belleville, "1 Tim," 90–91; Knight, *PE*, 207; Marshall, *PE*, 653; Witherington, *Letters*, 258. Towner argues that behind this instruction is the assumption that the reader of Scripture in public worship, Timothy in this case, was a proficient and effective reader ("The Public Reading of Scripture," 44–53). Paul's command for Timothy to give himself to the "reading" may, therefore, indicate Timothy's task to re-read, that is, to perform the 1 Timothy letter again for the audience as part of their corporate worship. For further discussion regarding the practice of reading aloud and performing letters in the first century, see volume 1, chapter 1.

132. Towner, *Letters*, 317–19.

faith," that is, "in Christ Jesus" (3:13), and the corresponding promise of life for the present and for the inevitable-coming (4:8b–9).[133]

Second, Timothy is to give himself to "the exhorting" (τῇ παρακλήσει). The term recalls Paul's own use of the verbal cognates earlier in the letter and leaves little room for misunderstanding. It is in the immediate context of both Paul's authority as an apostle of Christ Jesus according to the command of God (1:1) and Timothy's identity as Paul's "child" under his authority (1:2) that the audience heard Paul's statement to Timothy: "As I exhorted (παρεκάλεσά) you to remain in Ephesus . . ." (1:3). Such an exhortation, therefore, would be understood as not as a suggestion but an authoritative command given from Timothy's father "in faith," Paul, who himself is under the authority of God our Savior (1:1), who is both the Savior of all humans and the one upon whom Paul and Timothy have hoped (4:10). Furthermore, in 2:1 the audience heard, "I exhort (παρακαλῶ), therefore, first of all to be-done supplications . . . on behalf of all humans." As in 1:3, the audience heard not an optional suggestion but an authoritative command by Paul—God's appointed proclaimer, apostle, and teacher (2:7)—for the men and women of God's household to follow. Here in 4:13, then, Paul's command for Timothy to give himself to "the exhorting" is not only an authoritative statement for Timothy to follow but also—and significantly—places the authority of Paul's own exhorting into Timothy's hands for the audience to follow. Thus Paul's emphasis on Timothy's authority and the

---

133. It is not unlikely that "the reading" of Scripture included the 1 Timothy letter itself. As noted, Paul viewed himself in the tradition of the OT prophets (see volume 1, chapter 3 regarding 1 Timothy 1:12). Paul, therefore, would have viewed his own words in the 1 Timothy letter as Scripture—God's words delivered through him—on par with the OT (the apostle Peter thought this way of Paul's letters, 2 Pet 3:15–16). Given the situation in Ephesus, it seems that Paul in 4:13 would be calling upon Timothy to read aloud the letter to repeatedly voice the apostle's call—thus God's—upon the audience to align with him and Timothy—thus with Christ Jesus. In effect, Timothy's public reading of the letter to the church would continue Paul's apostolic presence until his arrival (4:13) (for Paul's apostolic presence in the performance of the letters, see volume 1, chapter 1). See Swinson, *Letters to Timothy*, 72–74.

In passing, it may be worth noting that the letter would initially be performed by the letter carrier rather than by Timothy (see volume 1, chapter 1). Questions may thus be raised as to whether Timothy, who was not present for Paul's dictation of the letter, would be equipped to perfom the letter in the same manner as Paul had dictated it or had written it while training the letter carrier to perform it. Yet, undoubtedly Timothy—Paul's "genuine child" who was raised "in faith" by Paul (1:2)—would be very familiar not only with Paul's apostolic teaching but also Paul's apostolic speaking—Paul's cadence, rhythm, tone, mannerisms, and delivery. Here, then, especially after hearing the letter performed by the letter carrier as Paul intended, it is most likely that Timothy would be capable, equipped, trained, and prepared to carrying out Paul's instructions in 4:13 to continue the reading of Scripture—including Paul's letter—to the Ephesian church.

sustained call for the audience's allegiance to Timothy is reiterated. Timothy is to provide authoritative exhortations to the audience concerning the words of the faith and training for godliness on the basis of the reading of the authoritative word of God (4:5), that is, the faithful word that Paul has repeatedly acclaimed as worthy of all acceptance (1:15; 4:9). Moreover, given that none must look-down-on Timothy but rather are to submit to him as a proven, qualified leader, it is further clarified that the audience's submission to Timothy is not only based on his qualification to lead but also on the basis that his exhortations are both from Paul's apostolic authority and from Scripture itself.

Third and finally, Timothy must hold-toward "the teaching" (τῇ διδασκαλίᾳ, 4:13). Paul's specification here is significant. Not only does Paul's reference to "the teaching" (τῇ διδασκαλίᾳ) identify a unique, singular teaching that was recognized and accepted by the Ephesian church, but it also recalls Paul's specific reference to "the (τῆς) commendable teaching (διδασκαλίας)" (4:6b) and "the (τῇ) sound teaching (διδασκαλίᾳ)" (1:10b) over and against the plural "teachings (διδασκαλίαις) of demons" (4:1) to which "some" are holding-toward.[134] That is, Timothy is to lead the audience—particularly when they gather for worship to hear the reading and the exhorting—to equally hold-toward "the sound teaching (διδασκαλίᾳ)" that accords with the gospel (1:10b–11) by Paul, a divinely appointed "teacher" (διδάσκαλος, 2:7). To be sure, then, the audience understand that "the teaching" in view would be fully consistent with "the reading" of Scripture and "the exhorting" that intends the audience to adhere to both. In sum, the net effect of the introductory "a" sub-element highlights a movement in the fourth microchiasm: it begins with the apostates's holding-toward "teachings" of demons (4:1), then moves to Timothy's individual nourishment in "the commendable teaching" (4:6b), and finally moves to the corporate attention of both Timothy and the Ephesian church toward "the teaching" when they convene for worship (4:13).

---

134. The deliberate contrast would further emphasize Paul's rhetorical use of "hold-toward" in 4:13:

A element: "holding-toward (πρόσεχοντες) . . . teachings (διδασκαλίαις) of demons" (4:1);

A' element: "hold-toward (πρόσεχε) . . . the teaching (τῇ διδασκαλίᾳ)" (4:13).

1 Timothy 4:14: Do Not Be Without-Concern,
The-Laying of Handsd of the Presbytery

("b" sub-element)

In the "b" sub-element (4:14), the audience hear a shift from Timothy's public duties for the church to his personal stewardship: "Do not be without-concern with the gift that is in you" (4:14a).[135] Towner observes that the verb "be without-concern" (ἀμέλει) is common for the kind of instruction from a superior to a subordinate.[136] As such, Paul qualifies his statement in 4:12, namely that while no one is to look down on Timothy, it does not mean that Timothy is not under authority. As Paul has underscored throughout the letter, just like the apostle himself is under Christ Jesus and God's authority (1:1, 12; 2:7), Timothy is under the authority of another, Paul. Still, the phrase "Do not (μή) be without-concern" would also be understood as a subtle allusion to the apostate false teachers who have consistently been associated with the negative particle "not" (μή).[137] The audience understand that the apostates are specifically those who are "not" concerned with Paul's instructions, effectively neglecting the concern for the entire household of God to preserve the teaching of the gospel and promote its corresponding missional godliness.[138] Furthermore, the command for Timothy to not be without-concern for "the gift that is in you" would further the sustained polemical contrast against the false teachers. That is, Timothy is to firmly reject the authority of those who look-down-on him (4:12) so that he may bring-about the household-law of God in faith (1:4). Indeed, he must continue to exercise his "gift" in full conviction that he is accountable to Paul, his father "in faith" (1:2), and ultimately to the living God upon whom they have hoped (4:10), that is, the Savior God who commanded Paul (1:1).

It is possible that the audience would understand the meaning of "gift" in various ways.[139] However, the progression and purposeful rhetoric

---

135. Given the focus of the third microchiasm on leaders's personal life in relation to their public office in the church (3:2–12), it is clear that Timothy's public responsibilities (4:13) are inextricably intertwined with the management of his private, personal dealings.

136. Towner, *Letters*, 321.

137. See above regarding 1 Timothy 4:12 in reference to "not" (e.g., 1:3, 4, 7, 20; 3:3, 6, 7, 8).

138. In view of Acts 20:28–30 the implication of Paul's statement here in 1 Timothy 4:14–15 may be significant and a direct polemic toward the false teachers of whom Paul foretold in Acts. See the following discussion regarding the Spirit's involvement with "the gift that is in you" (4:14).

139. See Marshall, *PE*, 564–65.

throughout the macrochiasm would likely orient the audience to understand the term in a common way. Several observations are worth noting. First, the term "gift" (χαρίσματος) recalls the cognate "grace" (χάρις) in 1:2 and 1:14 of the first microchiasm, which the audience heard as a salvific blessing directly from God the Father and Christ Jesus, and recalls the responsive "grace" (χάριν) in 1:12 that Paul holds to Christ Jesus for empowering him. Thus, the "gift" in view is clearly understood to be divine in nature. Second, the specification of the gift "that is in you" specifies the location of the gift—"in you" (ἐν σοί). Significantly, then, Paul is likely highlighting the other side of what it means to be "in faith," that is, "in Christ Jesus" (1:2, 4; 2:15; 3:13; 4:12): as much as Timothy is "in Christ Jesus" and thus "in Spirit" (3:16), so too is Christ Jesus and the Spirit "in Timothy."[140] To be sure, that Paul has in mind the Spirit is not only evident from the parallelism between the introductory A and concluding A' elements of the fourth microchiasm—functioning to introduce the theme, then advance it in the conclusion—but also from the analogous, sustained polemical contrast between Timothy and the false teachers—the Spirit versus deceitful spirits (4:1). In other words, Timothy and the audience are to understand that the "gift that is in you"—the Spirit—derives from a fundamentally different source than that which has led "some" to apostasy from the faith—deceitful spirits.[141]

Third, given the sustained emphasis on Timothy's unique, authoritative role—Paul's "genuine child" (1:2) who was entrusted by Paul to carry out the charge in Ephesus against "some" (1:18), was raised by Paul to know how to behave in God's household (3:15), nourishes himself in the words of the faith and of the commendable teaching (4:6), and is to be an example of those of the faithful (4:12)—the audience understand that the function of the "gift that is in you" is specific and uniquely assigned to Timothy for the preservation and promotion of the teaching and godliness in God's missional household over and against "some" who are false-teaching overseers

---

140. See e.g., 2 Timothy 1:13-4.

141. In Acts 20:28, Paul addresses the original overseers of the Ephesian church: "Hold-toward yourselves and all the flock, in which the Holy Spirit has appointed you-all overseers to care-for the church of God . . ." Where Paul's statement here in 1 Timothy 4:14 is understood as a polemic against the "fierce wolves"—the false teachers in 1 Timothy—whom Paul predicted will arise "from you-all yourselves" (Acts 20:29-30), that is, from the original overseers, the implication forceful. Whereas "the Spirit" (τὸ πνεῦμα) in Acts 20:28 appointed the original overseers, namely those whom Paul commands to "Hold-toward (προσέχετε) yourselves and all the flock," in stark contrast it is evident that "the Spirit" (τὸ . . . πνεῦμα) in 1 Timothy 4:1 did not appoint the false-teaching overseers in Ephesus who are "holding-toward" (προσέχοντες) deceitful "spirits" (πνεύμασιν) and teachings of demons (4:1). In other words, "some" who teach-different as overseers in the Ephesian church do not have that which Timothy has, namely "the gift that is in you" (4:14).

in the Ephesian church. In contrast to the false teachers who forbid to marry and teach others to avoid foods, Timothy is to instruct that everything in creation is to be received with thanksgiving by the faithful (4:3-4). In contrast to the apostates who lead others to fixate on vile and silly myths, Timothy must be an example in word, behavior, love, faith and purity (4:12) in accordance with the reading, the exhorting, and the teaching of the faithful word concerning Christ Jesus and the inclusive offer of salvation to all humans, which is brought about by the proper household-law of God (1:15; 3:1; 4:9). In sum, the audience hear Paul's statement with a common understanding that "the gift" in view finds its origin in God, is realized through the indwelling Spirit, and is given to Timothy for the sake of preserving the teaching and promoting godliness in the missional church of the living God (3:15), who is the Savior God upon whom Timothy has hoped (4:10).

Continuing the "b" sub-element, Paul states that the gift "was given to you consistent-with prophecy with the-laying of hands of the presbytery" (4:14). The verb "was given" (ἐδόθη) recalls Christ Jesus in the second microchiasm, who "gave (δούς) himself as ransom on behalf of all" (2:6). Here, then, the audience understand that Timothy's gift not only has a divine origin but also is associated with Christ Jesus. The connection would both strengthen the force of Paul's prior statement concerning the gift—as it were, "in Timothy"—and enhance its implications. In short, not only is God's gift "in you" (ἐν σοί, 4:14a) but it is also "to you" (σοι, 4:14b).[142] Furthermore, where the verb "was given" (ἐδόθη) in 4:14 also recalls Paul's activity with regard to Hymenaeus and Alexander—"whom I have given-over (παρέδωκα) to Satan" (1:20)—the polemical constrast is evident: whereas the gift in Timothy "was given" by God (4:14), the false teachers who oppose "the sound teaching, according to the gospel of the glory of the blessed God" (1:10b-11a) have been "given-over" to Satan, that they might be-disciplined not to blaspheme" (1:2). Emphatically, Paul intends the audience to understand that Timothy—not "some"—is qualified and has the authority to lead the Ephesian church until Paul comes (4:13).

It is unlikely that the prepositional phrase "consistent-with prophecy" (διὰ προφητείας) was heard by the audience to indicate that Timothy's gift came by means of prophecy.[143] Rather, where the preposition "consistent-with" (διά) recalls its prior occurrences throughout the letter connoting "in keeping with," it is evident to the audience that Paul intends the same

---

142. Knight, *PE*, 208: "Aorist passive ἐδόθη indicates that the gift 'was given' by God." In this way, the "gift" (χαρίσματος) that was given to Timothy is certainly to be understood in light of the "grace" (χάρις) received by Timothy directly from God the Father and Christ Jesus in 1:2.

143. Cf. discussion in Marshall, *PE*, 565-66.

meaning here. In 1:16 Paul declared that "consistent-with" (διά) his status as the first, lead of sinners (1:15b, 16a) and the fact that Christ Jesus came to save sinners (1:15a), he was granted-mercy; in 2:10 Paul specified that women are to cosmetic themselves in that which is "consistent-with" (δι') their profession of godliness, namely good works; and in 2:15, Paul stated that women will be-saved "consistent-with" (διά) a missional lifestyle that evidences their existence "in faith" (2:15). In the same way, therefore, the audience understand that "the gift in you, which was given to you consistent-with prophecy" conveys that the gift was accompanied by the activity of prophecy, the sense being "in keeping with prophecy."

The term "prophecy" (προφητείας) recalls its earlier occurrence in the first microchiasm where Timothy was encouraged to war the commendable war against the false teachers according to the "prophecies" (προφητείας) preceding upon him (1:18). In effect, Paul reminds Timothy here in 4:14 that Timothy's calling to lead the household of God in Ephesus over and against the false-teaching overseers is certainly accompanied by and in keeping with a prophetic word.[144] As such, Paul's use of the preposition "consistent-with" (διά) would be affirmed for the audience.[145] The net effect of Paul's reminders in 1:18 and 4:14 would not be insignificant: both Timothy and the entire audience are to understand that Timothy functions as a prophet against the false teachers, that is, a leader to bring about what was prophesied, precisely because he was commissioned through prophecy itself. Undoubtedly, Paul's point is to further the contrast between Timothy and the apostates, as heard throughout the fourth microchiasm and particularly here through the implications of 4:14 in the "b" sub-element.

The gift in Timothy is correlated "with the-laying of hands of the presbytery." While it is possible that Paul's statement was heard as identifying that Timothy's gift came via the-laying of hands, it is more likely that the audience understood "the-laying of hands" as an expression to recognize God's anointing of Timothy.[146] That is, because "the gift" in view was

---

144. In support of this interpretation, Towner insightful notes: "Prophecy itself will not have been the 'means' or cause of conveyance; the passive verb 'was given' indicates the action of God/the Spirit. It is probably rather a reference to words of the Spirit spoken by a prophet(s) that confirm and identify Timothy's giftedness and thereby authorize his ministry in the community" (*Letters*, 322–23).

Again, the relevance of Acts 20:28–30 comes into view; Paul clearly foretold—in effect, prophesied—the eventual rise of the false-teaching overseers in Ephesus. See volume 1, chapter 1.

145. See volume 1, chapter 4 regarding 1 Timothy 2:15; see also above regarding 1 Timothy 4:5.

146. In support of the latter, Knight says that the phrase "indicate[s] the public testimonies to that internal work [the gift] of God" (*PE*, 208).

given from and originated from God, and because the "prophecy" in view functioned to affirm the use of Timothy's gift in Ephesus rather than as a medium through which the gift was conferred, it seems that the audience would understand that "the-laying of hands" (ἐπιθέσεως τῶν χειρῶν) was similarly a form of public recognition in light of God's gifting.[147] Moreover, the term "the-laying" (ἐπιθέσεως) here in 4:14 recalls Paul's cognate use of the particle "Instructing" (ὑποτιθέμενος) in 4:6 of the parallel A element. In this way, where the term also recalls Paul's statement in 1:18, "This charge I entrust (παρατίθεμαί) to you," the audience understand that "the-laying" (4:14)—in the same way as "Instructing" (4:6)—carries the connotation of authority. Thus as much as "the-laying of hands" was a public recognition of God's activity in Timothy's life, it was simultaneously an authoritative gesture by "the presbytery."

The term "the presbytery" (τοῦ πρεσβυτερίου)—literally, "the elders"—references an authorized church council comparable to the highest of Jewish councils.[148] That this authorized "presbytery" is identified as the agent of "the-laying of hands" reiterates to the audience that Timothy's gifting—in contrast to the the apostate false teachers—was officially sanctioned by the leaders of the church at large.[149] Unsurprisingly, in view of Paul's preceding

---

147. Marshall, *PE*, 566: "The phrase with μετά has the force 'accompanied by'; it may qualify ἐδόθη or διὰ προφητείας."

In passing, it may be worth noting a connection to Paul's earlier instructions for the men to pray "lifting reverent hands" (χεῖρας) (2:8). Given the missional context of 2:1–15, the repeated reference to "hands" (τῶν χειρῶν) in 4:14 may imply the salvific importance of the gift that was given to Timothy, namely to preserve the teaching and truth of the inclusive offer of salvation to all humans by coming to have-faith upon Christ Jesus (1:16).

148. Marshall, *PE*, 567: "πρεσβύτριον is used elsewhere in the NT to mean a 'council of elders', namely the Sanhedrin (Lk 22.64; Acts 22.5), and then it came to refer to a Christian group of elders."

149. Witherington, *Letters*, 259: "We do get a glimpse here of the structure of a Christian community, and involves something like a board of elders, or like the *gerousia* of a synagogue or the *presbyterion* of the Greco-Roman collegium." Ibid. underscores (1) that the laying on of hands was "the human recognition by church leaders that God had done something in Timothy's life" but (2) that the laying on of hands was not—in contrast to some commentators (e.g., Barrett)—an ordination of sorts bringing Timothy into the fold of elders. Wall with Steele, *1 & 2 Timothy*, 124: "The congregation's acceptance of Timothy's divine authorization . . . is made public by a liturgical gesture, the imposition of hands. This gesture . . . indicates that the elders provide public testimony to the prophecy's expected fulfillment . . . Especially in an apostolate shaped by Jewish tradition . . . the responsibility of the most revered (and typically most senior) group of leading men would include public recognition of those charged with administering the congregation's affairs." Marshall, *PE*, 567: "The vast majority of scholars assume that this is the meaning here: a group of elders laid their hands on Timothy."

In passing, it may be worth noting that Paul's laying of hands on Timothy in 2

imperatives for Timothy to charge and teach (4:11), to let none—namely "some"—look-down-on him (4:12a), to be an example of those of the faithful (4:12b), and to lead the church in worship (4:13), Paul is emphasizing the simple but important point to the audience that Timothy has the authority to do all these-things—not only as authorized by Paul's apostolic authority (1:3, 18) but also by that of "the presbytery." Indeed, for this reason Timothy must not be without-concern with the gift that was given by God, that is consistent-with prophecy, and that was publically recognized by the qualified men who govern the church.[150]

1 Timothy 4:15: These-things Be Concerned With, Manifest Your Progress to All

("b'" sub-element)

In the "b'" sub-element (4:15) Paul restates the parallel "b" sub-element in positive terms: "These-things be concerned with; be in them." The terms "these-things" (ταῦτα) and "them" (τούτοις) recall their prior occurrences in reference to what precedes.[151] In effect, then, the audience understand that Paul has in view the previous imperatives for Timothy to be an example, lead the church in worship, and use his gift as expected. Furthermore, the term "be concerned" (μελέτα) recalls its negative cognate "Do not be without-concern (ἀμέλει)" in 2:14 of the parallel "b" sub-element.[152] Thus rather than being "without-concern" (2:14), Timothy is to "be concerned" (4:15), namely with his example in word, in behavior, in love, in faith, in purity (4:12), his leading in regard to the reading, the exhorting, and the teaching (4:13), and his concern for the publically attested gift that was given to him by God (4:14). The rhetorical juxtaposition of the negative and positive injunctions would likely be reminiscent of Paul's rhetorical strategy to cover

---

Timothy 1:6 does not involve any sort of contradiction to 1 Timothy 4:14. One is not mutually exclusive of the other, and it is also possible that Timothy may have undergone separate consecrations for different missions. For further discussion, see Marshall, *PE*, 569–69.

150. See Collins, *1 & 2 Tim*, 119.

151. See 1:18; 3:14; 4:6, 11. Knight, *PE*, 210: "ταῦτα, as in vv. 6 and 11 . . . refers to the preceding items." Marshall, *PE*, 570: "ταῦτα is somewhat vague, but must refer to the various things that must be done according to vv. 12–13. The reference of ἐν τούτοις will be the same."

152. Towner, *Letters*, 326: "The first imperative (*meleta*) forms an assonant link to the immediately preceding imperative of v. 14 (*mē amelei*) that reinforces the continuity of the whole subsection."

the full orb of leadership qualifications—an overseer is to be "kind, without-fighting" (3:3).[153] Still, from the parallelism between the "b" and "b'" sub-elements, the audience would likely perceive another of Paul's rhetorical strategies: in light of the gift for which Timothy has received public affirmation with the-laying of hands of the presbytery—the indicative—Timothy must "be concerned" with these-things—the imperative.[154]

The verb "be concerned" (μελέτα) itself carries the connotation "to cultivate" or "to think carefully and deeply about."[155] To be sure, the backdrop to this command has in view the apostates who are clearly "without-concern" for "these-things" to which Timothy must "be concerned"; indeed, the young-plant false-teaching overseers (3:6) are disregarding the gift that is in Timothy by looking-down-on his youth (4:12), are holding-toward deceitful spirits and teachings of demons rather than the teaching of the church (4:1, 13), are accepting vile and silly myths (4:7a; cf. 1:4), and are devoted to ascetic bodily training rather than training for godliness (4:7b-8). Over and against the false teachers and in line with the sustained polemical contrast throughout the fourth microchiasm, Timothy is to "be concerned" with leading the church toward godliness (4:7b, 8b) by instructing the brothers with the commendable teaching (4:6) regarding the living God who is the Savior of all humans (4:10). In short, Timothy is to disallow anyone—particularly "some"—from looking-down-on him because of his youth (4:12) because he—unlike the young-plant false teachers (3:6)—is concerned, purposeful, and dedicated to the things that are both appropriate for those of the faithful and for worship (4:12-13). Such will

---

153. Although the pairing of "kind, without-fighting" (ἐπιεικῆ ἄμαχον) are not cognate terms, their conceptual juxtaposition would be apparent; see chapter 2.

154. Towner suggests a similar interpretation: "Verse 15 appears at first to be superfluous since it adds no new content. Its function is to repeat the command of v. 14, which was cast in terms of the Spirit's gifting, and to shift the focus to Timothy's dedication" (*Letters*, 325). For further discussion on Paul's use of the "indicative-imperative" dynamic, see Burridge, *Imitating Jesus*, 105-7; Ridderbos, *Paul*, 254-58; Dunn, *Theology of Paul the Apostle*, 630-31; Gaffin, *By Faith*, 77-85.

155. MacArthur, *Master's Plan for the Church*, 188: "(*meletaō*) conveys the idea of thinking through beforehand, planning, strategizing, or premeditating." Knight, *PE*, 210: "μελετάω (also in Acts 4:25) 'can signifiy either *to study* or *practice*, and which to choose in this context is a puzzle' (Simpson; see also MM). If the word means 'practice,' then the previous reference to exercise is reiterated"; regarding the latter meaning, see e.g., Iovino, *Lettere a Timoteo*, 116.

Spencer suggests several OT allusions: "it was also used for meditative pondering in the Old Testament, for example, 'in his law *will he meditate* [μελετήσει] day and night' (Ps 1:2) . . . Thus, *meletaō* in 4:15 includes an inward aspect of 'meditative pondering' . . ." (*1 Tim*, 118). Such a nuance seems appropriate to Paul's command here.

be consistent-with prophecy and the-laying of hands of the presbytery that recognized his gift to do so (4:14).

For those in the audience familiar with the OT, the related imperative "be in them" (ἐν τούτοις ἴσθι) would likely echo LXX Proverbs 23:17: "Do not let your heart envy sinners but rather in the fear of the Lord be (ἐν φόβῳ κυρίου ἴσθι) all the day." Given the situation in Ephesus, the allusion to the proverb certainly would be appropriate as an emphasis for Timothy. On the one hand, he is to be without-concern with the things of the apostate false teachers such as their relative measure of success to influence the church; after all, according to the lawful use of the commendable law, "some" are still "the without-godly and sinners" (1:8–9), who do not have-faith upon Christ Jesus's ransom on their behalf (1:16; 2:7). On the other hand, Timothy is to focus "all the day" in regard to the things of Christ Jesus—the Lord (1:2, 12, 14)—such as the faithful word and the reading, the exhorting, and the teaching that would direct God's missional household to lead-through a life in all godliness (2:2) for the sake of attracting all humans to Christ Jesus. Literally, the imperative "be in them" demands Timothy to immerse his life and thought—to saturate himself—in fulfilling the charge to preserve the the teaching and promote godliness in the Ephesian church.

In the conclusion of the "b'" sub-element, Paul identifies the explicit purpose for Timothy's diligence: "that your progress might be manifested to all." The pronoun "your" (σου) here in 4:15 recalls its earlier occurrences in the current A' element of the microchiasm (σου, 4:12; σοί, 4:14; σοι, 4:14). Where the repeated pronoun is intentional, the rhetorical effect was likely heard to both highlight Timothy over and above "some" and reiterate his proactive role to maintain his qualification to lead the church. Here, then, the earlier emphasis for Timothy to "train yourself toward godliness" (4:7b) would be strengthened: like an athlete dedicated to victory, Timothy is to saturate and soak himself in all activities of godliness (4:12–14). Yet, rather than being a strictly private matter, Paul specifies that Timothy's "progress might be maniftested to all." In the context of such training, the term "progress" (προκοπή) would convey the fine-tuning of an advanced athlete. That is, the audience understand that Timothy's progress as an example of those of the faithful (4:12) and his leadership in worship activities (4:13) ought to be getting progressively better as he pushes himself to have a tighter grasp on the faith (1:18; 3:9).[156] Moreover, the public aspect of Timothy's

---

156. Paul would not intend for "progress" to be understood as perfection. Indeed, Barcley articulates the very essential nuance of such "progress": "True Christian godliness is seen not in a sinless life, but in one's growth in holiness. The irony is that growth in godliness brings with it an increased awareness of our own sinfulness" (*1 & 2 Tim*, 146). Similarly, drawing out Barcley's implication, Edwards highlights the relational

progress is intended to be "manifested"—that is, evident or obvious—to all. Undoubtedly, the verb "manifested" (φανερά) recalls its prior use in reference to Christ Jesus who "was manifested (ἐφάερώφη) in flesh" (3:16). As such, it seems that by immersing himself in the things of Christ—the preservation of the teaching and its resultant godliness—Timothy's life will itself be missional, in effect manifesting the life of Christ Jesus "to all" (πᾶσιν, 4:15).[157] Still, that Timothy is to attract "all" to Christ Jesus through his own commitment to his progress in godliness, the audience understand Paul's twofold emphasis. On the one hand, the essential, missional character of a qualified leader is highlighted: Timothy is not only to have a commendable standing (3:13) but also a commendable testimony from those-outside (3:7). On the other hand, therefore, Paul is underscoring the subsequent result of Timothy's qualified, missional leadership: at the very least, the entire household of God in Ephesus will be trained by Timothy to manifest their progress to those-outside, thus attracting all humans to Christ Jesus. To be sure, the missional quality of Paul's commands for Timothy to maniftest his progress to "all" (πᾶσιν) aligns with the living God, who is the Savior of "all" (πάντων) humans (4:10) and desires "all" (πάντας, 4:15) humans to be-saved (2:4a).[158] In sum, particularly in relation to 4:12 within the current A' element, the audience understand that Timothy's plain and visible qualification as an authorized leader of the teaching and of godliness in God's missional household should not only stop the false-teaching overseers but also reinforce that the faithful in the Ephesian church indeed are correct to follow Timothy—by doing so, they will manifest Christ Jesus to all.

---

compenent of such "progress," namely that whenever he saw sin in others, it provided an occasion for him to be aware of and repent for his own sins ("Resolution no. 8," xx).

It may be worth noting these observations are reminiscent of Paul's statement concerning deacons in 1 Timothy 3:13 who acquire "much confidence in faith that is in Christ Jesus": by an awareness of their own sin, deacons gain confidence that Christ Jesus came specifically for them (1:15), thereby acquiring greater confidence in both their act of trusting upon Christ and being in a relationship with him; see chapter 2.

157. It is possible to translate "to all" (πᾶσιν) as "in all matters"—e.g., in all matters of godliness. However, both the immediate context of 4:12 ("the faithful") and the reference to Christ's manifestation in 3:16 have humans in view. For sure, the audience would hear the term in reference "to all [people]." See Marshall's discussion (*PE*, 571).

158. Cf. Knight, *PE*, 210: "πᾶσιν (see 2:1, 2, 4, 6) indicates all those before whom Timothy lives." Yet, given both Paul's missional emphasis and God's inclusive scope pertaining to "all humans" throughout the macrochiasm (2:1, 4a, 6; 4:10), it seems unlikely Paul has only the Ephesian congregation in view.

1 Timothy 4:16: Strongly-hold Yourself and
The Teaching, Salvation

("a'" sub-element)

The concluding "a'" sub-element and final statement of the A' element (4:16) ends the fourth microchiasm: "Strongly-hold yourself and the teaching, strongly-remain in them; for doing this you will save yourself and those who hear you." The audience hear 4:16 of the A' element as a bookend to 4:1 in the parallel A element. The concluding imperative for Timothy to "Strongly-hold (ἔπεχε) . . . the teaching (τῇ διδασκαλίᾳ)" here in 4:16 of the A' element recalls the opening statement of the microchiasm regarding "some" who are "holding-toward (προσέχοντες) deceitful spirits and teachings (διδασκαλίαις) of demons" in 4:1 of the parallel A element. Thus here at the climax of the microchiasm, Paul not only continues the polemical contrast between Timothy and "some" but also amplifies how Timothy's devotion to "the teaching" (τῇ διδασκαλίᾳ) of the church (4:16)—"the (τῇ) sound teaching (διδασκαλίᾳ)" (1:10b) by Paul the "teacher" (διδάσκαλος, 2:7); "the (τῆς) commendable teaching (διδασκαλίας)" (4:6); "the teaching" (τῇ διδασκαλίᾳ, 4:13)—is antithetical to the apostates's devotion to "teachings" (διδασκαλίαις) of demons (4:1), which is the reason why "some" "teach-different" (ἑτεροδιδασκαλεῖν, 1:3), namely some-thing different that lies-opposed to the sound teaching (1:10b). Still, as much as the negative polemic against the false teachers is heard, so too is the positive assertion for Timothy to actively ensure that he himself is continuously being-nourished in "the commendable teaching" (4:6b). Furthermore, given that "apostasy from the faith" is in view (4:1)—swerving-from faith (1:6), having become-shipwrecked regarding the faith (1:20)—the audience clearly understand that salvation is at stake. On the one hand, Timothy must "Strongly-hold"—"pay attention to"—the teaching to avoid apostasy himself.[159] On the other hand, by strongly-holding the teaching, he will be able to lead the faithful among the audience to live out their salvation; subsequently, the apostates might observe his progress, no longer look-down-on him, and begin to follow him and "the teaching" (4:13, 16).

In addition to the contrast against the false teachers in 4:1, the verb "Strongly-hold" (ἔπεχε) in the "a'" sub-element would also remind the audience of the parallel "a" sub-element wherein Timothy was commanded to "hold-toward" (πρόσεχε) . . . the teaching (4:13). While a clear connection

159. As an intransitive that does not take a direct object, the imperative verb "Strongly-hold" (ἔπεχε) would connote "to pay attention to." See Knight, *PE*, 210; Marshall, *PE*, 571.

is in view, the audience would understand that the command for Timothy to "Strongly-hold" in 4:16 is not meant to be heard as a rhetorical contrast to the parallel command "hold-toward" in 4:13. This is certain not only by the different rhetorical strategy of 4:13, which is irony similar to Paul's use of "youth" in 4:12, but also by the shared term that connects 4:13 and 4:16 together and grounds their definitive contrast against the false teachers: "the teaching" (τῇ διδασκαλίᾳ, 4:13, 16). Here, then, as one and the same command, the audience understand that "Strongly-hold (ἔπεχε) yourself and the teaching (τῇ διδασκαλίᾳ)" in the "a'" sub-element (4:16) is an emphatic, parallel repetition of the "a" sub-element to "hold-toward (πρόσεχε) . . . the teaching (τῇ διδασκαλίᾳ)" (4:13). At the same time, the progression of the minichiasm from the "a" sub-element to the "a'" sub-element would carry with it the implications of the "b" and "b'" sub-elements. That is, Timothy must "Strongly-hold . . . the teaching" (4:16) in light of the gift that was given by God and is consistent-with prophecy and the public recognition of the authorized leaders of the church (4:14); he is to do this so that all might see the tangible result (4:15) of what it means to "hold-toward . . . the teaching" (4:13).[160]

Furthermore, Paul also commands Timothy to strongly-hold "yourself." The term "yourself" (σεαυτῷ) in 4:16 recalls its earlier occurrence in 4:7b wherein Timothy was commanded to "train yourself (σεαυτόν) for godliness." Certainly the audience hear Paul's emphasis on Timothy's responsibility to pay close attention to himself in view of his training regimen: as Timothy strongly-holds himself to live in line with "the teaching," so too will he train himself in view of "godliness." In short, the audience understand that "Strongly-hold yourself and the teaching" intends a tangible action—training (4:7b)—which itself results in progress that is clearly manifested to all (4:15).

In full, the concluding juxtaposition of Timothy's personal life— "yourself" (σεαυτῷ)—and "the teaching" in the A' element would reinforce and advance the sustained theme of the macrochiasm, namely the inseparable relationship between truth and lifestyle. Beginning with the A unit of the macrochiasm, the first microchiasm identified the fundamental

---

160. Here, it may be helpful to visualize the arrangement of the minichiasm, indicated by the linguistic parallels:
"a". "hold-toward . . . the teaching" (πρόσεχε . . . τῇ διδασκαλίᾳ) (4:13);
   "b". "be without-concern" (ἀμέλει) (4:14);
   "b'". "be concerned" (μελέτα) (4:15);
"a'". "Strongly-hold . . . the teaching" (ἔπεχε . . . τῇ διδασκαλίᾳ) (4:16).
Rhetorically, the introductory imperative in the "a" sub-element (4:13) advances the central imperatives in the "b" and "b'" sub-elements (4:14–15) into the concluding imperative in the "a'" sub-element (4:16).

importance of the sound teaching that accords with the gospel, thus exhibiting God's glory and resulting in blessings toward him (1:10b–11, 17). Progressing to the B unit, the second microchiasm identified that the missional impetus of a life in all godliness derives from a knowing-embrace of the truth concerning the testimony about the one God who desires all humans to be-saved and the one mediator Christ Jesus who gave himself as a ransom on behalf of all (2:2–6). Moving forward to the C unit, the third microchiasm identified that such a missional lifestyle of godliness also flows from qualified men who are able to lead the church to uphold the confessedly great truth concerning the mystery of godliness, Christ Jesus (3:1–7, 8–13, 15–16). Now in the C' unit, the fourth microchiasm identifies that godliness flows from and aligns directly with a knowing-embrace of truth, namely the teaching (4:3b, 6, 13, 16). Specifically, the relationship between truth and godliness was expressed both negatively and positively. Negatively, Paul identifies the failure of "some" to knowingly-embrace the truth (cf. 4:3b) because they are holding-toward teachings of demons (4:1), which have led them to practice ascetic bodily training rather than training for godliness (4:7–8). Positively, as an example of those of the faithful who have knowingly-embraced the truth (4:3b, 10b, 12), Timothy is to lead the audience toward godliness through the reception of God's creation and proper worship. Here, then, in the concluding, climactic statement of the C' unit, it is only fitting for Paul to summarize and advance all that the audience have heard, in effect: "Strongly-hold yourself to promote godliness as you strongly-hold the teaching to preserve it."

Still, Paul states another imperative for Timothy: "strongly-remain in them" (4:16). Aurally, the command to "strongly-remain" (ἐπίμενε) would be heard as an alliterative parallel of Paul's command to "Strongly-hold (ἔπεχε) yourself" (4:16).[161] The rhetorical effect would strengthen the force of the Paul's commands; the audience are to understand that Timothy will adhere to the apostle Paul's instructions by continuously devoting himself to commendably leading the church. Consequently, therefore, in the same way that Timothy adheres to the apostle Paul's instructions (1:3, 18; 4:16) and the apostle Paul adheres to God and Christ Jesus's commands (1:1, 12; 2:7), the audience understand their own call to adhere to Timothy, thus to Paul, thus to God and Christ Jesus.

Moreover, the verb "strongly-remain" (ἐπίμενε) recalls Paul's initial exhortation in the first microchiasm for Timothy "to remain" (προσμεῖναι) in Ephesus in order to charge "some" not to teach-different (1:3). What is more, "stongly-remain" (ἐπίμενε) in 4:16 also recalls Paul's statement to

---

161. The ἐπί prefix on both verbs would be apparent.

the women in the second microchiasm who will be-saved if they "remain (μείνωσιν) in faith" (2:15). In both instances, the dangerous and influential presence of the false teachers was in view, both upon the entire Ephesian church (1:3) and specifically upon the women in the church (2:15). As such, Paul's instructions in 4:16 for Timothy to "strongly-remain" would certainly carry the sense of persevering amidst opposition, namely amidst "some" who teach some-thing different that lies-opposed to the sound teaching (1:3, 10b) and who apostasy from the faith (4:1; cf. 1:6, 20). Also, "strongly-remain" in 4:16 would be heard with the cumulative effect of the entire macrochiasm. The false teachings of "some" (A unit), their influential presence upon the men and women in the congregation (B unit), their inability to lead as overseers (C unit), and the danger of their false teachings upon missional godliness and the inclusive offer of salvation to all humans (C' unit) function as a buiding force to highlight the extremely difficult situation with which Timothy is confronted in Ephesus. For Timothy to "strongly-remain," therefore, would undoubtedly require much nourishment (4:6b), much training (4:7b), much toiling and agonizing (4:10), much hope upon God (4:10), much assertion of authority (4:11–12), and much devotion to every aspect of his leadership (4:13–15). At the same time, for the Ephesian audience listening to the performance of the letter, certainly the apostle Paul would be calling them to rally behind Timothy's leadership. In short, by heeding Paul's command to "strongly-remain," Timothy will lead the audience to align themselves with God and Christ Jesus and thus to follow in the difficult path of preserving the teaching and promoting godliness as part of God's missional household.

The specification that Timothy is to strongly-remain "in them" (αὐτοῖς) in 4:16 echoes "be in them" (τούτοις) in 4:15b of the immediately preceding "b'" sub-element. In this way, it is possible that the pronoun "them" (4:16) would be heard in reference to the activities implied "in them" (4:15b). Yet, given that "strongly-remain" (4:16) was heard as a rhetorical reference to "Strongly-hold yourself and the teaching" (4:16), it is more likely that the phrase "continue in them" (4:16) would be understood as part of Paul's rhetorical emphasis on his climactic, concluding commands to Timothy in 4:16. To be sure, here at the conclusion of the fourth microchiasm, Paul's point is to intensify and elevate the sustained movement that the audience have just heard. From the outset of the microchiasm, the apostle made clear that in keeping with what the Spirit says, "some" have already apostatized from the faith and are leading others in God's household to do the same (4:1–3a). Given this reality, Timothy is to be instructing the brothers who have knowingly-embraced the truth by being-nourished in the commendable teaching that he has followed (4:3b–6). Specifically, he is to train himself for the accompaniment of the teaching—godliness—and lead the church according to the gift that was given to him by God, which was recognized through the laying of hands by the governing authority of the presbytery (4:7–15). The force, then, of this closing imperative in 4:16 is that Timothy must "strongly-remain in them" even as "some" persist to influence others in the Ephesian church. In short, Timothy is commanded by Paul to not give up.

Paul's final words explain why Timothy must strongly-remain: "for doing this you will save yourself and those who hear you" (4:16). As heard throughout the macrochiasm and repeatedly in the present microchiasm, the conjunction "for" (γάρ) has an explanatory force, providing the basis for the preceding statement. In effect, the audience understand that Timothy must strongly-hold himself and the teaching, that is, strongly-remain in them, because "doing this you will save yourself and those who hear you." In this way, too, it would be clear for the audience that "this" (τοῦτο) refers to the same preceding actions that Timothy must do—"Strongly-hold yourself and the teaching, strongly-remain in them."[162] Moreover, the combined phrase "for . . . this" (τοῦτο γάρ, 4:16) recalls its earlier occurrence "for . . . this" (τοῦτο γάρ, 4:10) in regard to Paul and Timothy's collaborative toiling and agonizing to preserve the teaching about the faithful word, the promise of life, and the universal offer of salvation because the living God is the Savior of all humans (4:9–10). The connection would draw out the soteriological significance of Paul and Timothy's actions: they are instruments of salvation.[163] In effect, the reason for Timothy's active response to Paul's commands in 4:16 is because salvation is at stake. At the same time, Paul's point sheds light on the urgency for Timothy's actions: "some" who are holding-toward teachings of demons are instruments of destruction.

In view of Paul's emphasis on salvation, the audience hear a significant shift of focus from God as the Savior (4:10) to the simultaneous reality of human involvement in salvation: "for doing this you will save yourself and those who hear you" (4:16). Paul indicates that it is by Timothy "doing" (ποιῶν)—strongly-holding himself and the teaching—that salvation will come. Here at the climax of the microchiasm, then, the audience understand that Paul's emphasis is *both* that the living God is the only Savior of humans *and* humans have a responsibility to actively respond to God as the Savior.[164] Here in the context of Paul's commands to Timothy, it is clear

162. See Knight, *PE*, 211.

163. Wieland, "Function of Salvation," 158: "Since salvation is linked to faith, one who teaches the Christian faith becomes an agent of God's saving."

164. Schreiner, *Paul*, 284: "Paul can hardly mean that Timothy is ultimately responsible for his own salvation or the salvation of his hearers. This would contradict Paul's insistence that salvation is of the Lord . . . Nor is it persuasive to argue that Timothy's

that such an active response is characterized by being in submissiveness to God's missional household-law in faith (1:4; cf. 3:1–13). That is, just as the apostle Paul submits to Christ Jesus and the command of God, so too must the "genuine child" Timothy submit to Paul. To be sure, the audience understand that they are to respond by being in submissiveness to Timothy, thus to Paul, thus to Christ Jesus and God.

The concluding emphasis on human responsibility is furthered by the term "yourself" (σεαυτόν). The term was already heard by the audience in 4:16, "Strongly-hold yourself" (σεαυτῷ); its immediate repetition again in 4:16 effectively doubles the force of Timothy's personal responsibility here at the high point of the microchiasm. Moreover, "yourself" (σεαυτόν) in 4:16 recalls Paul's command for Timothy to "train yourself (σεαυτόν) for godliness" in 4:7b. As such, the audience would likely hear a twofold nuance in relation to 4:16. On the one hand, as in 4:7b, Timothy's personal responsibility is elevated, the sense being: "No one else will do it for you." On the other hand, as in 4:7b, Timothy's accountability is placed within the context that Paul raised him (1:1, 18); Timothy's "doing" has in view that which Paul prepared him to do. The audience understand that Timothy's actions are to be trusted for salvation.

The verb "you will save" (σώσεις) is reminiscent of prior cognates throughout the macrochiasm.[165] In the current A' element of the fourth microchiasm, Paul articulated that the living God is the "Savior" (σωτήρ) of all humans (4:10). There, the clear implication was that humans cannot save themselves but rather it is only possible to be-saved by the "Savior of all humans." Undoubtedly, then, the verb "you will save" in 4:16 would be understood by the audience within this overall framework, namely that God is the ultimate source of salvation, not Timothy. Moreover, at the climactic conclusion of the second microchiasm, Paul stated that a woman "will be-saved" (σωθήσεται, 2:15). There, the focus was on the missional lifestyle of

---

actions have no role in the salvation of his hearers or himself. In that case the wording of the text is jettisoned altogether! Salvation is ultimately of the Lord, for it is his work. And yet the actions of human beings are significant and crucial as well."

165. The future aspect of the verb in the phrase "you will save (σώσεις) yourself" does not suggest that Timothy is not already saved. Throughout the letter, Paul has articulated past (justification, 1:9; 2:6), present (sanctification, 4:5, 9), and future (glorification, 3:16; 4:9) nuances of salvation.

It may be worth noting that some commentators interpret the verb "you will save" without ultimate salvific significance. However, such an interpretation of 4:16 cannot be supported due to Paul's consistent and interconnected use of "save"—along with its adjectival cognates—throughout the 1 Timothy macrochiasm in reference to eternal salvation from sin (1:1, 15; 2:3, 4, 15; 4:10, 16). See analysis below. For further discussion, see Schreiner, *Paul*, 284; Knight, *PE*, 211.

women who remain "in faith" to bring more people into the familial household of God, thus evidencing their existence "in faith" and, therefore, that they "will be-saved" (σωθήσεται, 2:15) by the "Savior (σωτῆρος) God, who desires all humans to be-saved (σωθῆναι)" (2:3-4a). To be sure, in the second microchiasm the audience understood that Paul was highlighting God's activity to save humans with the nuance that those whom God has saved will live a corresponding missional lifestyle of godliness (2:2, 10). So, too, in light of Timothy's salvation—his existence "in faith" (1:2) and his hope upon the living God, who is the Savior (4:10)—Paul's statement "for doing this you will save yourself and those who hear you" underscores Timothy's corresponding, missional lifestyle of godliness as a twofold nuance. On the one hand, by "doing," Timothy evidences his salvation and the fact that others will be-saved by God's doing. On the other hand, Timothy's refusal to actively respond to Paul's commands will evidence his lack of salvation and refusal to participate in God's missional activity.

Still, the verb "you will save" (σώσεις) in 4:16 recalls Paul's statements in the first microchiasm that Christ Jesus came into the world "to save" (σῶσαι) sinners (1:15) and that Paul is an apostle of Christ Jesus according to the command of "God our Savior (σωτῆρος)" (1:1). In full, then, the audience understand that where "God our (σωτῆρος) Savior" (1:1), that is, "our Savior (σωτῆρος) God" (2:3), who is the "Savior" (σωτήρ) of all humans (4:10), desires all humans "to be-saved" (σωθῆναι, 2:4a), and that for this reason Christ Jesus came "to save" (σῶσαι) sinners (1:15), the clear implication is that Timothy's salvation in 4:16 is fundamentally rooted in the desire and activity of the Savior God and Christ Jesus; the same applies to Paul's salvation in 1:16 and to salvation for "all humans" (2:4a, 6; 4:10). Given that Timothy has already received the salvific blessings from God the Father and Christ Jesus that are available "in faith" (1:2), the audience understand beyond any doubt that Timothy is already saved.[166]

Yet, even in light of Paul's emphasis on the Savior God's ultimate sovereignty to save humans and Paul's surety of Timothy's salvation, the onus of the fourth microchiasm has clearly been on human responsibility, namely on Timothy's responsibility (4:6-16). Thus the climactic force of Paul's statement "for doing this you will save yourself and those who hear you" in 4:16 is that what a person does absolutely matters. In effect, as for the women in 2:15, the sense for Timothy in 4:16 would be: "By living according to your salvation, you will evidence your salvation." What is more, even Paul—who raised Timothy to be a qualified leader—evidences his human responsibility in

---

166. Certainly there are other implications that Timothy is already saved—e.g., Paul's collective references that include Timothy: "our hope . . . our Savior" (1:1); "we know . . . that for the just the law is not laid" (1:8-9); etc.

matters of salvation; he commands and encourages Timothy to strongly-hold himself and the teaching, that is, to strongly-remain "in faith" for the sake of Timothy's salvation and those in Ephesus (4:16).[167] To be sure, the audience understand that while God is the Savior of all humans, humans play a crucial role in their own salvation and in the salvation of others.[168]

The present tense of the participle "those who hear" (ἀκούοντάς) is significant. Undoubtedly, it would be a reminder to Timothy that his leadership has a direct bearing on the salvation of specific people—with names and faces—among the audience in Ephesus.[169] At the same time, Timothy hears Paul shift his attention toward the audience: they themselves are directly challenged to consider whether they are listening to "you" (σου), that is Timothy, or to the "some."[170] In this sense, as much as the focus has been uniquely on Timothy (4:6–16), here in the climax of the fourth microchiasm the audience realize Paul's sudden rhetorical move: everything that has been said throughout the microchiasm could be understood from the perspective of "those who hear." The audience understand that Paul is not only requiring Timothy's active response as evidence of salvation; rather, Paul expects his audience to actively respond to everything that he has said about Timothy, namely that Timothy is their authorized, publically recognized leader. In effect, the shift of Paul's focus to "those who hear" would carry the sense of, "By listening to Timothy, you [the audience] will evidence your salvation." Thus in climactic fashion, Paul highlights that participatory human responsibility is part and parcel of the salvation

---

167. Witherington, *Letters*, 260–61: "the granting of the grace gift does not guarantee its responsible use, which Paul must also encourage." Similarly, see Bassler, *1 & 2 Tim*, 89.

168. In orthodox theology, this distinction is sometimes described in terms of "definitive sanctification" contrasted with "progressive sanctification." Frame, *Systematic Theology*, 986: "The first is a single act of God that happens at a single point in time. The second is a continuing work of God with which he calls us to cooperate. This distinction reflects the fact . . . that for the believer holiness is both a fact and a command." See Murray, *Collected Writings*, 2:277–304; Köstenberger, *Excellence*, 60–61; Vickers, *The Cross*, 96.

169. See Fee, *1 & 2 Tim*, 69–70. Howard helpfully nuances the implications of Paul's command to Timothy in 4:16 regarding "those who hear": "while the believer's holiness is the result of the finished work of Christ on the cross, there is a consistent and pervasive aspect in Scripture wherein the believer lives out that holiness within the context of community such that they grow in their spiritual maturity—an aspect of progressive sanctification. As such, holiness was defined as the unique status given by God to the redeemed for the purpose of impacting others for his glory" (*Paul, the Community*, 183).

170. It may be worth noting that Paul is placing himself under the same scenario as Timothy. As the letter is performed for the audience in Ephesus, it is functionally Paul who is speaking to the audience in Ephesus (see volume 1, chapter 1). To be sure, Paul's challenge to the audience is equally whether they are listening to him.

offered by and received from the Savior God. Not just Timothy, nor just the faithful among the audience, but anyone—even "some"—are called to actively respond and participate according to the missional household-law of the living God who is the Savior of all humans.

In summary of the fourth microchiasm, those who have apostatized from the faith in the A element are holding-toward deceitful spirits and teachings of demons (4:1) rather than to the recognized practices of the church in the parallel A' element—the reading, the exhorting, and the teaching (4:13). Over and against the false teachers who reject God's commendable creation, the faithful in the A element who have knowingly-embraced the truth (4:3) are called to view Timothy as their example in the parallel A' element (4:12). By rejecting vile and silly myths and the little profitability of ascetic bodily training in the B element (4:7–8a), Timothy and the audience are to pursue godliness training, thus accepting the definite promise of its all profitability in the parallel B' element, namely life for the present and for the inevitable-coming (4:8b). The contrast is clear, and the war to preserve the teaching and promote godliness as God's missional household is certain. The audience must decide whether they will adhere to the apostle Paul and his qualified representative Timothy, or to the apostate "some" who effectively represent deceitful spirits and demons. As the C' unit of the macrochiasm narrows to a conclusion, the scope of Paul's final statement expands: all in the Ephesian church must strongly-hold themselves and the teaching, for by doing this, they will evidence their salvation. Indeed, Paul is speaking; the question is: are "those who hear" listening? Where salvation is at stake, the audience must be fully aware of the eternal ramifications of accepting or rejecting Paul's call for their allegiance to Timothy, to himself, and thus to Christ Jesus and God.

Bibliography

Volume 2

Akin, Daniel L. "The Mystery of Godliness Is Great: Christology in the Pastoral Epistles." In *Entrusted with The Gospel: Paul's Theology in the Pastoral Epistles*, edited by Andreas J. Kostënberger and Terry L. Wilder, 137–52. Nashville: B&H, 2010.
Arichea, Daniel C., Jr "Who Was Phoebe? Translating *Diakonos* in Romans 16.1." BT 39 (1988) 401–15.
Barcley, William B. *1 & 2 Timothy*. Webster, NY: Evangelical, 2005.
———. "1 Timothy." In *A Biblical-Theological Introduction to the New Testament: The Gospel Realized*, edited by Michael J. Kruger, 357–75. Wheaton, IL: Crossway, 2016.
Barrett, C. K.. *The Pastoral Epistles*. NCBNT. Oxford: Clarendon, 1963.
Bartchy, S. Scott. *First-Century Slavery and 1 Corinthians 7:21*. Eugene, OR: Wipf & Stock, 1973.
Bassler, Jouette M. *1 & 2 Timothy and Titus*. ANTC. Nashville: Abingdon, 1996.
Bauer, Walter, et al. *A Greek-English Lexicon of the New Testament and Other Early Christian Literature* (BDAG). 3rd ed. Revised by F. W. Danker. Chicago: University of Chicago Press, 2000.
Beale, G. K., and Benjamin L. Gladd. *Hidden But Now Revealed: A Biblical Theology of Mystery*. Downers Grove, IL: InterVarsity, 2014.
Belleville, Linda L. "1 Timothy." In *1 Timothy, 2 Timothy, Titus, Hebrews*, edited by Philip W. Comfort, 25–60. CBC 17. Carol Stream, IL: Tyndale, 2009.
———. "Christology, Greco-Roman Religious Piety, and the Pseudonymity of the Pastoral Letters." In *Paul and Pseudepigraphy*, edited by Stanley E. Porter and Gregory P. Fewster, 221–44. PS 8. Boston: Brill, 2013.
———. "Teaching and Usurping Authority: 1 Timothy 2:11–15." In *Discovering Biblical Equality: Complementarity Without Hierarchy*, edited by Ronald W. Pierce and Rebecca Merrill Groothuis, 205–23. Downers Grove, IL: InterVarsity, 2005.
Betsworth, Sharon. *The Reign of God Is Such as These: A Socio-Literary Analysis of Daughters in the Gospel of Mark*. New York: T. & T. Clark, 2010.
Blass, F., and A. Debrunner. *A Greek Grammar of the New Testament and Other Early Christian Literature* (BDF). Translated by R. W. Funk. Chicago: University of Chicago Press, 1961.

Bockmuehl, Markus. "Das Verb φανερόω im Neuen Testament: Versuch einer Neuauswertung." *BZ* 32 (1988) 87-99.
Bufe, Chaz. *Provocations: Don't Call Them Libertarians, AA Lies, and Other Incitements.* Tuscon: See Sharp, 2014.
Burridge, Richard A. *Imitating Jesus: An Inclusive Approach to New Testament Ethics.* Grand Rapids: Eerdmans, 2007.
Burton, E. D. W. *Syntax of Moods and Tenses in New Testament Greek.* 3rd ed. Edinburgh: T. & T. Clark, 1976.
Carson, D. A., and Douglas Moo. *An Introduction to the New Testament.* 2nd ed. Grand Rapids: Zondervan, 2005.
Cochran, Matthew E. *As Though It Were Actually True: A Christian Apologetic Primer.* Eugene, OR: Resource, 2010.
Coleman, Roche. *Connecting the Chasm.* Bloomington, IN: WestBow, 2013.
Collins, John N. *Diakonia Studies: Critical Issues in Ministry.* New York: Oxford University Press, 2014.
Collins, Raymond F. *1 & 2 Timothy and Titus: A Commentary.* NTL. Louisville: Westminster John Knox, 2002.
Cook, Christopher C. H. *Alcohol, Addiction, and Christian Ethics.* New York: Cambridge University Press, 2006.
Couser, Greg A. "The Sovereign Savior of 1 and 2 Timothy and Titus." In *Entrusted with The Gospel: Paul's Theology in the Pastoral Epistles*, edited by Andreas J. Köstenberger and Terry L. Wilder, 105-36. Nashville: B&H, 2010.
Dalton, William Joseph. *Christ's Proclamation to the Spirits: A Study of 1 Peter 3:18—4:6.* 2nd ed. Rome: Editrice Pontificio Istituto Biblico, 1989.
DeConick, April D. *Holy Misogyny: Why the Sex and Gender Conflicts in the Early Church Still Matter.* New York: Continuum, 2011.
Deichgräber, Reinhard. *Gotteshymnus und Christushymnus in der frühen Christenheit.* Göttingen: Vandenhoeck & Reprecht, 1967.
Denaux, Adelbert. "Stranger on Earth and Divine Guest: Human and Divine Hospitality in the Gospel of Luke and the Book of Acts." In *Strangers and Pilgrims on Earth: Essays in Honour of Abraham van de Beek*, edited by E. Van der Borght and P. van Geest, 87-100. Boston: Brill, 2012.
Deppe, Dean B. *All Roads Lead to the Text: Eight Methods of Inquiry into the Bible.* Grand Rapids, Eerdmans, 2011.
Dibelius, Martin, and Hans Conzelmann. *A Commentary on the Pastoral Epistles.* Philadelphia: Fortress, 1972.
Dionson, Herman. "1 Timothy 4:6-16: Towards a Theology of Encouragement." *AJPS* 18/2 (2015) 7-21.
Doxiadis, Apostolos, and Michalis Sialaros. "Sing, Muse, of the Hypotenuse: Influence of Poetry and Rhetoric on the Formation of Greek Mathematics." In *Writing Science: Medical and Mathematical Authorship in Ancient Greece*, edited by Markus Asper, 367-410. Boston: de Gruyter, 2013.
Dunn, James D. G. *Jesus and the Spirit: A Study of the Religious and Charismatic Experience of Jesus and the First Christians as Reflected in the New Testament.* Grand Rapids: Eerdmans, 1975.
———. "Jesus—Flesh and Spirit: An Exposition of Romans 1.3-4." *JTS* 24 (1973) 40-68.
———. *The Theology of Paul the Apostle.* Grand Rapids: Eerdmans, 1998.

Dupont, J. "Σὺν Χριστῷ." In L'union avec le Christ selon saint Paul. Paris: Louvain, 1952.
Edwards, Jonathan. "Resolution no. 8." In The Works of Jonathan Edwards 1. Carlisle, PA: Banner of Truth Trust, 1979.
Ellingworth, Paul. "'Men and Brethren . . .' (Acts 1.16)." BT 55 (2004) 153–55.
———. "The 'True Saying' in 1 Timothy 3,1." BT 31 (1980) 443–45.
Ellis, E. Earle. "Paul and His Co-Workers." NTS 17 (1971) 437–52.
Fay, Ron C. "Greco-Roman Concepts of Deity." In Paul's World, edited by Stanley E. Porter, 51–80. Boston: Brill, 2008.
Fee, Gordon D. 1 & 2 Timothy, Titus. NIBC 13. Peabody, MA: Hendrickson, 1988.
———. God's Empowering Presence: The Holy Spirit in the Letters of Paul. Peabody, MA: Hendrickson, 1994.
Fiore, Benjamin. "Paul, Exemplification, and Imitation." In Paul in the Greco-Roman World: A Handbook, edited by J. Paul Sampley, 228–57. New York: Trinity, 2003.
Fiorenza, Elisabeth Schüssler. "Missionaries, Apostles, Coworkers: Romans 16 and the Reconstruction of Women's Early Christian History." Word & World 6/4 (1986) 420–33.
Fowl, Stephen E. The Story of Christ in the Ethics of Paul: An Analysis of the Function of the Hymnic Material in the Pauline Corpus. JSNTSup 36. Sheffield: Sheffield Academic, 1990.
Frame, John M. Systematic Theology: An Introduction to Christian Belief. Phillipsburg, NJ: P&R, 2013.
Gaffin, Richard B., Jr. By Faith, Not By Sight: Paul and the Order of Salvation. 2nd ed. Phillipsburg, NJ: P&R, 2013.
———. "'Life-Giving Spirit': Probing the Center of Paul's Pneumatology." JETS 41/4 (1998) 573–89.
Gench, Frances Taylor. Encountering God in Tyrannical Texts: Reflections on Paul, Women, and the Authority of Scripture. Louisville: Westminster John Knox, 2015.
———. Faithful Disagreement: Wrestling with Scripture in the Midst of Church Conflict. Louisville: Westminster John Knox, 2009.
Goodwin, Mark J. "The Pauline Background of the Living God as Interpretive Context for 1 Timothy 4.10." JSNT 61 (1996) 65–85.
Gundry, R. H. "The Form, Meaning and Background of the Hymn Quoted in 1 Timothy 3:16." In Apostolic History and the Gospel: Biblical and Historical Essays Presented to F. F. Bruce on His Sixtieth Birthday, edited by W. Ward Gasque and Ralph. P. Martin, 203–22. Grand Rapids: Eerdmans, 1970.
Heil, John Paul. The Letters of Paul as Rituals of Worship. Eugene, OR: Cascade, 2011.
Ho, Chiao Ek. "Mission in the Pastoral Epistles." In Entrusted with The Gospel: Paul's Theology in the Pastoral Epistles, edited by Andreas J. Kostënberger and Terry L. Wilder, 241–67. Nashville: B&H, 2010.
Howard, James M. Paul, the Community, and Progressive Sanctification: An Exploration into Community-Based Transformation within Pauline Theology. New York: Peter Lang, 2007.
Hughes, R. Kent, and Bryan Chapell. 1-2 Timothy and Titus: To Guard the Deposit. Wheaton, IL: Crossway, 2012.
Hutson, Christopher E. "Ecclesiology in the Pastoral Epistles." In The New Testament Church: The Challenge of Developing Ecclesiologies, edited by John P. Harrison and James D. Dvorak, 164–88. McMBSS. Eugene, OR: Pickwick, 2012.
Iovino, Paolo. Lettere a Timoteo, Lettera a Tito. Milan: Paoline, 2005.

Jamir, Lanuwabang. *Exclusion and Judgment in Fellowship Meals: The Socio-historical Background in 1 Corinthians 11:17-34*. Eugene, OR: Pickwick, 2016.

Jeffers, James S. *The Greco-Roman World of the New Testament Era: Exploring the Background of Early Christianity*. Downers Grove, IL: InterVarsity, 1999.

Jeon, Paul S. *To Exhort and Reprove: Audience Response to the Chiastic Structures of Paul's Letter to Titus*. Eugene, OR: Pickwick, 2012.

Jeremias, Joachim. *Die Briefe an Timotheus und Titus*. NTD 9. Göttingen: Vandenhoeck & Ruprecht, 1963.

Jewett, Robert. "Paul, Phoebe, and the Spanish Mission." In *The Social World of Formative Christianity and Judaism: Essays in Tribute to Howard Clark Kee*, edited by Jacob Neusner, 142–61. Philadelphia: Fortress, 1988.

Jipp, Joshua W. *Divine Visitations and Hospitality to Strangers in Luke-Acts: An Interpretation of the Malta Episode in Acts 28:1-10*. Boston: Brill, 2013.

Johnson, Luke Timothy. *Contested Issues in Christian Origins and the New Testament*. SNT 146. Boston: Brill, 2013.

———. *Letters to Paul's Delegates: 1 Timothy, 2 Timothy, Titus*. New York: Bloomsbury Academic, 1996.

———. "The New Testament's Anti-Jewish Slander and the Conventions of Ancient Polemic." *JBL* 108 (1989) 419–41.

Karris, R. J. *The Pastoral Epistles*. NTM 17. Wilmington, DE: Michael Glazier, 1979.

Keegan, Terence J. *First and Second Timothy, Titus, Philemon*. NCBC 9. Collegeville, MN: Liturgical, 2006.

Kelly, J. N. D. *A Commentary on the Pastoral Epistles*. HNTC. Peabody, MA: Hendrickson, 1987.

Kierspel, Lars. *Charts on the Life, Letters, and Theology of Paul*. Grand Rapids: Kregel, 2012.

Knight, George W., III. *The Pastoral Epistles: A Commentary on the Greek Text*. NIGTC. Grand Rapids: Eerdmans, 1992.

Koenig, John. *New Testament Hospitality: Partnership with Strangers as Promise and Missions*. Eugene, OR: Wipf & Stock, 2001.

Köstenberger, Andreas J. *Excellence: The Character of God and the Pursuit of Scholarly Virtue*. Wheaton, IL: Crossway, 2011.

———. "Hermeneutical and Exegetical Challenges in Interpreting the Pastoral Epistles." In *Entrusted with The Gospel: Paul's Theology in the Pastoral Epistles*, edited by Andreas J. Kostënberger and Terry L. Wilder, 1–27. Nashville: B&H, 2010.

Krause, Deborah. *1 Timothy*. RNBC. London: T. & T. Clark, 2004

Kyle, Donald G. *Athletics in Ancient Athens*. 2nd ed. New York: Brill, 1993.

Kynes, Bill. "The Church: A Hidden Glory (1 Timothy 3:14–16)." *Themelios* 35/1 (2010) 30–36.

Lohfink, Gerhard. *Die Himmelfahrt Jesu: Untersuchungen zu den Himmelfahrts–und Erhöhungstexten bei Lukas*. SANT 26. Munich: Kösel, 1971.

Long, Thomas G. *1 & 2 Timothy and Titus*. BTCB. Louisville: Westminster John Knox, 2016.

Longenecker, Bruce W. *Rhetoric at the Boundaries: The Art and Theology of the New Testament Chain-Link Transitions*. Waco, TX: Baylor University Press, 2005.

López, René A. "A Study of Pauline Passages with Vice Lists." *BSac* 168 (2011) 301–16.

MacArthur, John. *1 & 2 Timothy: Encouragement for Church Leaders*. Nashville: Nelson, 2007.

———. *The Master's Plan for the Church*. Chicago: Moody, 2008.

MacDonald, Margaret Y. *The Pauline Churches: A Socio-historical Study of Institutionalization in the Pauline and Deutero-Pauline Writings*. New York: Cambridge University Press, 1988.

Madigan, Kevin, and Carolyn Osiek, eds. *Ordained Women in the Early Church: A Documentary History*. Baltimore: Johns Hopkins University Press, 2005.

Madsen, Thorvald B., II. "The Ethics of the Pastoral Epistles." In *Entrusted With The Gospel: Paul's Theology in the Pastoral Epistles*, edited by Andreas J. Köstenberger and Terry L. Wilder, 219-40. Nashville: B&H, 2010.

Macy, Gary, et al. *Women Deacons: Past, Present, Future*. New York: Paulist, 2011.

Malherbe, Abraham J. "Overseers as Household Managers in the Pastoral Epistles." In *Text, Image, and Christians in the Graeco-Roman World: A Festschrift in Honor of David Lee Balch*, edited by Aliou Cissé Niang and Carolyn Osiek, 72-88. PTMS 176. Eugene, OR: Pickwick, 2012.

Marshall, I. H. *The Pastoral Epistles*. ICC. Edinburgh: T. & T. Clark, 1999.

Martin, Brice L. "1 Timothy 3:16—A New Perspective." *EQ* 85/2 (2013) 105-20.

Matera, Frank J. *God's Saving Grace: A Pauline Theology*. Grand Rapids: Eerdmans, 2012.

Merkle, Benjamin L. *40 Questions about Elders and Deacons*. Grand Rapids: Kregel, 2008.

———. "The Biblical Qualifications for Elders." In *Baptist Foundations: Church Government for an Anti-Institutional Age*, edited by Mark Dever and Jonathan Leeman, 253-70. Nashville: B&H, 2015.

———. "Eccesiology in the Pastoral Epistles." In *Entrusted with The Gospel: Paul's Theology in the Pastoral Epistles*, edited by Andreas J. Kostënberger and Terry L. Wilder, 173-98. Nashville: B&H, 2010.

———. *Why Elders? A Biblical and Practical Guide for Church Members*. Grand Rapids: Kregel, 2009.

Metzger, Bruce M. *A Textual Commentary on the Greek New Testament (TCGNT)*. 2nd ed. Stuttgart: Deutsche Bibelgesellschaft, 1994.

Mihoc, Vasile. "The Final Admonition to Timothy." In *1 Timothy Reconsidered*, edited by Karl Paul Donfried, 135-52. COP 18. Leuven: Peeters, 2008.

Moo, Douglas J. *The Epistle to the Romans*. NICNT. Grand Rapids: Eerdmans, 1996.

Mounce, William D. *Pastoral Epistles*. WBC 46. Nashville: Thomas Nelson, 2000.

Muddiman, John, and John Barton, eds. "The Pastoral Epistles." In *The Pauline Epistles*, edited by John Muddiman and John Barton, 244-62. OBC. New York: Oxford University Press, 2001.

Murray, John. *Collected Writings of John Murray*. Vol. 2. Carlisle, PA: Banner of Truth Trust, 1977.

Nauck, Wolfgang. "Probleme des frühchristlichen Amtsverständnisses (1 Ptr 5,2f.)." *ZNW* 48 (1957) 200-220.

Ngewa, Samuel M. *1 & 2 Timothy and Titus*. ABCS. Grand Rapids: Zondervan, 2009.

Oberlinner, Lorenz. *Die Pastoralbriefe. Erste Folge: Kommentar zum Ersten Timotheusbrief*. HTKNT 11/2. Freiburg: Herder, 1994.

Oden, Thomas C. *First and Second Timothy and Titus*. Interpretation. Louisville: Westminster John Knox, 1989.

O'Gorman, Kevin D. "Dimensions of Hospitality: Exploring Ancient and Classical Origins." In *Hospitality: A Social Lens*, edited by Conrad Lashley et al., 17–32. New York: Elsevier, 2007.

Ollrog, Wolf-Henning. *Paulus und seine Mitarbeiter: Untersuchungen zu Theorie und Praxis der paulinischen Mission*. WMANT 50. Neukirchen-Vluyn: Neukirchener, 1979.

Patterson, Dorothy Kelley, and Rhonda Harrington Kelley, eds. "1 Timothy." In *Women's Evangelical Commentary: New Testament*, edited by Dorothy Kelley Patterson and Rhonda Harrington Kelley, 654–90. Nashville: B&H, 2006.

Payne, Philip B. *Man and Woman, One in Christ: An Exegetical and Theological Study of Paul's Letters*. Grand Rapids: Zondervan, 2009.

Quinn, Jerome D. *The Letter to Titus: A New Translation with Notes and Commentary and an Introduction to Titus, I and II Timothy, The Pastoral Epistles*. AB 35. New York: Doubleday, 1990.

Quinn, Jerome D., and William C. Wacker. *The First and Second Letters to Timothy: A New Translation with Notes and Commentary*. Grand Rapids: Eerdmans, 2000.

Resseguie, James L. *Narrative Criticism on the New Testament: An Introduction*. Grand Rapids: Baker, 2005.

Richardson, Peter. "From Apostles to Virgins: Romans 16 and the Role of Women in the Early Church." *TorJT* 2 (1986) 232–61.

Ridderbos, Herman. *Paul: An Outline of His Theology*. Translated by John Richard De Witt. Grand Rapids: Eerdmans, 1975.

Roloff, Jürgen. *Der Erste Brief an Timotheus*. EKK 15. Zürich: Neukirchener, 1988.

Sandelin, Karl-Gustav. *Attraction and Danger of Alien Religion: Studies in Early Judaism and Christianity*. WUNT 290. Tübingen: Mohr Siebeck, 2012.

Schottroff, Luise. *Lydia's Impatient Sisters: A Feminist Social History of Early Christianity*. Translated by Barbara and Martin Rumscheidt. Louisville: Westminster John Knox, 1995.

Schreiner, Thomas R. "Overseeing and Serving the Church in the Pastoral and General Epistles." In *Shepherding God's Flock: Biblical Leadership in the New Testament and Beyond*, edited by Benjamin L. Merkle and Thomas R. Schreiner, 89–118. Grand Rapids: Kregel, 2014.

———. *Paul, Apostle of God's Glory in Christ: A Pauline Theology*. Downers Grove, IL: InterVarsity, 2001.

Schreiner, Thomas R., and Ardel B. Caneday. *The Race Set Before Us: A Biblical Theology of Perseverance and Assurance*. Downers Grove, IL: InterVarsity, 2001.

Seeberg, D. Alfred. *Der Katechismus der Urchristenheit*. Leipzig: Deichert, 1903.

Simpson, E. K. *The Pastoral Epistles: The Greek Text with Introduction and Commentary*. London: Tyndale, 1954.

Smith, Claire S. *Pauline Communities as "Scholastic Communities": A Study of the Vocabulary of "Teaching" in 1 Corinthians, 1 and 2 Timothy and Titus*. WUNT 2/335. Tübingen: Mohr Siebeck, 2012.

Solevåg, Anna Rebecca. *Birthing Salvation: Gender and Class in Early Christian Childbearing Discourse*. Leiden: Brill, 2013.

Spencer, Aída Besançon. *1 Timothy: A New Covenant Commentary*. NCCS. Cambridge: Lutterworth, 2013.

Spicq, C. *Saint Paul: Les Épîtres Pastorales*. 2 vols. EBib. Paris: Gabalda, 1969.

———. *Theological Lexicon of the New Testament (TLNT)*. Translated by J. D. Ernest. Peabody, MA: Hendrickson, 1994.
Sproul, R. C. *The Holiness of God*. Wheaton, IL: Tyndale, 1985.
Stanley, David Michael. *Christ's Resurrection in Pauline Soteriology*. Rome: Editrice Pontificio Istituto Biblico, 1961.
Stenger, W. *Der Christushymnus 1 Tim 3,16: Eine Strukturanalytische Untersuchung*. RST 6. Frankfurt: Peter Lang, 1977.
Stiefel, Jennifer H. "Women Deacons in 1 Timothy: A Linguistic and Literary Look at 'Women Likewise . . .' (1 Tim 3:11)." In *Women Deacons? Essays with Answers*, edited by Phyllis Zagano, 13–29. Collegeville, MN: Liturgical, 2016.
Strobel, August. "Der Begriff des 'Hauses' im griechischen und römischen Privatrecht." *ZNW* 56 (1965) 91–100.
Swinson, L. Timothy. *What Is Scripture? Paul's Use of* Graphe *in the Letters to Timothy*. Eugene, OR: Wipf & Stock, 2014.
Tellbe, Mikael. *Christ-Believers in Ephesus: A Textual Analysis of Early Christian Identity Formation in a Local Perspective*. WUNT 242. Tübingen: Mohr Siebeck, 2009.
Thatcher, Tom. "The Deacon in the Pauline Church." In *Christ's Victorious Church: Essays on Biblical Ecclesiology and Eschatology in Honor of Tom Friskney*, edited by Jon A. Weatherly, 53–67. Eugene, OR: Wipf & Stock, 2001.
Thielman, Frank. *Theology of the New Testament: A Canonical and Synthetic Approach*. Grand Rapids: Zondervan, 2005.
Torjesen, Karen Jo. *When Women Were Priests: Women's Leadership in the Early Church and the Scandal of Their Subordination in the Rise of Christianity*. New York: HarperSanFransisco, 1993.
Towner, Philip H. "The Function of the Public Reading of Scripture in 1 Timothy 4:13 and the Biblical Tradition." *SBJT* 7 (2003) 44–53.
———. *The Goal of Our Instruction: The Structure of Theology and Ethics in the Pastoral Epistles*. JSNTSup 34. Sheffield: JSOT, 1989.
———. *The Letters to Timothy and Titus*. NIGTC. Grand Rapids: Eerdmans, 2006.
Trebilco, Paul. *The Early Christians in Ephesus from Paul to Ignatius*. Grand Rapids: Eerdmans, 2004.
Trummer, Peter. "Einehe nach den Pastoralbriefe: Zum Verständnis der Termini μιᾶς γυναικὸς ἄνδρα υνδ ἑνὸς ἀνδρὸς γυνή." *Bib* 51 (1970) 471–84.
Verner, David C. *Household of God: The Social World of the Pastoral Epistles*. SBLDiS 71. Chico, CA: Scholars, 1983.
Vickers, Douglas. *The Cross: Its Meaning and Message in a Postmodern World*. Eugene, OR: Wipf & Stock, 2010.
Wall, Robert W., with Richard B. Steele. *1 & 2 Timothy and Titus*. Grand Rapids: Eerdmans, 2012.
Wieland, George M. "The Function of Salvation in the Letters to Timothy and Titus." In *Entrusted with The Gospel: Paul's Theology in the Pastoral Epistles*, edited by Andreas J. Kostënberger and Terry L. Wilder, 153–72. Nashville: B&H, 2010.
Wijngaards, John. *The Ordained Women Deacons of the Church's First Millennium*. Norwich, UK: Canterbury, 2011.
Wilson, Walter T. *Pauline Parallels: A Comprehensive Guide*. Louisville: Westminster John Knox, 2009.

Witherington, Ben, III. *Letters and Homilies for Hellenized Christians.* Vol. 1, *A Socio-Rhetorical Commentary on Titus, 1–2 Timothy and 1–3 John.* Downers Grove, IL: IVP Academic, 2006.

Yarbrough, Mark M. *Paul's Utilization of Preformed Traditions: An Evaluation of the Apostle's Literary, Rhetorical, and Theological Tactics.* New York: T. & T. Clark, 2009.

Young, Frances. *The Theology of the Pastoral Letters.* New York: Cambridge University Press, 1994.

www.ingramcontent.com/pod-product-compliance
Lightning Source LLC
Chambersburg PA
CBHW051740230426
43670CB00012B/2096